THE MISHNAH
Oral Teachings of Judaism

THE MISHNAH

Oral Teachings of Judaism

Selected and Translated by

EUGENE J. LIPMAN

Schocken Books • *New York*

First SCHOCKEN PAPERBACK edition 1974
Second Printing, 1976
Copyright © 1970 by the B'nai B'rith Commission on Adult Jewish Education
Library of Congress Catalog Card No. 72–12621
Published by arrangement with The Viking Press, Inc.

This volume is part of The B'nai B'rith Jewish Heritage Classics, SERIES
EDITORS: DAVID PATTERSON, LILY EDELMAN. Published in Cooper-
ation with The Commission on Adult Education of B'nai B'rith.

Manufactured in the United States of America

To the memory of

Reb Aryeh Levine
"Father of the Prisoners"

Teacher in Israel, counselor and comforter of the afflicted and the imprisoned, heroic fighter for Israel's freedom, man of infinite compassion and love.

Contents

The Third Order: *Nashim* (Women)

The Fourth Order: *Nezikin* (Civil and Criminal Law)

The Fifth Order: *Kodashim*   (Sacred Things)   239

The Sixth Order: *Tohorot*   (Ritual Purity)   267

Preface

The purpose of this brief selection of Mishnaic material is to present to serious readers some interesting and relevant passages with a straightforward, traditional commentary. The hope is that it will illustrate the role of this classic in the evolution of *Halakhah* *— Jewish law—and of Judaism in general.

The volume is intended for the general public. No attempt has been made to deal with any of the scholarly problems related to the Mishnah.

The translation from the Hebrew is my own. It is not literal, though an effort has been made to retain the intent of the original Hebrew and to express it in modern English. It contains many words which are implicit in the Hebrew text but which require being made explicit in the English translation to facilitate comprehension. To avoid confusion with regard to certain words, I have adopted the following procedure: The word *Mishnah* (plural *Mishnayot*) is used to mean either one paragraph of the text or the entire Six Orders of the Mishnah. The word *Massekhet* is translated as "book," one of the sixty-odd divisions of the Mishnah text. The word *volume* is used in referring to this specific study collection of the Mishnah.

The criteria employed in the selection of material for this volume are as follows:

1. Some *Mishnayot* are basic to specific areas of Jewish law. For example, the details of tasks prohibited on the Sabbath have their genesis in the thirty-nine categories listed in the Mishnah. The

* The *kh* transliteration of Hebrew is pronounced like the *ch* in the German word *ach*.

Gemara and later literature expanded them further, but the thirty-nine have remained basic.

2. Some *Mishnayot* contain statements concerning ritual procedures still followed by Jews in general. The Passover *Seder* includes several paragraphs from the Mishnah, verbatim.

3. Some *Mishnayot* include examples of the hermeneutic rules by which the rabbis and scholars of Judaism used Biblical texts to reach conclusions in Jewish law. The Mishnah informs us, for example, how they determined that ten men constitute the proper quorum for collective worship.

4. Some *Mishnayot* contain historical material of great interest or value, even though the circumstances of Jewish practice may have changed; e.g., the operation of the Sanhedrin, aspects of cult in the ancient Temple, etc.

5. Some *Mishnayot* comprise Aggadic material of great philosophical, psychological, or even sermonic worth which remains useful to this day.

I am grateful for three kinds of assistance which have been essential. The first has been literary. The English translation has been prepared with two works constantly at hand: Herbert Danby's historic translation (Oxford, 1933) and the magnificent Soncino edition of the Babylonian Talmud. The commentary is dependent primarily on two traditional commentators on the Mishnah: R. Ovadya of Bertinora, Italy (c. 1450–c. 1510) and R. Yomtov Lipmann Heller (1579–1654).

The second relates to editorial aid. Dr. Eugene B. Borowitz read the first draft of this book; both his suggestions and encouragement have meant a great deal. Dr. Chaim Etrog read a later draft with great care; his corrections and recommendations have been of significant help.

In its final stages, the manuscript was carefully read by Dr. Louis L. Kaplan and Rabbi Chaim Pearl. Out of their erudition have come many invaluable suggestions.

The General Editor of the Jewish Heritage Classics series, Professor David Patterson of Oxford University, has graciously and good-humoredly carried on many months of transatlantic correspondence about the manuscript. Both style and content have benefited from his devotion.

Mrs. Lily Edelman, the Managing Editor, has had just the right combination of literary sensitivity, gentle stubbornness about pruning, and genial impatience to help a weary author produce a readable and completed book.

This whole project would never have gotten under way without Mrs. Vivian Mendeles' willingness patiently to put together, with scissors and staples, the Mishnah selections from which the first draft was prepared.

Just before the manuscript went to press, I was deeply saddened to learn of the death of Reb Aryeh Levine of Jerusalem. For many months Reb Aryeh had sat patiently with me and taught me details of Jewish law and practice. He was a true teacher in Israel, and his life shone day by day with his determination to live what he learned and taught. Reverently and gratefully this book is dedicated to his memory.

I would like to thank the Morris Adler Publications Fund of B'nai B'rith's Commission on Adult Jewish Education for making the Jewish Heritage Classics Series possible as a memorial to the late Rabbi Morris Adler, former Chairman of that Commission.

Introduction

What is Mishnah?

"Ḥevra Mishnayis. . . . Ḥevra Shass."

Generations of Jews have used these phrases daily.

The *Ḥevra Mishnayis* was a small group of men seated around a wooden table, a few candles dimly lighting the books of Mishnah on which they were concentrating. The rabbi sat with them, reading and explaining the text, chanting each word. The men listened, asking questions, raising objections, swaying and nodding agreement or shrugging dissent with pursed lips and tugs at their beards. They clinched their arguments with a swinging thumb.

The *Ḥevra Mishnayis* could be found in every synagogue, in every village, town, and city where enough Jews lived to form a community. And their text was always the Mishnah (literally, "teaching" or "repetition"), the general name for the first great compilation of Oral Law.

The *Ḥevra Shass* comprised a similar group of men, seated at the same tables, studying with the same motions. Only the book was different. The text was not a *Mishnayis* book; it was a Gemara, a commentary on and further elaboration of the Mishnah.

Between the afternoon and evening services each day, and on Saturday afternoons, the men would sit and study together as a group, as a *Ḥevra*. They were not scholars but simple men—shopkeepers and laborers, wagon-drivers and craftsmen. And like all men, they had their dreams. Of course, they dreamed of being wise like Solomon, and, even more important, of becoming famous in the Jewish world for some ingenious new interpretation of passages in either the Mishnah or the Gemara.

In the meantime, they eked out a meager living, raising large families and making sure that each of their sons received a good education in Bible, Mishnah, and Gemara. Their joy was great if those sons, at the age of thirteen or fourteen, were able to go away to one of the great *yeshivot,* or Talmud academies, there to become scholars, perhaps even rabbis! For their daughters, the supreme achievement was to be married off to promising students, boys who might one day become rabbis in Israel. As for the men themselves, they sat studying on those hard benches during much of their leisure time. Whether for an hour after a long day's work, or two hours on Saturday afternoon, they sat and "learned" sections of the Talmud, the Mishnah, and the Gemara.

The custom remains, though the setting has changed. The towns have given way to metropolitan centers; the small, bare rooms have been replaced by great synagogues, colleges, universities; the students have become professional men, leaders of government, business tycoons, writers, and thinkers; the teachers have been transformed into sophisticated professional rabbis with Ph.D. degrees. But for some Jews, at least, there still exists the joy of studying, on a Saturday afternoon, a *perek Mishnayis,* a chapter of the Mishnah, or a *blatt Gemora,* a page of the Gemara. In every country where Jews live, in every community where they engage in any serious study of Judaism, Mishnah and Gemara remain the central pillars in the lifelong education of the Jew.

Why Mishnah and Gemara? Why Talmud? What magic lies hidden in those words? What has given those books their central place in the educational, cultural, and religious life of Jewry for more than fifteen hundred years?

The Mishnah (popularly known as *Mishnayis*) is a collection of Jewish legal material. Compiled in Palestine between 160 C.E. * and 200 C.E., it is arranged into six major Orders (*Seder,* plural *Sedarim*). Hence the Hebrew *Shishah Sedarim* (Six Orders) or

* Common Era.

Shass (which is also used as a familiar abbreviation for the Talmud).

The Six Orders are as follows:

1. *Zera'im* ("Seeds"), dealing with the laws of agriculture. The first book of this Seder, however, is called *Berakhot* (literally, "praises" or "blessings") and deals with prayers.

2. *Mo'ed* ("Appointed Time"), dealing with the laws of the Sabbath and the Festivals.

3. *Nashim* ("Women"), dealing with the laws pertaining to marriage, divorce, and family relationships.

4. *Nezikin* ("Damages"), dealing with civil and criminal statutes and court procedures.

5. *Kodashim* ("Sacred Matters"), dealing with laws of sacrifice and the Temple cult.

6. *Tohorot* ("Purities"), dealing with laws of ritual uncleanliness.

The Mishnah is a selective compilation. The men (*Tanna'im*) who compiled it did not utilize all the information available to them. As soon as its text became available, scholars began to discuss it critically. They would quote teachers or sages whose statements on a given subject had been omitted from the Mishnah. Such a statement was called a *Baraita* (plural *Baraitot*), and it was accorded due respect. Some collections of *Baraitot* were written down and called *Tosefta* ("additions" or "supplements").

By these and other techniques, succeeding generations of scholars, or *Amora'im,* subjected the Mishnah text to searching criticism, commentary, and supplementation. New situations gave rise to new ideas, and spirited discussions took place in the academies of Palestine and Babylon. The rabbis sought truth: they strove to know what God *really* told His people at Mount Sinai, and explored every possible implication of the written Torah. In part, their quest was practical; they had decisions to make as judges. In addition, they had to teach Torah to the people. For some, the ongoing search was mystical; they probed the inner secret meanings of God's revelation. Finally, their quest became involved with the concept of *Torah Lishma*—Torah for its own sake, study for the love of study and the deepening of the intellect.

Ultimately, two collections of these widely varied, richly colored responses to the Mishnah text were written down. One, the shorter, was compiled in Palestine toward the end of the fourth century C.E. It is known as the Palestine or Jerusalem Gemara. The longer, and by far the more important, was compiled in Babylon a century later, and is known as the Babylonian Gemara. The Mishnah and the Gemara commentaries together constitute the two Talmuds, the Palestinian and the Babylonian.

The first and shorter part, the simpler part of the Talmud—the Mishnah—is our principal concern in this book. In order to ascertain its central role in Jewish teaching, a brief review of the concepts on which Judaism rests is in order.

Judaism begins with God and the covenant. The date, place, and circumstances of its beginning are unclear because more than one covenant situation is mentioned in the Bible.

God entered into a covenant with Noah. Whether or not Noah lived as an historic personage or whether there are one or two covenant descriptions in Genesis (Chapters 8 and 9) are irrelevant here. What is important is that Jews firmly believed that God entered into a covenant with Noah, as we learn from the Bible.

God also entered into a covenant with Abraham, with Isaac, and with Jacob. It is clear that Jews believed that these personages were the patriarchs of their people and that God entered into a covenant with each of the three in turn.

Then God entered into a covenant relationship with the entire Jewish people. At Mount Sinai He covenanted with that people, present and future. Down through the centuries, the Jewish people have considered themselves a covenant people, in sacred relationship to God. It dates that covenant from Mount Sinai. It has groped and struggled to determine the precise content of the covenant. It has dedicated its corporate existence to fulfilling the covenant both in its collective expressions and in the lives of its individual members. Indeed, the purpose of Israel as a people and of Jews as individuals is fulfillment of covenant.

The covenant is Judaism's answer to the question of life's purpose. Each person must try to develop himself to the utmost as a partner of the living God in fulfillment of the covenant. Every Jew lives within the fold of the Jewish people, which functions collectively for the same covenantal purpose. The ultimate aim of the covenant, and consequently of the life work of the individual Jew and the Jewish people, is the creation of the universal kingdom of God on earth, the perfect human society.

The content of the covenant is therefore of supreme importance in Judaism, and the determination of that content the most complex problem a serious Jew faces. For it requires the impossible: a sure knowledge of the divine will. What did God say at Mount Sinai? What did He reveal as His will? What did He require of His covenant people? Jewish thinking has devoted itself to such questions over the centuries.

Torah is a core word in Judaism. It is the totality of God's instructions to His people, the totality of the covenant's content. In a real sense, Torah means revelation, but it must be thought of in three separate ways.

First, we speak of *The* Torah. This is the first writing down of Torah, a specific literary work, comprising the Five Books of Moses: Genesis, Exodus, Leviticus, Numbers, Deuteronomy. The Pentateuch is the literary foundation for all subsequent activity by which Jews have attempted to ascertain the content of the covenant. It is viewed differently by different groups of Jewish thinkers, but its centrality as a source of Judaism is beyond question.

Second, Torah is the process by which Jewish thinkers have tried to determine the specific commands of God at Mount Sinai. They continue to believe that the Sinaitic revelation was not recorded in its entirety (some would say it was not completed at that time and place). Over the subsequent centuries, procedures evolved by which the additional commandments of God could be discovered in the text. These procedures have been incorporated as a vital aspect of Torah.

Third, the decisions made by individuals and schools of thought were ultimately written down in a voluminous literature of wide scope and diversity. This literature too is Torah.

As Judaism developed out of the experiences of the Jewish people, Torah took two forms, *Aggadah* and *Halakhah*. Aggadah (an Aramaic word similar to the Hebrew *Haggadah,* from a root which means "tell" or "talk about") consists of interpretations of Biblical passages in story form, sermons, folklore, theology, speculative inquiry of all sorts. It subsequently expanded to include all such interpretive thinking, even that not based on Biblical sources. Aggadah has never been "official" or dogmatized, and interpretations vary widely. It warmed the heart of the Jew even as it sharpened his intellect, bringing him closer to God and the covenant. It added emotional depth and intensity to his search for God's law. It gave compelling force to his determination to live God's way.

Halakhah, the other form of Torah, is derived from the Hebrew root meaning "walk," meaning the way to go, the things to do, Jewish law. Essentially, Judaism is a system of law as it evolved from the written Torah to the action required of Jews today. Every act of every Jew in every generation can be characterized, at least in theory, as an act of obedience to God's command, or of disobedience to the divine law as revealed by way of Torah. Every act is either a *mitzvah* ("obedience") or an *averah* ("disobedience").

In each generation, scholars have studied intensively the heritage of Aggadah and Halakhah. They have used systematic rules to provide answers to new problems which have arisen, and to expand the heritage further through their own insights and speculations. Great religious authority adheres to the major literary works of the heritage. In the Orthodox Jewish tradition, this authority is derived directly, in an unbroken line, from Mount Sinai. For the non-Orthodox, authority is less clearly defined.

The Orthodox position found its first written expression in *Pirke Avot* (*Ethics of the Fathers*), a short collection of rabbinic maxims and proverbs composed by the same generations of scholars who created the Mishnah. *Pirke Avot* is appended to the Fourth Order of the Mishnah, and begins: "Moses received Torah from Sinai and transmitted it to Joshua; and Joshua to the Elders; and the Elders to the Prophets; and the Prophets transmitted it to the Men of the Great Assembly. . . ." The text continues by informing us that authoritative Torah was then transmitted to Simeon the Righteous, and then to a series of pairs of scholars, each pair presumably consisting of the president (*Nasi*) of the Sanhedrin, the Great Court at Jerusalem, and his deputy (*Av Bet Din*). According to tradition, the Sanhedrin was the authentic interpreter of Torah.

Thus, tradition has it, there was a divinely determined chain of authority for the transmission of the knowledge of God's will to His covenant people, as well as for the correct manner of interpreting Torah in order to learn more of Torah. Eventually both institutions and a literature arose to direct the process and guide the continuing quest for authentic Torah. The institutions, the literature, and the great teachers were granted authority by the Jewish community.

Jewish scholars, Orthodox and non-Orthodox alike, are aware that the history of Halakhah is complicated. The complications begin within the text of the written Torah. Many scholars believe that the Torah's text was transmitted orally and written down over a period of seven centuries or more, and that it contains within itself evolutionary steps and changes in Halakhah. These scholars maintain that the text of the written Torah, as transmitted to us, was probably fixed about the time of Ezra, during the third quarter of the fifth century B.C.E.*

The prophetic books of the Bible, and the miscellaneous writings which constitute the third section of the Bible, contain little material pertaining to Halakhah. Some narrative sections of these books reflect the mores and customs of contemporary society; but in subsequent centuries, Halakhic decisions were not based on this material.

As soon as the Jewish people settled down after the first Babylonian exile (which ended officially in 538 B.C.E., although maximum resettlement in Palestine took another century to be completed), they used scholars and scribes to make decisions in cases which arose in their communities and were not covered directly in Torah law. This process continued uninterrupted for five centuries, coupled with regular study of Torah in the local synagogues of Palestine and the expanding Diaspora. The decisions of the scholars were transmitted orally from generation to generation, and served as precedents for the growing corpus of Halakhah.

* Before the Common Era.

The overall approach to the oral interpretation of the written Torah was called *Midrash* (from the Hebrew *darash*, "to interpret"). Both Aggadic Midrash and Halakhic Midrash were collected and written down during the last two pre-Christian centuries and the first century of the Common Era. The major collections of Halakhic Midrash which have come down to us are: *Mekhilta*, a Halakhic interpretation of Exodus; the *Sifra*, interpreting Leviticus; and the *Sifre*, on Numbers and Deuteronomy. There is no Halakhic Midrash collection on Genesis because the first book of the Torah contains very little such material.

By the time the Temple was destroyed in 70 C.E., the body of Halakhic discussion and decision was enormous. Most of it had not been written down. But there was great anxiety among the scholars and sages about the future of Judaism. The majority of Jews had been living outside Palestine for some generations. They had been kept faithful to Judaism by their continuous contacts with the Temple and with the Sanhedrin. Now, even though the latter continued to function at the Yavneh Academy established by Joḥanan ben Zakkai, there was a deep anxiety that all the precedents might not be accurately remembered, and new decisions might be made in faraway places which might distort the intent of God and violate the covenant. The historic response of the scholars was to begin to write down post-Biblical Halakhah in systematic form.

Several collections were apparently undertaken. We know of one by Rabbi Akiba and one by his pupil, Rabbi Meir. Then the Nasi (Sanhedrin president) Rabbi Judah decided to compile an authoritative and "complete" corpus of Halakhah. A group of scholars set to work on the task, which continued for many years. Though we do not know exactly when they began or finished, it can be said with some certainty that the finished work—the Mishnah—was completed before 200 C.E. There is some disagreement among scholars about the exact form of the final work— whether it was actually written or merely organized orally for systematic consideration by scholars in Palestine and Babylon, the two centers of Jewish learning at that time.

Next to the Bible, the Talmud is undoubtedly the most important literary work in the history of Judaism. The entire structure of Halakhah, which kept Judaism alive over the centuries in all the countries of the dispersion, grew directly from the text of the Talmud—thousands of commentaries, elaborations, systematic collections, codes, questions and answers, scholarly probings of all kinds, which are still being written in our day. If the written Torah is the wellspring of Jewish law, then the Talmud must be considered its most vital reservoir.

It would be inaccurate to convey the impression that the Talmud has been universally accepted since its completion more than fourteen hundred years ago. Even before the writing down of either the Mishnah or the Gemara, groups of Jews had rebelled against the whole idea of oral Torah. (In fact, one group, the Samaritans, rebelled against the written Torah itself, refusing to accept many of its fundamentals in the fifth pre-Christian century and leaving Judaism at that time.) The entire complex Sadducean schism was expressed chiefly in the refusal of the Sadducees to accept any Halakhah except the written Torah. Centuries later, in Babylon, beginning about 760 c.e., the Karaites refused to accept the concept of oral Torah. Certainly the history of Reform Judaism reflects a similar refusal to accept the authority of the Talmud and of the *Shulḥan Arukh* (the sixteenth-century code of Halakhic decisions which has become authoritative in Orthodox Judaism). Conservative Judaism too, while affirming the authority of the Talmud, has been proposing changes in Jewish practice contrary to Halakhah.

The questions asked by students of Mishnah and Gemara are different today. They reflect the new science, the new humanities, the new social sciences, the new philosophies of our time. They reflect, too, the new Jews—the emancipated, sophisticated, free Jews of the second half of the twentieth century in Israel, and in America and elsewhere in the Diaspora. The vocabulary and the emphases are different. The needs too are different, except for the fundamental need, the one which animates the whole process: the need for Jews to know what constitutes a mitzvah and what God requires of man. What must man do as His partner in fulfilling the covenant? Answers to these questions must be sought within the framework of values related to the history of Judaism and the literary heritage of the Jewish people. To the extent that Jews make decisions in ignorance of the literary sources of Judaism and especially of Halakhah, the heritage is distorted and the covenant denied. Through study, and only through study of Torah in its broadest sense, can Jews understand the nature of the covenant and the meaning of Jewish existence.

That is why those men, generation after generation, sat at those simple wooden tables in villages, towns, and cities from Spain to China, from Estonia in the north to Yemen in the south and from the United States to the land of Israel. And wherever they are still permitted to do so, many Jews continue to drink from the endlessly deep, ever-sweet waters of the Mishnah and the Gemara, and feel themselves closer to God and more determined to live their lives in accordance with His will.

The First Order

ZERA'IM

Seeds: The Laws of Agriculture

INTRODUCTION

Zera'im was made the First Order, according to Maimonides, because food is the first essential to living; therefore, laws concerning its production and use should stand at the beginning of the Mishnah. To express our gratitude to the Creator for these gifts, the one non-agricultural tractate which opens this order is *Berakhot*—"Benedictions and Prayers."

The agricultural laws set forth are applicable only to the Land of Israel; Syria is included because much of that country was conquered by King David. There is no Gemara in the Babylonian Talmud to the ten agricultural tractates because these laws did not apply in Babylon. There is, however, a Palestinian Gemara to every book in this Order.

Zera'im is permeated with one profoundly spiritual note: the Land of Israel is like no other land, its soil is no ordinary soil, farming there is not like farming elsewhere. For not only does God own the land, with the Israelites as His "sharecropping" partners; God Himself lives there in a mystical sense. Long after God's universality was accepted as basic teaching, Jews continued to feel His presence in a special way in His special land.

BERAKHOT—BLESSINGS

Introduction

Berakhot means "praises" or "blessings." Because so many Jewish prayers begin and/or end with the phrase: *"Barukh attah adonay,* Praised be Thou, O Lord," the book of the Mishnah dealing with prayer is called *Berakhot*.

Private and public prayer have great merit in the hierarchy of *mitzvot* in Judaism. The origins of this form of communication with God are lost in the mists of antiquity. There are occasional prayers in the Torah, but there seems to have been little *organized* public prayer before the destruction of the First Temple in 586 B.C.E. Public fasts with prayer were known to have taken place in times of great national danger, but regular public prayers unrelated to Temple sacrifice went unrecorded, if they occurred at all.

Pious tradition ascribes two different origins to Jewish liturgy. In the Gemara (*Berakhot* 26b), we are told the Patriarchs composed the three daily services: Abraham the *Shaḥarit* ("morning"); Isaac the *Minḥah* ("afternoon"); and Jacob the *Ma'ariv* ("evening").

Other early sources tell us that the prayer services were originated to replace animal sacrifice during the Babylonian Exile (586–538 B.C.E.). This is questionable. Though an intimate connection between the daily sacrifices in the Temple and the time of daily prayers did develop later, there is evidence that some blessings predated the Exile and that prayer developed more fully in local synagogues in Palestine at the time when animal sacrifice was taking place at the central shrine in Jerusalem. The Second Temple apparently had a synagogue in which daily prayers were conducted.

The only clear Biblical statement about set daily prayer occurs in Daniel (6:11), the last of the books of the Bible to be written, probably at the beginning of the second century B.C.E. The passage reads:

> And when Daniel knew that the writing was signed, he went into his house—now his windows were open in his upper chamber toward Jerusalem—and he kneeled upon his knees three times a day and prayed, and gave thanks before his God, as he did aforetime.

Several details of importance are to be noted. Prayer in the direction of Jerusalem was already traditional. Praying three times a day was not new with Daniel or his generation ("as he did aforetime"). In addition, there is a clear statement of the origin of the word *berakhah.* Daniel knelt—*barekh al birkhhee*—and he prayed. Praise to God was expressed while kneeling, and the word *barekh*—"kneel"—became the word for blessing, the brief prayer thanking God for the opportunity to perform a specific mitzvah.

Two English words have been used in translating *berakhah.* That man can praise God is clear; but can man bless God? In the traditional Priestly Blessing, did the priests in fact bless the people or did they invoke God's blessing? The word *berakhah* has been consistently translated as "blessing" because no other abstract English noun is suitable. But *barukh* is translated as "praised."

Berakhot deals with three major areas of prayer: the Shema and its accompanying blessings; public prayer in general—the time of the service, the content of the liturgy, the attitude of the worshipper, and, finally, the blessings to be said before eating specific foods and at the close of a meal.

It was necessary to begin with *Berakhot,* wrote Maimonides in his Mishnah commentary, for the same reason that a doctor prescribing for his patient will begin with rules of diet. Man's eating arrangements are fundamental. And before one can eat, one must say a word of praise and thanks to God. Having decided that blessings connected with eating should be discussed in the Mishnah before the laws about growing the food itself, it was logical to include all blessings together. Since so many Jewish prayers involve blessings, it was logical for all prayer laws to be grouped together. The result: *Berakhot.*

But why begin the book with the Shema? asked Maimonides. His answer: It is the only mitzvah regularly required each day at a set time. Therefore, it should be discussed at the very beginning. Maimonides was not concerned with those modern views that see the Shema as the core prayer of the Jewish faith, the "watchword of Judaism," or its "credo." He properly took a logical Halakhic view.

Biblical Sources for Berakhot

Hear, O Israel! The Lord is our God, the Lord alone. You must love the Lord your God with all your heart and with all your soul and with all your might. Take to heart these words with which I charge you this day. Impress them upon your children. Recite them when you stay at home and when you are away, when you lie down and when you get up. Bind them as a sign on your hand and let them serve as a symbol on your forehead, inscribe them on the doorposts of your house and on your gates. (Deuteronomy 6:4–9)

SEE ALSO

> Deuteronomy 8:10, 11:18–20
> Psalms 55:18
> Daniel 6:11

Berakhot 1:1

What is the earliest time in the evening that the Shema [1] may be recited? From the time the priests [2] enter their living quarters to eat the heave-offering [3] until the end of the first watch.[4] This is the opinion of R. Eliezer. But the Sages say: until midnight. Rabban Gamaliel says: until dawn. His sons once returned after midnight from a feast. They said: We have not yet recited the evening Shema. He said: If the dawn has not yet risen, you are required to recite it. Moreover, wherever the Sages prescribe "until midnight," the duty lasts until dawn. Why then did the Sages say: until midnight? To keep a man far from transgressing.[5]

---

1. The Torah requirement to recite the Shema each evening and morning is found in Deuteronomy 6:4 ff. Commentators agree that, from early times, the Shema, the *Ve'ahavta* (Deuteronomy 6:5–9), and Deuteronomy 11:13–21 were recited together twice daily. After the destruction of the Temple in 70 C.E., the Rabbis discussed other

possible times for the recitation of the Shema; e.g., when taking out the Torah.

2. After being purified by bathing, priests who were ritually defiled had to wait until evening to re-enter the Temple area. See Leviticus 22:7.

3. There are many Biblical sources for the laws of the heave-offering: Numbers 18:8–11; 8:19; Leviticus 7:30, 34, 8:27–29, 9:21, 10:14–15, 14:12, 23:9–12, 23:20.

4. The night was considered to be twelve hours in length, and was divided into three watches of four hours each.

5. It is a fundamental principle of rabbinical law to protect people from the non-performance of a mitzvah which has a time limit by virtue of the human habit to delay. This principle is part of the larger concept of "building a fence around the Torah" (*Avot* 1:1).

Berakhot 1:5

The story of the Exodus from Egypt is recited at night.[1] R. Eleazar b. Azariah said: I am as [2] one seventy years old, yet I could not prove why the Exodus should be recited at night, until Ben Zoma explained it: It is written, "that you may remember the day when you came forth out of the land of Egypt all the days of your life." The "days of your life" means the days only; but *all* the days of your life" means the night as well. The Sages say: "The days of your life" means this world only, but *all* the days of your life" includes the days of the Messiah.[3]

---

1. This statement stems from the fact that the third paragraph following the Shema and considered an integral part of it mentions the Exodus (Numbers 15:37–41).

2. Why "as" one seventy? Tradition tells us that Eleazar b. Azariah was a very young man (some say eighteen) when he was elected Nasi, president of the Sanhedrin. Overnight, his hair and beard are said to have turned gray, giving him the appearance of an elder. Respect for age is deep-seated in Judaism.

3. This entire paragraph is part of the traditional Haggadah read at the Passover Seder. Though the Mishnah is primarily concerned with

Halakhah, the laws of conduct, no Jewish text can ignore theology, philosophy, and folklore (Aggadah). The interpretations of the Biblical text in this paragraph are entirely in the realm of Aggadah.

Berakhot 2:1

If a man was reading the verses of the Shema in the Torah for purposes of study and the time came to recite the Shema, if he directed his heart [1] he has fulfilled the mitzvah; otherwise, he has not fulfilled it. Between the paragraphs of the three which follow the Shema itself he may salute a man and return a greeting out of respect.[2] But in the middle of a paragraph he may salute a man and return his greeting only out of fear of him. This is the opinion of R. Meir. R. Judah says: In the middle he may salute a man out of fear and return a greeting out of respect; between the paragraphs he may salute a man out of respect and return the greeting of any man.[3]

---

1. Is it enough to fulfill a mitzvah unconsciously or by accident? The Rabbis were divided. The statement here reflects the majority view that consciousness of the mitzvah to be performed, concentration, and dedication of self are essential in fulfilling a mitzvah between man and God. Only occasionally did a rabbi express a view akin to the concept of Roman Catholicism: *ex operare operate,* sacraments are of grace automatically when they are properly performed, regardless of intent. The Rabbis held overwhelmingly, however, that in mitzvot between a man and his fellow man, the action itself is important. According to tradition, if such a mitzvah is performed with concentration, it counts as two mitzvot.
2. Respect is due one's father or teacher, a rabbi, a great scholar, etc. Fear is due to one who might cause harm if he does not receive a proper greeting: e.g., a nobleman or other politically powerful person.
3. Several mitzvot are in conflict here, and the Mishnah must establish a pyramid of values. When does concentration on prayer as a mitzvah get overbalanced by courtesy and respect, or by self-preservation, which are also mitzvot? The Rabbis are not in agreement, but all treat the subject seriously.

Berakhot 2:3

If a man recites the Shema so softly that he himself cannot hear, he has nevertheless fulfilled the mitzvah. R. Jose says: He has not fulfilled it.[1] If he recites it without pronouncing the words distinctly, R. Jose says he has fulfilled the mitzvah; R. Judah says he has not.[2] If a man recites the paragraphs in wrong order, he has not fulfilled the mitzvah. If he recites it and makes a mistake, he must go back and recite it again.[3]

---

1. R. Jose's view was not accepted as law. The Gemara (*Berakhot* 15a) gives another interpretation: Vocalizing is not essential, comprehension is. If he said the Shema in any language he could "hear," i.e., understand, he has fulfilled the mitzvah. This is one of many Talmudic statements accepting prayer as valid in any language, not just in Hebrew.
2. R. Jose's view was accepted as law. In both situations, the liberal tendency was accepted.
3. Both the Gemara and the commentators concerned themselves in great detail with this paragraph. It was not enough to pray, even with concentration. The right prayers have to be said, clearly and completely. The liturgy was more than a guide to help the Jew fulfill the mitzvah of prayer. The liturgy itself became a mitzvah. This concept is connected with the idea of the corporate Jewish group and the values to be found in corporate Jewish prayer.

Berakhot 2:4

Craftsmen may recite the Shema on the top of a tree or on top of a stone wall, which they may not do when they say the *Tefillah*.[1]

---

1. The *Tefillah* (*"the* prayer") is the *Amidah*, the traditional petitions said silently while standing (*Amidah* means "standing up"). They are also known as the *Shemoneh Esray*, the Eighteen Blessings, formerly the number in the traditional daily morning service. Because the *Tefillah* contains the major petitionary prayers of the lit-

urgy and is the core of the whole service, it requires even more concentration than the Shema itself. Therefore, it cannot be said properly in a dangerous position, while the Shema can be.

Berakhot 2:5

A bridegroom is exempt from the mitzvah of reciting the Shema on the first night of the marriage [1] or until the end of the next Sabbath if he has not consummated the marriage before then.[2] When Rabban Gamaliel married, he recited the Shema the first night. His disciples said, when they learned of this: Master, didn't you teach us that a bridegroom is exempt from reciting the Shema on the first night? He said: I will not listen to you to cast off the yoke of the Kingdom of Heaven even for one hour.[3]

---

1. Only if his bride is a virgin. Their intercourse is a mitzvah and requires his full concentration. In addition, the groom must concentrate his attention after intercourse on determining whether or not his bride was a virgin. R. Yomtov Lipmann Heller added the more romantic view that the groom must concentrate all his attention on lovemaking to be tender with his inexperienced bride if she is a virgin, and to comfort her if he discovers that she is not, since she then faces an ordeal of automatic divorce and disgrace.
2. A total of four nights, since virgins were traditionally married on Wednesday.
3. The attitude of Rabban Gamaliel is quoted not as exemplary but as unusually zealous. Jewish law generally takes the view that marriage and its joys are of unparalleled importance.

Berakhot 3:3

Women,[1] slaves,[2] and minors [3] are exempt from reciting the Shema and from putting on phylacteries. But they are obliged to say the Tefillah,[4] to perform the mitzvot of affixing and kissing a mezuzah,[5] and to say the blessings after meals.[6]

---

1. Women are exempt from the Shema and many other mitzvot which have a time limit upon their performance. This exemption is based

upon the constancy and unpredictability of their household and motherly duties and was never intended to be a demeaning of the status or role of women.

2. This refers to non-Jewish slaves only. They are expected to obey only the seven Noahidic laws.

3. Minors are exempt from all positive commandments. Minors include boys up to the age of thirteen, and girls up to twelve-and-a-half, a rabbinical generalization regarding the time of puberty.

4. Again we see the emphasis on the importance of the petitionary prayers. No one can be exempt from prayers for forgiveness, health, peace, etc.

5. One might think women should be exempt from the duty of affixing a mezuzah to a doorpost and kissing it when entering or leaving the house, since, as Bertinora reminds us, this mitzvah is closely related to that of Talmud Torah, or study, from which women are exempt. But since the mitzvot of mezuzah have no time limits, women must obey them. (Study does have a time limit; it is required day and night!)

6. Because this mitzvah is a specific Torah injunction and there is no clause limiting its applicability to men. "You shall eat, be satisfied, and praise the Lord your God" (Deuteronomy 8:10).

Berakhot 5:1

One stands up to say the *Tefillah* only in a serious mood. Zealous men used to wait an hour before they said the *Tefillah,* so that they might direct their hearts toward God.[1] Even if the king greets a man during the *Tefillah* he may not return the greeting.[2] Even if a snake was twisted around his heel, he may not interrupt it.[3]

---

1. They waited an hour after entering the synagogue "to rid their hearts of their business affairs" (Albek).

2. Compare *Berakhot* 2:1 (p. 34), where we learned that the Shema can be interrupted to return a greeting. Without doubt, the Rabbis considered the *Tefillah* the core of the liturgy. Incidentally, Bertinora adds that only a Jewish king can be ignored. A non-Jewish king must be greeted, interrupting even the *Tefillah,* lest he be insulted and kill the worshipper.

3. The commentators correctly add: only if he was sure the snake was

not one poisonous to men. In the latter case, he interrupted his prayers, as he did if a scorpion or other dangerous insect came near him.

Berakhot 6:1

What blessing is said before eating fruits? [1] Over the fruit of trees, one says: Praised be Thou . . . who creates the fruit of the tree. Wine is the exception. Over wine, a man says: . . . who creates the fruit of the vine. Over the fruits of the earth, one says: . . . who creates the fruit of the ground. Bread is the exception. Over bread, one says: . . . who brings forth bread from the earth.[2] Over vegetables, one says: . . . who creates the fruit of the ground. R. Judah says: . . . who creates various kinds of herbs.[3]

---

1. It is forbidden to enjoy the earth or its produce without praising God, its Creator. The laws are derived from Psalms 24:1.
2. Bread and wine are so important to man that they merit special blessings.
3. R. Judah's view was not accepted as law.

Berakhot 6:4

When a man is about to eat many different varieties of food, R. Judah says: If one of the seven kinds [1] is among them, he must say the blessing over that one. But the Sages say: He may say the blessing over whichever one he wishes.

---

1. The seven food products for which ancient Israel was praised: wheat, barley, grapes, figs, pomegranates, olives, and dates (see Deuteronomy 8:8). The honey referred to in the Biblical verse was made from dates. The view of the Sages was accepted as law.

Berakhot 7:2

Women or non-Hebrew slaves or minors may not be included in counting the necessary number [1] for the blessings after the meal.[2] How much must one eat to be included in the group? An olive's bulk. R. Judah says: an egg's bulk.[3]

---

1. The first paragraph of Chapter 7, not included here, indicates that when three or more persons eat together the blessings after the meal are said corporately. In all Jewish worship, though individual prayer is certainly a mitzvah, there is extra merit in corporate prayer.
2. Bertinora takes the opportunity here to discuss various rabbinical definitions of a minor. There are three:

    a. Thirteen years of age for a boy, twelve-and-a-half for a girl. The Bar Mitzvah ceremony as we know it postdated the Talmud by nearly ten centuries, but the rabbinic teaching about the age of moral and ritual responsibility was so clear that the thirteenth year was the obvious time for the Bar Mitzvah ceremony.

    b. Individual pubescence: in the words of the Sages, "when two genital hairs appear."

    c. When the child understands "whom one praises" when one says a blessing; that is, when he is old enough to understand an abstract concept like God as the Source of all blessings.
3. R. Judah's view was not accepted as law.

Berakhot 8:1

With regard to a meal, the schools of Shammai and Hillel differ: [1] The school of Shammai says that on a Sabbath or a festival day one says the blessing first over the day [2] and then over the wine.[3] The school of Hillel says that one says the blessing first over the wine and then over the day.[4]

---

1. These differences of opinion continue throughout Chapter 8.
2. The blessing which ends: . . . who sanctifies the Sabbath or Israel and the Festivals.

3. Because the day is the reason behind saying the Kiddush.
4. Because the wine is the agent of sanctification, and until the blessing over it is said the day is not sanctified and requires no special blessing. In all the disputes in this chapter, the view of the school of Hillel was accepted as law.

Berakhot 8:5

The school of Shammai says: The order in which the blessings are said at the end of Sabbath is the lamp, the food, the spices, and the Havdalah.[1] The school of Hillel says: the lamp, the spices, the food, and the Havdalah. The school of Shammai says: The blessing over the lamp reads . . . who did create the light of fire. The school of Hillel says: . . . who creates the lights of fire.[2]

---

1. The order of the blessings after the final Sabbath meal is in dispute. Havdalah, the ritual for ending the Sabbath, is said directly after the third traditional Sabbath meal. The school of Hillel felt— and this became law—that the two blessings over the candle and the spices belonged together, their intent being directed toward the ritual ending of the Sabbath, and both being short. The longer *Birkat Hamazon* ("blessing after meals") can then be said in gratitude for the third festive meal of the Sabbath; then the Sabbath can be concluded with the Havdalah blessing.
2. There is an important theological difference between Shammai and Hillel here. Shammai believed that the word *created* in the prayers refers only to the original creation of the world; therefore, he used the past tense and the singular. Hillel took the view that God's creativity is active and constant. Jewish thinkers generally agree with Hillel.

Berakhot 9:3

If a man builds a house or buys new vessels [pots, pans, dishes], he should say: Praised be He who has given us life.[1] A man should praise God for a misfortune regardless of any consequent good, and for good fortune regardless of any consequent evil.[2] If a man cries out to God over what is past, his prayer is vain. Thus if his wife is pregnant and he says: May it be Thy will that my wife should have a boy, this prayer is vain. If he is returning from a journey, hears sounds of lamentation in the city, and says: May it be Thy will that they who lament be not of my house, this prayer is vain.

---

1. An abbreviation for the full blessing . . . who has given us life and sustained us and brought us to this season.
2. The Gemara takes this position and cites examples. Albek cites a valuable suggestion from the commentators: If something evil occurs, one should not say a prayer for good tidings in order to coerce God into causing good to arise from the evil. When something good happens, one should not say the blessing for an evil tiding in fear that evil may yet result. These would be vain prayers.

PE'AH—EDGE OF THE FIELD

Introduction

Though this book, Pe'ah (edge or corner of the field), names one means of providing food for the poor, it deals with all such procedures. Five were listed in the Torah: Pe'ah, gleanings, forgotten sheaves, forgotten clusters of grapes, and the poor tithe, paid instead of the second tithe in the third and sixth years of the seven-year cycle (see p. 61 f.).

Theoretically, Pe'ah had to be given only on grain products. But the Rabbis extended it to include grapes and the fruit of trees, as they did with gleanings.

The word Pe'ah is known to contemporary Jews because of its plural, Pe'ot, the ritual locks of uncut hair worn over the ears by some traditionalist Jews.

Biblical Sources for Pe'ah

When you reap the harvest of your land, you shall not reap all the way to the edges of your field, or gather the gleanings of your harvest. You shall not pick your vineyard bare, or gather the fallen fruit of your vineyard; you shall leave them for the poor and the stranger: I the Lord am your God. (Leviticus 19:9–10)

SEE ALSO

> Leviticus 23:22
> Deuteronomy 14:28–29, 24:19–22, 26:12

Pe'ah 1:1

For these things no limited quantities are prescribed: [1] *Pe'ah,*[2] first fruits,[3] the Festival offering,[4] deeds of loving-kindness, and the study of Torah. These are things whose fruits a man enjoys in this world while the capital is saved for him in the world-to-come: honoring father and mother, deeds of loving-kindness, making peace between a man and his fellow; and the study of Torah is equal to all of them combined.[5]

---

1. And the more of them that are done the better, in terms of mitzvah. The verse refers to Torah commandments. As we shall see in the next Mishnah, the Rabbis did, in fact, prescribe minimum limits in some cases.
2. See Leviticus 19:9 and 23:22. The size of the *Pe'ah,* the corner of the field to be left for the poor, is not specified: the bigger the better.
3. See Deuteronomy 26:1 ff. The amount of the *Bikkurim,* or first fruits, is not specified. On the Festival of Shavuot the individual brought as much as he liked to the priests at the Temple in Jerusalem.
4. Sacrifices were brought by the pilgrims who went up to Jerusalem on Pesaḥ, Shavuot, and Sukkot, in fulfillment of the commandment:

"And they shall not face the Lord empty-handed" (Deuteronomy 16:16–17). The number of sacrifices varied according to the individual's wealth and willingness to give.

5. Each of these religious principles is supported by specific Biblical commands:
    1. Honoring parents: Exodus 20:12 and Deuteronomy 5:16.
    2. Deeds of loving-kindness: Proverbs 21:21.
    3. Peacemaker: Zechariah 8:12 ff.
    4. Study of Torah: Proverbs 8:18 ff.

Pe'ah 1:2

Pe'ah should be no less than one-sixtieth of the harvest. And although it has been stated that no measure is prescribed for *Pe'ah* [1] it should always be given in accordance with the size of the field, the number of the poor, and the yield. [2]

---

1. This is a classic example of the rabbinic "fence around the Torah," in which Torah regulations are buttressed by rabbinic extension to ensure minimum compliance.
2. No procedure is established for determining these factors, except by the individual himself. In a relatively simple society with a small population, this was possible. Though our policy is more complex, the principle of religious responsibility for every Jew remains unchanged.

Pe'ah 2:6

R. Simeon of Mitzpah once sowed his field in this way [1] and came before Rabban Gamaliel. [2] They went up to the Chamber of Hewn Stone [3] to inquire. Nahum the Scribe said: I have received a tradition from R. Measha, who received it from his father, who received it from the *Zugot*, [4] who received it from the prophets as a Halakhah given to Moses at Sinai: [5] If a man sowed his field with two kinds of wheat and made them up into one threshing floor, he gives one *Pe'ah*. But if he set up two threshing floors, he must give two *Pe'ot*.

---

1. With two kinds of wheat. The previous Mishnah, not included here, indicated that all grain except wheat required a gift of two *Pe'ot* if two varieties were sown, then harvested simultaneously on the threshing floor. Wheat requires only one *Pe'ah* gift under such circumstances. Our Mishnah does not give a logical reason, but relies on that final authority: direct tradition going back to Moses.
2. Gamaliel the First, or the Elder. He was Nasi of the Sanhedrin in the first century c.e., and was either the son or grandson of Hillel. He is not to be confused with his grandson, Gamaliel II, Nasi of the Sanhedrin at Yavneh some decades later, who was temporarily deposed because of his authoritarian attitude.
3. The Sanhedrin met in this chamber, which was within the Temple precinct.
4. The "pairs," each a Nasi and *Av Bet Din* (president and vice-president) of the Sanhedrin. Their names are listed in order in *Avot*, Chapter 1.
5. This phrase is the ultimate legal authority in rabbinic literature. A rabbi who based a legal position thus was theoretically obligated to trace the tradition back to Moses, as was done in this Mishnah. In post-Talmudic rabbinic literature, the phrase was used less and less for new legal positions. In a real sense, however, all of Halakhah was revealed to Moses at Mount Sinai, for traditional Judaism, and this concept is basic to the authority of the Halakhic system.

Pe'ah 4:5

The poor may make three searches for *Pe'ah* each day,[1] in the morning, at noon, and just before sunset.[2] Rabban Gamaliel says that this ruling is made only to prevent searching less often.[3] Rabbi Akiba says it was made only to prevent searching more often.[4] The people of Bet Namer used to reap with a rope [5] and leave *Pe'ah* in every furrow.[6]

---

1. The same ruling applied to gleaning in the fields.
2. Why at these specific times? Bertinora wrote: early in the morning

for nursing mothers, since the infants take a morning nap; at noon for youngsters, "whose way it is to go out then"; late afternoon, just before sunset, for the elderly, who walk slowly and cannot reach distant fields until late afternoon.

3. Insensitive landowners might not want the poor on their property so often and might try to limit searches to one or two a day.
4. Insensitive landowners might insist that the Pe'ah receivers and gleaners remain in the fields all day in the hot sun, following the harvesters at every moment even though their share was not large enough to justify that much time.
5. Marking clearly the dividing line between harvest and Pe'ah or gleaning.
6. Apparently, this practice both enlarged the Pe'ah area and avoided controversy, and was considered noble by the Rabbis.

Pe'ah 4:10

What are considered gleanings? [1] Whatever drops down at the moment of reaping. If a reaper cuts an armful or plucks a handful, then is pricked by a thorn and what he holds falls to the ground, this belongs to the owner. [2] Whatever falls from within the hand or the sickle belongs to the poor. [3] Whatever falls from the back of the hand or the sickle belongs to the owner. [4] When something falls from the top of the hand or the sickle, R. Ishmael says: It belongs to the poor. R. Akiba says: to the owner. [5]

---

1. The right of the poor to glean is stated in Leviticus 19:9–10; 23:22.
2. The grain does not fall to the ground at the moment of cutting or plucking, but only when the worker is hurt by the thorn.
3. If the stalk falls from the sickle to the ground, having missed the hand altogether, or is fumbled momentarily in the hand and falls to the ground, it is a gleaning.
4. If, in cutting one sheaf or grabbing one, the back of the hand or the sickle bangs into another and knocks it down, this is not a gleaning, for the latter sheaf or stalk did not fall at the moment of cutting.
5. The stalk was being held between the fingertips or was hit by the head of the sickle. Is this situation comparable to 3 or 4 above? R. Akiba's view was accepted as law. These details were not trivial

to the Rabbis. Sustenance for the poor and right and wrong were involved, and every detail was important.

DEMAI—DOUBTFUL CROPS

Introduction

Demai is the name given to agricultural products with regard to which there is doubt whether the proper tithes have been given. (For tithe laws, see pp. 60 ff.) It is the function of this book to help the Jew to avoid transgressing the law because of a lack of conscientiousness on the part of other Jews.

No one knows the origin of the word *demai*. Aramaic and very old, it seems to be connected with root words expressing question or doubt, but this is speculative.

There are no direct Biblical sources for the material in this book. Its regulations flow from the normative laws about tithes and offerings.

Demai 2:2

A man who wishes to be trustworthy will give tithes from what he eats and from what he sells and from what he buys to resell. He will not be the guest of an *am ha'aretz*.[1] R. Judah says: Even if he is the guest of an *am ha'aretz,* he may be considered trustworthy. His students [2] said: If he isn't trustworthy in what concerns himself, how can he be considered trustworthy in dealing with that which belongs to others? [3]

---

1. Literally "the people of the land," the peasants. The phrase came to mean the ignorant generally, and rabbinic literature contains many unpleasant restrictions and sayings about the *am ha'aretz*. One of the strongest is: "The *am ha'aretz* cannot be righteous" (*Avot* 2). This Mishnah is limited in its implications, however; one may not eat at the table of an *am ha'aretz* because there is always the sus-

picion that he did not tithe his crops and the meal is *demai*.
2. The text says *they*, frequently used in the Mishnah to refer to the students of the teaching rabbi, or to fellow scholars.
3. There is a constant emphasis in rabbinic literature on the importance of one's ethical status in the community. Consistently, the "greatest crown is the good name" (*Avot* 4:13).

Demai 3:5

If a man gives food to be cooked to the mistress of an inn, he must tithe both what he gives her and what he receives back from her, since she must be suspected of exchanging it.[1] R. Jose said: We are not responsible for deceivers. He must tithe only what he receives back from her.[2]

---

1. If she likes the guest, she may cook better food, but without tithing it. If she does not know or like him, the Sages assumed she would switch the foods to items of lesser-quality—and would not tithe those either.
2. R. Jose accepts the problem of food-switching, but suggests that the guest need not be concerned about the tithe on the food he gives the innkeeper but does not get back; that is her moral responsibility. But R. Jose's view was not accepted as law. There was always a tendency in the direction of zealousness rather than slackness in these matters.

Demai 3:6

If a man gives food to be cooked to his mother-in-law, he must tithe both what he gives her and what he receives back from her, since she must be suspected of changing what is spoiled.[1] R. Judah said: She would desire the well-being of her daughter and would feel ashamed before her son-in-law.[2] R. Judah concedes that if a man gave food to his mother-in-law which is legal to eat in the

Seventh Year, she need not be suspected of changing it and giving her daughter forbidden Seventh Year food to eat.[3]

---

1. In the process of cooking. She would take of her stock and serve her daughter and son-in-law only tasty dishes.
2. He might think she had spoiled the food on purpose because she did not approve of him. The mother-in-law problem is very old!
3. R. Judah's views aroused strong opposition, according to the Jerusalem Gemara. He then used the Seventh Year argument as an exception to his earlier statement, to soften its impact. Foods which grew during the Seventh Year were not to be eaten; the people were to live from surpluses accrued over the first six years (see pp. 54 ff.). This matter was so serious that R. Judah could not imagine even a disapproving mother-in-law transgressing it. His view was accepted as law.

KILA'YIM—DIVERSE KINDS

Introduction

Five forms of "diverse kinds" are discussed in the Mishnah: seed plants, plants and vines, animals for breeding, animal for work, fibers for fabric. Within each, the mixing of the various species is prohibited.

The Torah does not explain why these laws were instituted. They appear to fall into the category of Ḥukkim, regulations which must be obeyed because God wants them obeyed, according to the Jerusalem Talmud. A number of commentators note that God's natural laws must not be tampered with and that such mixing of natural species is "unnatural." This concept is so out of harmony with our scientific approach that it is not widely obeyed. Even in Orthodox circles in Israel, tree grafting and hybridization of grains are widely practiced.

The two forms of species-mixing still widely avoided are crossbreeding of animals or working with two different animals, and the wearing of sha'atnez, the mixed fibers of wool and linen.

Biblical Sources for Kila'yim

You shall not let your cattle mate with a different kind; you shall not sow your field with two kinds of seeds; you shall not put on cloth from a mixture of two kinds of material. (Leviticus 19:19)

SEE ALSO

Deuteronomy 22:9–11

Kila'yim 1:3

The turnip and the radish,[1] the cabbage and the cauliflower, the beet and the *orach* [2] are not considered diverse kinds. R. Akiba added: garlic and wild garlic, onions and wild onions,[3] lupine and wild lupine [4] do not constitute diverse kinds.[5]

---

1. Albek translates it as "cabbage turnip," making the relationship even closer.
2. Other names are found for this vegetable: *rumex* and *sonel,* for example. No more familiar name can be found.
3. Shallots or scallions. The origin of this English word is worth noting. When the Crusaders conquered Palestine, they found these wild onions growing at Ashkelon, which they called *Ascelon.* They named the onions *Ascelons.* The *a* dropped, and the word became *scallions* in English, *shallots* in French.
4. Apparently an extinct member of the bean family.
5. In all these cases, the botanical family relationships are considered sufficiently close for these vegetables not to be called *kila'yim,* and consequently they could be planted in the same field.

Kila'yim 1:7

One kind of fruit tree may not be grafted onto another kind,[1] nor one kind of vegetable onto another kind, nor a tree to a vegetable, nor a vegetable to a tree. R. Judah permits the grafting of a vegetable to a tree.[2]

---

1. Of fruit tree. A fruit tree and a non-fruit tree may not be grafted together, but two non-fruit trees may be, since no edible produce is involved. Strangely enough, the fruit of grafted trees is kosher and may be eaten.
2. The view of R. Judah was not accepted as law.

Kila'yim 2:6

If a man wants to lay out his field in plots, each containing a different kind of crop, the school of Shammai says: Between each kind he must leave a space equal to three furrows of plowed land.[1] The school of Hillel says: the width of a Sharon yoke.[2] The opinion of the one is close to the opinion of the other.

---

1. Then each section can be considered a separate field, with no danger of *Kila'yim.*
2. The Jerusalem Talmud indicates that both involve about two *amot,* or approximately a yard.

Kila'yim 8:2

One kind of cattle with another, one kind of wild animal with another, cattle with a wild animal, a wild animal with cattle, one kind of non-kosher (see Leviticus 11:1–8) animal with another, one kind of kosher animal with another, a non-kosher animal with a kosher, a kosher animal with a non-kosher: in all these cases it is forbidden to plow or draw with them, or drive them.[1]

---

1. An animal which is *drawn* is one which is led or directed while being ridden, such as a camel. Other commentators suggest that the word refers to forms of traction, not plowing, which require two or more animals to be yoked together to pull a load. An animal which is *driven* is one which must be forced into moving, such as a donkey. *Drive* may also mean yoking two animals together while moving them from one place to another.

   This is a good example of the care taken by the writers of the Mishnah to try to foresee every possible alternative, combination, or contingency.

Kila'yim 9:1

Only wool and linen may not be mixed for clothing under the law of diverse kinds, just as wool and linen alone become non-kosher by being touched by a person with symptoms of leprosy. When the priests minister in the Temple they wear only wool and linen. If camel's hair and sheep's wool have been combed together and the greater part is camel's hair, it is permitted to mix them with linen. But if the greater part is sheep's wool, it is forbidden. If they are in equal parts it is forbidden. The law is the same if hemp and flax have been combed together.[1]

---

1. If there is more hemp than flax, the mixture can be combined with wool for clothing. Otherwise, it is forbidden.

Kila'yim 9:2

Silk and coarse silk are not included in the law of diverse kinds, but they are still forbidden for appearance's sake.[1] Mattresses and cushions do not come under the law of diverse kinds provided a man's flesh does not touch them directly. Diverse kinds may not be worn even momentarily, and they may not be worn over ten other garments, even to escape customs duty.[2]

---

1. Legally, silk could be combined with wool or linen for clothing fabric. The law of *Mar'it Ayin* ("appearances") was invoked here: silk looked like linen, coarse silk like wool. This is an important principle in Halakhah. For two reasons, technically legal matters are prohibited for appearance's sake: first, lest the individual's reputation suffer because others might think he was breaking the law; and second, lest others actually break the law because the reputable Rabbi so-and-so had apparently done so. There are many examples in Halakhah of the operation of this principle. One of the best involves the rabbinic decision that fowl may not be cooked in. milk or eaten simultaneously with milk foods. Technically, fowl is not meat—any more than fish is meat. But, among other reasons, because it looks so much like meat, *Mar'it Ayin* is invoked.

2. This statement has a contemporary ring. Then, as now, clothes worn by an individual were not usually subjected to customs duty. The Hebrew word in the text is well-chosen: *lignov*, "to steal from customs." There is, however, another aspect. There were taxes imposed solely on Jews by the Romans, for example, and Jews would wear *kila'yim* as one device among others to avoid being recognized. Many manuscripts and printed editions of the Mishnah do not contain this phrase, because of either non-Jewish censorship or self-censorship.

Kila'yim 9:8 [1]

Only spun and woven fabrics are forbidden under the law of diverse kinds, as it is written: "You shall not wear *sha'atnez;* (Deuteronomy 22:11); i.e., that which is *shu'a* ("combed"), *tavui* ("spun"), and *nuz* ("woven").[2] R. Simeon b. Eleazer says: The verse means that he who wears *sha'atnez* is estranged and estranges his Father in heaven against him.[3]

---

1. This paragraph is a fine exercise in the rabbinic practice called *Notarikon*—the deducing of legal decisions from words, parts of words, and puns on words—with attendant complications. The word

sha'atnez is unrelated to any normative Hebrew word. The Rabbis took pieces of the words meaning "to comb," "to spin," and "to weave" and spun them into the word *sha'atnez,* and found the limitation on *Kila'yim* in this verbal combination. It exempts all embroidered, knitted, and other garments from this law.

2. Typical among the complications arising from this unique rabbinic logic is the problem of the *tzitzit,* the ritual fringe worn on garments in ancient times, and now confined to the *tallit.* If the *nuz* part of *sha'atnez* means merely to intertwine two spun threads (as in plaiting) then the *tzitzit* are *Kila'yim.* But this is an impossibility, since the *tzitzit* originate in direct Torah law (see Numbers 15:37–41). But the Rabbis got out of this difficulty in various ways, without invalidating the basic requirement of *nuz,* by adding weaving requirements of numerous threads, or requiring the mixing of wool and linen in the spinning process before *Kila'yim* can be declared. With today's technical processes, the matter is moot, and *sha'atnez* is clearly definable to those who choose not to wear it, especially since in some places *sha'atnez*-free garments are so labeled.

3. Not to be outdone, R. Simeon connected the word *sha-atnez* with the verb *luz,* "to estrange." He made a good sermonic point, unrelated to etymology.

SHEVI'IT—THE SEVENTH YEAR (SHEMITAH)

Introduction

The Torah, in its several statements about the *Shemitah* or Seventh Year, gives no clear reasons for the regulations which are promulgated, though the laws themselves are relatively clear. They fall into three categories: prohibited forms of agricultural labor during the Seventh Year; the use or non-use of food plants and fruits which grow without human care; and the remission of debts.

Commentators give a number of reasons for the "Sabbath of the Soil":

1. The number *seven* is a special number: the seven days of Creation, Shavuot (seven weeks), etc. Consequently, from a mystical standpoint, the seventh year requires special rules.

2. The land required a rest for its renewal. The remission of debts preserved economic stability by preventing the development of great fortunes side by side with abject poverty. (Nineteenth-century socialists looking for Biblical "justifications" frequently cited these laws.)

3. These laws promoted the sense of God's mastery and man's dependency. Like the Sabbath day, one year in seven was to be devoted, not to labor and the usual pursuits, but to God.

When Jewish farmers began to cultivate the soil of the Land of Israel for the first time in many centuries at the end of the nineteenth century, they faced the problem of *Shemitah*. The rabbinate had no difficulty in making calculations which determined *when* the Seventh Year would occur. Some authorities held that the traditional law had to be obeyed. Other rabbis permitted the fictional "sale" of the land to a non-Jew during the Seventh Year. A document of sale was written, a nominal price was paid, and at the end of the year the land was repurchased. During the year it could be worked by Jews who were technically tenants of the non-Jew. There was heated controversy about the matter. Gradually, however, the latter opinion prevailed, and it is almost universally followed in contemporary Israel.

Biblical Sources for Shevi'it

Six years you shall sow your land and gather in its yield; but in the seventh you shall let it rest and lie fallow. Let the needy among your people eat of it, and what they leave let the wild beasts eat. You shall do the same with your vineyards and your olive groves. (Exodus 23:10–11)

SEE ALSO

Leviticus 25:1–7
Deuteronomy 15:1–3, 9–10
Nehemiah 10:32

Shevi'it 1:1

Until when may an orchard be plowed in the year before the Seventh Year? [1] The school of Shammai says: as long as this work benefits the produce of the sixth year. The school of Hillel says: until Shavuot.[2] And the opinion of the one is close to the other.

---

1. At what point does work in the fields cease to benefit sixth-year crops, as permitted, and begin to benefit Seventh Year crops—which is forbidden? What constitutes an orchard is defined in careful detail in subsequent paragraphs, not included here.
2. For purposes of *Shemitah* counting, the year began with Rosh Hashanah. Shavuot then came only three months before the end of the sixth year. The school of Hillel's opinion should therefore be almost the same as that of the school of Shammai. Bertinora tells us that one of the Rabban Gamaliels ignored this whole discussion and permitted all work to be done with trees until the day before Rosh Hashanah of the *Shemitah* year.

Shevi'it 2:1

Until when may a "white field" [1] be plowed in the year before the Seventh Year? Until the ground has dried [2] or as long as plowing is being done for the planting of cucumbers and gourds.[3] R. Simeon said: You are putting the law into each man's hand! [4] A "white field" may be plowed until Pesah and an orchard until Shavuot.[5]

---

1. A field for grain, without trees: "white" because sun-baked.
2. After the spring rains in Israel, or toward the end of February and the beginning of March.
3. Both late crops. The farmer would surely have the Seventh Year in mind by then, not the sixth-year crops.
4. Because the fields of different farmers would dry at different times for topographical and other reasons. In addition, how dry is "dry"?

This kind of loose terminology was repugnant to the Rabbis.
5. The orchard could be plowed later because its purpose was not preparation for planting, only the loosening of soil to permit moisture to sink deeper around the roots. No firm legal decision is given here among the varying views because the differences are slight, but the view of Hillel's school was considered to prevail in these matters.

Shevi'it 3:8

After the rains have ceased in the sixth year, steps may not be built up the sides of ravines, for this would be preparation for the Seventh Year.[1] But they may be built during the Seventh Year after the cessation of the rains, since this is preparation for the eighth year. They may not be blocked in with earth, but only made in a loose embankment.[2] Any stone which can be taken by merely stretching out a hand may be removed.

1. Visitors to Israel marvel at the profusion of these old stone walls, many of them still in excellent condition after centuries of disuse, as well as sluices constructed without stone, especially in the Negev. Their purpose was to retain the scant rainwater and guide it into proper channels in the fields.
2. To fill in the walls might indicate an intention to hold back the Seventh Year rains for Seventh Year planting purposes. This is another case of *Mar'it Ayin*.

Shevi'it 4:3

Newly-plowed land may be rented in the Seventh Year from a non-Jew, but not from a Jew.[1] Non-Jews may be encouraged when they labor in the fields in the Seventh Year, but not Jews.[2] Greetings are offered to non-Jews in the interests of peace.[3]

1. For purposes of eighth-year (i.e., first year of new cycle) planting. The land may not be rented from a Jew, for he would be disobeying

the Torah by plowing during the *Shemitah* year.
2. By a kind word, "may your strength increase," even though the work goes on during the *Shemitah* year.
3. Bertinora adds: "even on their holy days." "In the interests of peace" is a major ethical principle of Judaism, always given the most serious consideration in rabbinic discussions, so long as some other vital principle is not sacrificed in the process.

Shevi'it 10:3

A loan secured by *prozbul* [1] is not canceled by the Seventh Year. When Hillel saw that people refrained from giving loans to one another, transgressing what is written in the Torah—"Beware lest there be a base thought in your heart" [2]—he instituted this law.

1. For the form of the *prozbul* document (from the Greek *prosbolé*) see the next Mishnah.
2. Because loans unpaid by the end of the sixth year were uncollectable, people refused to lend money toward the end of each cycle. Since this harmed the poor, who needed the money for seed, implements, and basic needs, Hillel created the legal fiction of the *prozbul*. It did away with the earlier Torah law, but was accepted as a legal *takkanah* because:
    a. It was couched in consistent language.
    b. Hillel quoted a solid Torah source (Deuteronomy 15:9) to justify it.
    c. Religious ethics required it.

Shevi'it 10:4

This is the formula of the *prozbul:* "I affirm to you, so-and-so and so-and-so, the judges in such-a-place, that, regarding any debt due me, I shall collect it whenever I wish." Either the judges or the witnesses [1] sign at the end.

1. Creditors had a right to use the courts to require payment of a debt. But this formula does more than put a court on notice that the

creditor intends to collect his debt no matter what. Some commentators say it has the effect of stating that the debt is already legally collected; only the transfer of the money at a later date is required. Others insist it is no more than a notice of intention to collect. Either way, the *prozbul* effectively "repealed" Seventh Year debt-cancellation rights.

TERUMOT—HEAVE-OFFERINGS

Introduction

Every Israelite was required to give the priests a free-will offering from the produce of the ground, including grain, fruit, wine, oil. (Even the Levites had to give *Terumah* to the priests from their tithe.) The amount of the free-will offering was not specified, but the Rabbis recommended from one-fortieth to one-sixtieth of the gross product, depending on the circumstances and generosity of the individual farmer.

There are many Biblical sources for this law. Since it was of deep concern to the priests as a major source of their sustenance, it is reiterated in each Torah document.

Biblical Sources for Terumot

Leviticus 20:10–14
Numbers 18:8, 11, 12, 25–32
Deuteronomy 12:6, 18:4
Nehemiah 10:38–40, 13:5–12

Terumot 1:1

Five persons may not give *Terumah,* and if they do so, their *Terumah* is not valid: a deaf mute; an imbecile; a minor; one who gives *Terumah* from that which is not his; and a non-Jew who gives *Terumah* from what belongs to an Israelite. Even if it was with the Israelite's consent his *Terumah* is not valid.[1]

---

1. These exceptions are based on Exodus 25:2, where the concept of free-will offering is enunciated: "Speak to the children of Israel that they take for Me an offering; of every man whose heart makes him willing you shall take My offering."

   "Children of Israel"—a non-Jew is exempt.

   ". . . of every man"—not children.

   ". . . whose heart makes him willing. . . ."—the mentally retarded and deaf-mutes were not considered as having conscious wills.

   Finally, a free-will offering would have to be given of one's own possessions, not of others'.

Terumot 8:11

Concerning both previous cases, R. Joshua said: This is not the category of *Terumah* about which I am cautioned lest I defile it, but only lest I eat it. What is the kind of *Terumah* concerning the defiling of which I am warned? A man was traveling from one place to another with loaves of *Terumah* in his hand, and a non-Jew said to him: Give me one of them to defile or I'll defile all of them. R. Eliezer said: Let him defile all of them, but the Jew must not turn one over for defilement. R. Joshua said: He should place one of them on a rock.[1]

---

1. Thus he would not personally transmit the loaf for defilement. The view of R. Joshua was accepted as law.

Terumot 8:12

Thus [1] if pagans said to a group of women: "Give us one from among you that we may defile her, and if not we shall defile you all," let them defile all of them, but let not one soul from Israel be turned over to them.[2]

---

1. This Mishnah is a digression resulting from the previous one. In an earlier instance, R. Joshua's view that it was better to give over the one loaf—as a relative protection of ritual purity—prevailed.
2. Here there is no disagreement because the betrayal of any human being is contrary to Jewish ethics. This matter became acutely real during the Nazi regime. After World War II, surviving Jews could not forgive other Jews who had betrayed their fellows, even when not for personal advantage but to try to save larger numbers of Jews. Community leaders who prepared lists of Jews for deportation were reviled, even though the alternative clearly was total destruction. Facile moral judgments have been drawn by persons personally uninvolved.

MA'ASEROT—TITHES

Introduction

This book of the Mishnah is really a continuation of *Terumot*. For the most part, the regulations enunciated with regard to *Ma'aserot* ("tithes") hold true for *Terumot* as well. The Mishnah text specifies when they do not.

Tithing has a long and complicated history. Tithes were brought before the establishment of the Temple in Jerusalem in the tenth century B.C.E. They were apparently collected by Levites around the countryside. By what may appear to be a curious change, they were collected, at least part of them, by priests at the Temple in Jerusalem during the Second Temple period (538 B.C.E. to 70 C.E.).

Actually, the history of tithing is inseparable from the complex history of the priesthood and the Levites. Priests were Levites (literally, "of the tribe of Levi"). Different groups of priests were rivals for leadership, and in fact varying priestly houses did rule at various times. There were both priests and Levites resident outside Jerusalem as well as in Jerusalem. During the Second Temple period, the *Ma'aser Rishon* ("first annual tithe") was split three ways: one-third to Levites outside Jerusalem, two-thirds brought to the Temple and there divided between priests and the Temple treasury.

The concept of the tithe has been incorporated into the religious practices of a number of Protestant denominations.

Biblical Source for Ma'aserot

And to the Levites I hereby give all the tithes in Israel as their share in return for the services that they perform, the services of the Tent of Meeting. Henceforth, Israelites shall not trespass on the Tent of Meeting, and thus incur guilt and die: only Levites shall perform the services of the Tent of Meeting; others would incur guilt. It is a law for all time throughout the generations. But they shall have no territorial share among the Israelites; for it is the tithes set aside by the Israelites as a gift to the Lord that I give to the Levites as their share. Therefore I have said concerning them: They shall have no territorial share among the Israelites. (Numbers 18:21–24)

Ma'aserot 1:1

There is a general rule about *Ma'aserot:* [1] Everything which is considered food and is watched over [2] and grows out of the soil [3] is subject to *Ma'aserot*. There is another general rule: Everything which is considered food both at the beginning and at the completion of its growth,[4] even though it is withheld from use to increase its quantity, is subject to *Ma'aserot* whether gathered early or mature. On the other hand, whatever is not considered food at the beginning of its growth but only in later stages [5] is subject to *Ma'aserot* only when it is considered food.[6]

---

1. Except when specified, the word *Ma'aserot* refers to both tithes and heave-offerings in this book. There were three tithes, only two of which were offered in any one year:

    Ma'aser Rishon ("first tithe"), given every year to the Levites, therefore known sometimes as *Ma'aser Levi*.

    Ma'aser Sheni ("second tithe"), given in the first, second, fourth, and fifth years of the seven-year cycle. This tithe was taken to Jerusalem, there to be eaten by the farmer and his family in a joyous sacrificial feast.

    Ma'aser Ani ("poor tithe") given in the third and sixth years of the cycle for distribution to the poor.
2. *Watched over* refers to private property. Only the produce of private property had to be tithed. Therefore, if one ate fruit along a public road, there was no concern about tithing. In addition, nothing eaten legally during the *Shemitah* or Seventh Year had to be tithed.
3. Therefore, foods like mushrooms were exempt, since they have no roots and grow on but not in the ground.
4. Like a carrot, which can be eaten as soon as the leaves sprout or can be left to grow maximally large before being eaten.
5. Like most fruits, which are edible not when they first appear on the tree but after they ripen.
6. The question is the timing of the act of tithing. The answer is clear: Food must be tithed, and consequently the amount is deducted only when the product has reached edible form.

Ma'aserot 2:7

If a man hires a worker to help him harvest figs, and the worker says: "on condition that I may eat figs," [1] he may eat them without tithing. But if the worker says: "on condition that I and my family may eat," or "on condition that my son may eat instead of my receiving a wage," [2] then he himself may eat and be exempt from

Ma'aserot, but if his sons eat, he is liable. If the worker says: "on condition that I may eat during the harvest and after the harvest too," then if he eats during the harvest he is exempt, but if he eats after the harvest he is liable, since he did not eat under circumstances prescribed in the Torah.[3] This is the general rule: If a man eats under circumstances prescribed in the Torah, he is exempt; but if he eats under circumstances not in the Torah, he is liable.[4]

---

1. He did not have to make this condition at all; he was entitled to eat all he wanted during the harvest, under the terms of Deuteronomy 23:25–6. Not all workers had this clear right, however. The matter is discussed in detail in the Gemara (*Bava Metzia* 87a ff.).
2. This addition makes the provisions at the end of Deuteronomy 23:25 applicable, according to the Rabbis.
3. The provisions of the Bible verse terminated after the harvest. Free eating took place only in the fields, and exclusively during the harvest.
4. In Chapter 3 of this Mishnah, other specific questions of harvest workers' rights are dealt with in this same spirit.

Ma'aserot 3:8

If a fig tree stands in a courtyard,[1] a man may eat figs from it one at a time and be exempt from *Ma'aserot.* But if he takes several at a time, he is liable.[2] R. Simeon says: At one time a man may have one fig in his left hand, one in his right, and one in his mouth, and be exempt. If he climbs to the top of the tree, he may fill his lap and eat.[3]

---

1. Earlier in this chapter, the Mishnah dealt in detail with the question: When are a courtyard's products subject to *Ma'aserot?* If the courtyard is private property, they are; if it is *hefker* ("unowned property") they are not. Various symbolic circumstances are adduced. The general conclusion tends in the direction of severity: Most courtyards are subject, including the courtyard referred to here.

2. The single fig cannot be divided for tithing; no single bit of food is subject. The question is: When does the tithable plural begin? "Several at a time" means, in effect, a handful.

3. So long as all the eating is done at the top of the tree. If he brings any figs down from the tree, those are subject. But the view of R. Simeon was not accepted as law.

MA'ASER SHENI—SECOND TITHE

Introduction

There are some major distinctions between *Ma'aser Rishon,* the first tithe, and *Ma'aser Sheni,* the second.

The first tithe was given every year. The second tithe was given in years one, two, four, and five of the seven-year cycle. In years three and six, the poor tithe (*Ma'aser Ani*) was given.

The first tithe was given to the Levites—or, in some eras, to the priests. The second tithe was consumed by the individual in Jerusalem. The first tithe could be eaten anywhere by its recipients.

The first tithe had to be brought to its recipients in its original form. The second tithe could be brought in money or another form.

The first tithe was not *kodesh,* or technically sacred, while the second was. The sacred nature of the tithe made it possible and necessary to redeem it for consumption by the individual, if it was brought to Jerusalem in non-edible form. But there was a 20-percent surtax to be paid for the privilege of redeeming it.

All the laws of tithes either appear in writings considered priestly in origin, or, in the case of Deuteronomy, they are laws written to strengthen the central sanctuary in Jerusalem. Especially before the Babylonian Exile, this was a problem. There were many cult centers in the Northern Kingdom, such as Beth El, Shiloh, and others. After the Exile, the Second Temple had little or no competition.

Biblical Sources for Ma'aser Sheni
Leviticus 27:30–31
Deuteronomy 14:22–27, 26:12–15

Ma'aser Sheni 1:1

Ma'aser Sheni [1] may be neither sold nor pledged nor bartered. It may not be used to weigh other produce. A man may not say to his fellow even in Jerusalem: "Here is wine; give me oil for it." This applies also to all other produce.[2] But persons may give it to one another as a gift.[3]

---

1. The second tithe could be given in its produce form or as its value in other products, including gold or silver, as decided by the individual who brought or sent it to Jerusalem. Once there, it had to be consumed, or, if it was in the form of money, other sanctified products had to be bought and consumed. The sanctity had to be preserved.
2. It may not be done with *Ma'aser Ani* ("poor tithe") either.
3. *Ma'aser Sheni* products are *kodesh* ("sacred") and may not be used for any secular purpose. A free gift, however, might be given without abusing the sanctity of the things. To invite guests to join freely in consuming the tithe in Jerusalem, for example, would be permitted.

Ma'aser Sheni 3:4

If one has unconsecrated produce in Jerusalem and *Ma'aser Sheni* money elsewhere,[1] he may say: "Let that money be exchanged for this produce." If he has *Ma'aser Sheni* money in Jerusalem and unconsecrated produce elsewhere, he may say: "Let this money be exchanged for that produce," so long as the produce is brought to and consumed in Jerusalem.

---

1. And he needs the money for other purposes. The produce becomes sacred, and is then subject to all the laws of *Ma'aser Sheni* produce.

Ma'aser Sheni 4:4

One may use a legal fiction with regard to *Ma'aser Sheni*.[1] How? A man may say to his grown-up son or daughter or to his Hebrew manservant or maidservant: "Here is money; redeem this *Ma'aser Sheni* for yourself." [2] But he cannot speak this way to a minor son and daughter or to his non-Hebrew slaves since their hand is as his hand.[3]

---

1. In order to avoid the additional tax of 20 percent of the tithe's value if the produce is redeemed instead of taken in original form for consumption in Jerusalem.
2. Because the *Ma'aser Sheni* money is not originally theirs, when they redeem it they do not have to pay the 20 percent. Two different mitzvot are involved, one from Leviticus 27:31 and the other from Deuteronomy 14:22–27. This rabbinic interpretation disconnecting the Leviticus passage from the Deuteronomy passage clearly changes the intent of the Torah, and permits the farmer to evade the additional tax.
3. That is, the slaves and minor children are chattels and have no unique legal existence apart from him.

ḤALLAH—DOUGH OFFERING

Introduction

According to the Torah, the priests were entitled to a total of twenty-four different offerings. *Ḥallah,* the dough offering, was one. As will be seen, its amount was not specified. Like *Pe'ah,* however, it was given a minimum quantity by rabbinic tradition.

We are not told, either in the Torah ordinance or in the Mishnah, how the offering was transported to the priests—whether it went only to the Temple in Jerusalem or to any priest resident anywhere, how often it had to be taken, etc.

It is clear that the offering had to be given only on dough prepared in Palestine. After the fall of the Second Temple, however, the Rabbis ruled that a symbolic *hallah* offering had to be made wherever bread was baked. Many Jews today can recall how their mothers took a pinch of dough before baking bread and burnt that small piece to ash, as their symbolic *hallah* offering.

The placement of this book in the Order is of interest: It is the anchor book, containing the transition from books dealing with all types of grain and food to those dealing with specific groupings. *Ḥallah* contains both.

Biblical Sources for Ḥallah

The Lord spoke to Moses, saying: Speak to the Israelite people and say to them:

When you enter the land to which I am taking you and you eat of the bread of the land, you shall set some aside as a gift to the Lord: as the first yield of your baking, you shall set aside a loaf as a gift; you shall set it aside as a gift like the gift from the threshing floor. You shall make a gift to the Lord from the first yield of your baking, throughout the generations. (Numbers 15:17–21)

SEE ALSO

> Ezekiel 44:30
> Nehemiah 10:38

Ḥallah 1:1

Five species of grain are subject to *ḥallah:* wheat, barley, spelt, oats, and rye.[1] These are subject to *ḥallah* and may be mixed or weighed together to make the minimum quantity for offering.

---

1. These are also the five species forbidden on Passover. The latter law is deduced by a *gezerah shava,* a hermeneutic rule which utilizes the same word in different contexts. In Deuteronomy 16:3, the word *leḥem* ("bread") appears in connection with Passover; in Numbers 15:19 the same word is used in the commandment to make a *ḥallah* offering, a gift of dough. Since this is a leavened dough, the same species forbidden on Passover, because they are leavenable, are included in the *ḥallah* offering here.

Ḥallah 2:7

The minimum measure of the *ḥallah* offering is one-twenty-fourth of the dough. If dough is being made for oneself, or for a son's banquet, the minimum measure is one-twenty-fourth. If a baker is preparing it to sell in the market, or if a woman makes it to sell in the market, it is one-forty-eighth. If the dough was rendered ritually non-kosher unwittingly or involuntarily, it is one-forty-eighth.[1] If the dough was rendered non-kosher deliberately, it is one-twenty-fourth, so that one who sins shall not profit thereby.[2]

---

1. The dough itself had to be burned, as fuel. So, too, the *ḥallah* portion.
2. That is, if the dough was made ritually non-kosher in order to evade the necessity of giving the larger *ḥallah* offering on it.

ORLAH—FRUIT OF THE TREES

Introduction

The word *Orlah* means the uncircumcised foreskin. In this book, however, it refers to the fruit put out by young trees in their first three years of life. It was absolutely forbidden to eat or derive benefit from such fruit. The fourth year's fruit had a special designation: *neta reva'i,* a plant in its fourth year. It was sacred, following the Torah's words: "Set aside for jubilation before the Lord" (Leviticus 19:24). It was to be eaten only in Jerusalem, in the same manner as the second tithe.

One peculiarity in the reckoning of the years should be noted. Though the Talmud itself speaks of a New Year of Trees (the fifteenth of *Shevat*), Rosh Hashanah, the first of *Tishri,* was the beginning of a new year for the reckoning of *Orlah.* If a tree was planted in *Elul,* to take an extreme example, it went into its second year on the first of *Tishri,* one month later.

Assuming that trees grew as they do today, little hardship was caused by the *Orlah* laws. Most major fruit trees put out no edible fruit for three to four years if they are planted as saplings. In Israel today, it is considered fortunate if a new orange tree produces edible oranges within four years.

Biblical Source for Orlah

When you enter the land and plant any tree for food, you shall regard its fruit as forbidden. Three years it shall be forbidden for you, not to be eaten. In the fourth year all its fruit shall be set aside for jubilation before the Lord; and only in the fifth year may you use its fruit—that its yield to you may be increased: I the Lord am your God. (Leviticus 19:23–25)

Orlah 1:1

If a fruit tree is planted to serve as a fence or only for timber, it is exempt from the law of *Orlah*.[1] R. Jose says: Even if he said, "let the inner side serve for food and the outer side for a fence," the inner side is subject to the *Orlah* laws and the outside is exempt.

---

1. The fruit may be eaten the first year it appears (and is edible), since the tree was not intended for food. Conscious intent is a vital concern in rabbinic law. As may be seen in civil cases (see pp. 201 ff.), it was as difficult to prove then as it is now.

Orlah 1:2

If, when our fathers came into the Land of Israel, they found a fruit tree already planted, it was exempt from the laws of *Orlah*. But if they planted a tree, it became subject to the law even though they had not yet conquered the Land.[1] If a tree was planted for the use of everyone, it is subject to the law. R. Judah says it is exempt.[2] If a tree was planted on public land, or if a non-Jew planted it,[3] or if a robber planted it,[4] or if it was planted on shipboard,[5] or if it grew by itself, it is subject to the law of *Orlah*.

---

1. The Land of Israel was only gradually subdued. When the land was "substantially conquered," the people were able to settle down to full-time agricultural pursuits. If trees were planted before that happy time, they were subject to the laws of *Orlah*.
2. Once again, R. Judah failed to convince his colleagues. His view was not accepted as law.
3. On land owned by a Jew.
4. On land he had stolen.
5. In a large pot. For a variety of purposes, rabbinic law considered shipboard as national territory, as we do today.

BIKKURIM—FIRST FRUITS

Introduction

The word *Bikkurim* comes from the same root as the word *bekhor,* "firstborn." It denotes the first fruits of the annual harvest. But it was not limited to fruit. Seven species were indicated by the Rabbis as being subject to the requirement that first fruits be brought to the Temple in Jerusalem in joyous procession. The seven species, which the Torah praised as the finest produce of the Land of Israel, were: wheat, barley, grapes, figs, pomegranates, olives, and dates for honey (Deuteronomy 8:8). In fact, the pilgrims to Jerusalem brought the first of other produce too, but this was not required.

The Mishnah does not tell us specifically when the *Bikkurim* were brought. The Apocryphal Book of Tobit (Chapter 1) connects the bringing of *Bikkurim* to Jerusalem with the three pilgrimage festivals of Pesaḥ, Shavuot, and Sukkot, when all males had to appear in the Temple in any case. Tradition tells us that *Ma'aserot* and *Terumot* were brought at those times as well, in order that additional long, difficult trips to Jerusalem might not be necessary. Much as the pilgrims appeared to have enjoyed the trip (see Chapter 3), it was a long way up the hills of Judea to Jerusalem—by foot.

In Israel today, the *Bikkurim* festival is a major one. It takes place on Shavuot. The processions both in the cities and in farm communities follow ancient customs quite closely. In Jerusalem, the courtyard of the Jewish Agency building serves as the terminal point of the children's parades. Mounds of fruit are left there for distribution to the poor or for sale.

Biblical Sources for Bikkurim

. . . and the feast of harvest, the first fruits of your labors, which you sow in the field; and the feast of ingathering, at the end of the year, when you gather in your labors out of the field. Three times in the year all your males shall appear before the Lord God.

You shall not offer the blood of My sacrifice with leavened bread; neither shall the fat of My feast remain all night until the morning.

The choicest first fruits of your land shall you bring into the house of the Lord your God. (Exodus 23:16–19)

OTHER SOURCES

    Exodus 34:26
    Leviticus 2:14; 23:17, 20
    Numbers 28:26

Bikkurim 1:1

There are some who bring *Bikkurim* and recite the statement in Deuteronomy 26:5–10. There are others who may bring *Bikkurim* but do not recite,[1] and there are some who may not even bring them at all. The following may not bring them: he who plants a tree on his own land but sinks a shoot of it so that it grows on another's land or on public land. Also, he who sinks a shoot from a tree planted on another's land or on public land so that it grows on his land. Or he that plants a tree on his own land and sinks it so that it still grows on his land but with a private or public road in the middle. Such persons may not bring *Bikkurim*.[2] R. Judah says: The last category may bring them.[3]

---

1. The next Mishnah specifies this category.
2. The tree must grow wholly on the individual's land.
3. R. Judah's view was not accepted as law.

Bikkurim 1:4

The following bring *Bikkurim* but may not recite the passage from Deuteronomy 26: The proselyte may bring them but he may not recite because he cannot say: "Which the Lord swore unto our fathers to give us" (Deuteronomy 26:3). But if his mother was an Israelite, he may both bring *Bikkurim* and recite.[1] When the proselyte prays privately, he should say: "O God of the fathers of Israel." When he is in the synagogue, he should say: "O God of your fathers." But if his mother was an Israelite, he says: "O God of our fathers." [2]

---

1. For he was really a Jew, since lineage was through the mother.
2. At the beginning of the *Tefillah*, the silent standing prayer.

Bikkurim 3:2

How are the *Bikkurim* taken up to Jerusalem? The men of all the small towns in the *Ma'amad* [1] assembled in the city of the *Ma'amad*, and spent the night in the town square. They did not go into any of the houses.[2] Early in the morning, the officer said: "Arise, and let us go up to Zion to the house of the Lord our God" (Jeremiah 31:6).

---

1. The Land of Israel was divided into twenty-four districts— *Ma'amadot*—which took turns supplying men to go to Jerusalem to symbolize "all Israel" for the daily sacrifice in the Temple, as required by the Torah. They also set up synagogues in the "capital" of each district during the Second Temple period, and took turns leading the reading of the Torah and conducting the evolving prayer liturgy.
2. Because there might be a corpse in one of the houses which would cause them to become unclean and therefore prohibited from entering the Temple precincts in Jerusalem, thus negating the entire purpose of the pilgrimage.

Bikkurim 3:3

Those who lived near Jerusalem brought fresh figs and grapes, while those from a distance brought dried figs and raisins. An ox led the procession; its horns were bedecked with gold and there

was an olive-wreath on its head.[1] The flute was played in front of
the procession until just before their arrival in Jerusalem. When
they neared Jerusalem, they sent messengers ahead, then arranged
their *Bikkurim* ornamentally. The governors [leaders of the
priests], chiefs [leaders of the Levites], and treasurers of the
Temple went out to meet them. Their number varied according to
the rank of the pilgrims. All the artisans of Jerusalem would rise
before them and greet them: [2] "Our brothers, men of such-and-
such a place, enter in peace."

---

1. This ox was later sacrificed as a peace offering.
2. Artisans at work are not required to rise even at the entrance of a
   scholar. Their gesture on this occasion evidenced the importance of
   the *Bikkurim* festival.

Bikkurim 3:4

The flute was played in front of them until they reached the
Temple Mount. When they reached the Temple Mount, even
King Agrippa would take a basket, place it on his shoulder, and
walk as far as the Temple Court.[1] When they reached the court,
the Levites sang the song: "I will extol Thee, O Lord, for Thou
has raised me up, and has not suffered my enemies to rejoice
over me" (Psalms 30).

---

1. In order that the priest might take the basket directly from his
   hand, as prescribed in Deuteronomy 26:4.

The Second Order

MO'ED

Festivals

INTRODUCTION

Mo'ed comes from the Hebrew root *ya'ad*, "to appoint" or "to fix a time for an appointment." In the Torah, where the word appears frequently, it is used in a variety of contexts, but specifically means "appointed times" or "recurring occasions."

Seder Mo'ed is the only one of the Six Orders of the Mishnah whose name is singular. Two reasons are given by tradition for this. First, the word is used in the Torah in the singular (Genesis 17:21, Deuteronomy 16:6, and Hosea 2:11). But more convincing is the argument that the whole Seder deals with one cycle of holy-day observances and should thus be designated in the singular.

The Torah itself prescribes six Festivals: Shabbat; the three Pilgrimage Festivals (Pesaḥ, Shavuot, Sukkot); the "time of the blowing of the Shofar," i.e., Rosh Hashanah; and Yom Kippur. By the time the Mishnah was written, most of the other festivals were already a routine part of the annual cycle. The chief exception was Simḥat Torah, which evolved later.

Various explanations are given for the order of the books in *Seder Mo'ed*. The one most frequently mentioned is that the books are listed in descending order of size, from *Shabbat,* with twenty-four chapters, to *Ḥagigah,* with only three.

The traditional calendar is an important aspect of all the books in this Seder, and a working knowledge of its intricacies is vital to a full understanding of the Mishnah. The calendar utilized in the Mishnaic period is essentially the same one by which Jewry lives today. It is a lunar-solar calendar; that is, it is based upon the time taken by the moon to encircle the earth, and it is calculated mathematically to reconcile the time gap between twelve such moon cycles (months), totaling 254 days, and the time it takes the earth to complete its orbit around the sun (a year), a total of 365¼ days.

The Hebrew calendar is calculated on a nineteen-year cycle. Twelve of those years consist of twelve months of twenty-nine or thirty days each. Seven of them consist of thirteen months. The last scholarly challenge to this calendar's accuracy took place in the tenth century, and was effectively answered by Saadia Gaon.

Jewish festivals are nature-oriented, tending to take place at full moon, at new moon, or at equinox or solstice. Seasonal changes are celebrated: spring (Pesaḥ), summer (Shavuot), and fall (Sukkot). In post-Biblical times, the fourth seasonal transition came to be marked by Ḥanukkah.

One major problem in handling any discussion of Jewish holy days is the elusive truth about the evolution of the Rosh Hashanah, Yom Kippur, and Sukkot festivals. If we accept the theory that the Torah contains more than one calendar system, then it is possible to understand the clustering of festivals around the New Moon preceding the fall equinox. A harvest festival at that time was inevitable. Superimposed on it was a New Year observance, then a penitential fast. Ultimately, these were separated out into three different events, and Sukkot proceeded to develop its own complexities: *Hoshanah Rabbah, Shemini Atzeret,* and Simḥat Torah. *Shemini Atzeret* was by far the earliest of these three, being of Torah origin (see Leviticus 23:36).

The Mishnah text makes it almost obligatory to accept some such approach to the "turn of the year" festivals.

The material about the three Pilgrimage Festivals should be studied in the context of the political rivalry between the North and the South before the Babylonian Exile, in which the Jerusalem Temple never succeeded in establishing itself as the central shrine of the people. After the Return, however, it had no competition. The Mishnah text reflects the Second Temple period and its attitudes.

SHABBAT—SABBATH

Introduction

Shabbat is the longest book of the Mishnah devoted to any single subject. In addition, *Eruvin,* the second book, is concerned solely with aspects of Sabbath observance. Even on this relatively superficial quantitative basis, there can be little doubt of the importance of Sabbath observance to the Talmudic teachers. This concern was a direct inheritance from Biblical teachers. There are more reminders about Sabbath observance in the Torah text than about any other matter, with the possible exception of idolatry.

The Sabbath is the greatest symbol of the spirit of Judaism. More than any other concept in the Jewish religious system, it raises the individual to his proper stature as the child and partner of God, co-creator of the world, being "but little lower than the angels." It is Judaism's prime statement about the uniqueness of the individual and his essential freedom of will.

In our day, too many Jews have the impression that Sabbath observance is comparable to the classic Puritan practices of seventeenth-century Europe and America: the stifling of all joy and gaiety, the outlawing of everything pleasant. Nothing could be further from the truth.

All Sabbath laws have as their purpose the lifting of the Jew out of the week's routine into a higher plane of existence. Each Sabbath, he receives, symbolically, an additional soul, a Sabbath soul. He is free to think, to feel, to attain spiritual heights, to refresh his soul.

The long evolution of Halakhah regarding Sabbath observance had its beginnings in a society whose economic and social bases were very different from our own. The forms of work prohibited in the Mishnah were appropriate for a farming and rural society. As elaborated in the Gemara and subsequent legal literature, the number of prohibitions increased, but in the same general direction. For the individual who accepts the divine origins and authority of all Halakhah, this evolution should pose no particular problems. For other Jews, a serious concern with the Sabbath concept and its practical implications is essential. The Sabbath remains the cornerstone of all Jewish observance.

Three kinds of Sabbath laws are included in the Mishnah:

1. The thirty-nine prohibited forms of labor, with their derivatives. These prevent mixing Sabbath action with normal weekday labor.

2. Laws called *shevut,* acts not considered truly labor, but not considered consistent with the sanctity of the Sabbath.

3. Laws called *muktzeh,* "set apart." The handling of certain items and articles was prohibited on the Sabbath, even though no labor was involved. Both *Mar'it Ayin* ("appearances") and the inner feelings of the individual were involved in these regulations.

Biblical Sources for Shabbat

The heaven and the earth were finished, and all their array. And on the seventh day God finished the work which He had been doing, and He ceased on the seventh day from all work which He had done. And God blessed the seventh day and declared it holy, because on it God ceased from all the work of creation which He had done. (Genesis 2:1–3)

SEE ALSO

> Exodus 17:22–26, 29–30; 20:8–11; 23:12; 31:12–17; 34: 21; 35:2–3
> Leviticus 19:3, 20; 23:3; 26:2
> Numbers 15:32–36
> Deuteronomy 8:12–15
> Isaiah 56:2, 58:13–14
> Jeremiah 17:21–22
> Ezekiel 20:12
> Nehemiah 10:32; 13:15–19

Shabbat 1:2

A man should not go to the barber just before the time of the afternoon *Tefillah* [1] unless he has already said it.[2] A man should not enter a bathhouse or a tannery,[3] nor should he begin to eat a meal or decide a lawsuit. But if any of these activities have been begun, they need not be interrupted. They must be interrupted to recite the Shema, but not for the *Tefillah*.[4]

---

1. This applies especially on Friday, but is true on the other days as well.
2. Lest he fall asleep and miss the service altogether. The nap in the barber's chair is very old indeed!
3. Symbolic of any business whose processes take a long time and cannot be accurately predicted.
4. The recital times of the *Tefillah*, the standing silent prayer, are not stipulated in the Torah. Those of the Shema are (see p. 32).

Shabbat 1:10

Meat and onions and eggs may not be roasted on Friday unless there is time for them to be finished before sundown. Bread may not be put into the oven when darkness has begun to fall, nor may cakes be put upon the coals unless there is time for a surface crust to form.[1] R. Eliezer says: only time enough to form a crust on the bottom surface.[2]

---

1. The purpose of all these regulations is to avoid the temptation to stir up the coals to complete the cooking process after the beginning of the Sabbath. The prohibition against lighting a fire on the Sabbath is most zealously guarded, for it is one of the Torah's two primary prohibitions, work being the other (Exodus 35:2–3).
2. R. Eliezer's view was not accepted as law. In connection with the Sabbath observance, the Rabbis clearly tended in the direction of rigorous interpretations rather than liberal ones. Two factors are

involved: the supreme importance of Sabbath observance as a mitzvah, and the ease with which an apparently minor matter can lead to a Sabbath violation.

Shabbat 2:5

If a man put out a lamp on Sabbath out of fear of non-Jews, or thieves, or an evil spirit, or to help a sick person go to sleep, he is not guilty of violating the Sabbath.[1] But if he did so to spare the lamp or to save oil or the wick, he is guilty. R. Jose says he is innocent in every case except saving the wick, because in that case he forms charcoal.[2]

---

1. It was not necessary to state these facts, since they are all covered under the principle of *pikkuah nefesh*—"mortal danger." (It is assumed that the person was dangerously sick.) The Mishnah reports these exemptions because they are followed by a statement of possible guilt, and the Rabbis did not want the latter prohibitions to be extended zealously into the former areas. *Pikkuah nefesh* transcends the Sabbath in the mitzvah hierarchy.
2. The charcoal would aid in rekindling the lamp later, as the other reasons for putting out the lamp would not. This rather weak argument did not persuade the Sages, for R. Jose's view was not accepted as law.

Shabbat 6:1

What may a woman wear when she goes out on the Sabbath and what may she not wear? [1] A woman may not go out with bands of wool or bands of flax or with her head-straps. She should not wear them in the *mikveh* unless she has loosened them.[2] She may not go out with a forehead-band or with head-bangles unless they are sewn on her headdress. Nor may she go out with a hairnet if she goes to a public place. She may not go out with a "golden city" [3] or a necklace or nose-rings [4] or with a ring that has no seal or with a needle that has no eye.⁵ Yet if she went out wearing any of these she is not liable to a sin-offering.⁶

---

1. What clothing and ornamentation are necessary and what unnecessary is a troublesome problem for the Rabbis. The most beautiful clothing should be worn on the Sabbath, to honor it. Ornamentation should be worn on the Sabbath. But too much of either violates the Sabbath. "Out" means "onto public property."
2. This detail has nothing to do with the Sabbath, and is included parenthetically. When a woman goes to the *mikveh* (the ritual bath) after her menstrual period or after childbirth, she must immerse herself totally. If she wore her headbands, some part of her hair would not contact the water directly.
3. A coronet on which was an engraving of the city of Jerusalem.
4. Earrings are permitted, however. No reason is given for the distinction.
5. A ring with a seal and a needle with an eye are obviously forbidden, since they are connected with labor. But even a ring without a seal and an eyeless needle for ornamental purposes are forbidden. The principle of *Mar'it Ayin* ("appearances") applies.
6. Since all these objects do have legitimate ornamental purpose, and she did not wear them deliberately to violate the Sabbath.

Shabbat 6:2

A man may not go out on the Sabbath wearing sandals shod with nails,¹ or with a single sandal if he has no wound on his foot,² or with *Tefillin*,³ or with an amulet unless it has been prepared by an expert,⁴ or with a breastplate, helmet, or greaves.⁵ But if he goes out wearing any of these he is not liable to a sin-offering.

---

1. Bertinora writes that an incident during the Roman War brought about this law. A group of Jews hid in a cave on the Sabbath. They heard a noise, thought it was the Romans, and began to panic. They ended up wounding and killing one another with the nails set into their sandals.
2. Lest he be suspected of carrying his other sandal hidden somewhere

within his clothing, a clear violation of the Sabbath.

3. Phylacteries, not worn for Sabbath prayers, and not to be used solely for ornamentation. *Tefillin* are not worn for Sabbath morning prayers because they are designated as an *ot*, a sign or symbol (Deuteronomy 6:8), and the Sabbath itself is already an *ot* (Exodus 31:17). Both are symbols of the covenant relationship between God and Israel.

4. So that he "is sure it will help." Amulets were worn as protection against spirits, to cure illnesses, or to bring good luck.

5. A military uniform is not considered normal clothing.

Shabbat 6:4

A man may not go out on the Sabbath [1] with a sword or a bow or a shield or a club or a spear. If he goes out with any of these he is liable to a sin-offering. R. Eliezer says: They are his adornments. But the Sages say: They are only a reproach,[2] for it is written, "And they shall beat their swords into plowshares, and their spears into pruning-hooks; nation shall not lift up sword against nation, neither shall they learn war any more." A garter is not susceptible to defilement [3] and they may go out with them on the Sabbath, but ankle-chains are susceptible to defilement and they may not go out with them on the Sabbath.[4]

---

1. Onto public property. The regulation assumes that a man is not under military orders, which would supersede the Sabbath.

2. This is a basic statement of Jewish ethical principle. In today's world, armaments appear unavoidable. Judaism has never taught absolute pacifism, though it respects the men who exemplify it. But the recognition of human failure to rise above the need for weapons remains a constant reproach to us as children of the God who showed the vision of peace quoted here to Isaiah (2:4).

3. Because it is not a garment, but an aid to stockings having, as it were, only a secondary existence.

4. Because they do have a primary physical relationship to the wearer.

Shabbat 7:1

An important general rule has been enunciated concerning the Sabbath: Any man who, having forgotten the principle of the Sabbath, performed many acts of work on many Sabbaths, is liable to bring only one sin-offering.[1] But if he was aware of the principle of the Sabbath, and still performed many acts of work on many Sabbaths, he is liable for every Sabbath which he profaned.[2] If he knew it was the Sabbath and performed many acts of work on many Sabbaths, he is liable for every main category of work which he performed.[3] If he performed many acts or work of one main category, he is liable to only one sin-offering.[4]

---

1. It is hard to imagine, but for legal purposes it must be considered theoretically possible that a man might never have learned or might have forgotten that the observance of the Sabbath is a law of the Torah, or that work is forbidden on the Sabbath.
2. He forgot that the Sabbath came the day after Friday, or, not knowing that it was the Sabbath, went to work.
3. He knew work was forbidden on the Sabbath, but did not know or remember that the types of acts he performed were in fact forbidden on the Sabbath.
4. The categories of work are enumerated in the next Mishnah.

Shabbat 7:2

There are thirty-nine main categories of work:[1] planting, plowing, reaping, binding sheaves, threshing, winnowing, cleaning crops, grinding, sifting, kneading, baking, shearing wool, washing, beating, or dyeing it, spinning, weaving, making two loops,[2] plaiting or braiding, separating two threads, tying (a knot), loosening (a knot), sewing two stitches, tearing in order to sew two stitches, hunting a deer or any other animal, slaughtering or flaying or salting the deer, curing its skin, scraping it or cutting it up, writing two letters,[3] erasing in order to write two letters,[4] building, pulling down, putting out a fire, lighting a fire, striking with a hammer, and taking anything from one domain to another.[5] These are the main categories of work, thirty-nine in all.[6]

---

1. These cateogries have sub-categories, or "offspring." Only four categories of work are mentioned directly in the Torah (lighting a fire, plowing, reaping, and gathering wood). In addition, there are acts prohibited on the Sabbath by rabbinic injunction which are not considered work, but the prohibition of which makes for more complete rest. See p. 80.
2. Making one loop, or performing one of any of the actions here requiring two persons for Sabbath violation, could be accidental.
3. Again, one letter could have been formed accidentally.
4. Erasing as such is not a forbidden action.
5. From private to public property, or vice versa. To carry within one's own house is not forbidden, depending on how heavy the burden is. See also *Shabbat* 11:1. The rest of this chapter and the next chapter of the book deal with specific acts. Do they or do they not fall within one of the thirty-nine categories, and under what circumstances?
6. These thirty-nine cateogries offer us a clear view of the kind of occupations in which the Jews engaged. We know that they were farmers in the simplest and most self-sufficient sense of the word.

Shabbat 9:3

Where [1] do we learn that a woman who emits semen on the third day [2] is ritually unclean? Because it is written, "And be ready for the third day, come not near a woman." [3] Where do we learn that they may bathe a circumcised child on the third day, even if it falls on a Sabbath? Because it is written: "And it came to pass on the third day when they were sore." [4] Where do we learn that they tie a strip of crimson fabric on the head of the scapegoat (see Leviticus 16)? Because it is written: "Though yours sins be as scarlet, they shall be white as snow" (Isaiah 1:18).

---

1. Whenever the Mishnah asks "where?," the question refers to a Biblical source. Theoretically, every Halakhah has a Torah source.

The oral Torah is an extension of the written Torah and not a separate revelation. This Mishnah is one of four (9:1–4) which have nothing to do with the Sabbath at all. The commentators indicate that these four *Mishnayot* were placed after 8:7 (not included here) because the type of Biblical proof adduced there by R. Meir was the same as the approach in these four paragraphs. This kind of digression happens only occasionally in the Mishnah. It occurs constantly in the Gemara, however.

2. The third day after intercourse. On the first and second days, then, she would certainly have been "ritually unclean" if she emitted drops of semen. After the third day, it was assumed by the Rabbis that the semen had lost its character and therefore could not cause ritual impurity. Medically speaking, the maximum life-span of sperm, after ejaculation, is estimated to be not more than eight hours.

3. Exodus 19:15, in the instructions Moses received before he went up to Mount Sinai.

4. Genesis 34:25, in the story of Dinah, daughter of Jacob.

Shabbat 13:6

If a deer enter a house [on the Sabbath] and a man shuts it in, he is guilty.[1] But if two people shut it in, they are not guilty.[2] If one alone was not able to shut it in, and two people shut it in [together], they are both guilty.[3] Rabbi Simon declares them not guilty.[4]

---

1. The act of shutting the deer in the house was considered to be hunting.

2. This is based on Leviticus 4:27: "And if one soul sin accidentally . . ." In this case, two souls committed one sin, and are therefore not guilty.

3. If the job was too great for one man, when the two accomplished it together, there was enough "sin" involved for each of them to be guilty of one.

4. R. Simeon's view was not accepted as law.

Shabbat 16:1

All sacred books may be saved from burning [1] whether they are read on the Sabbath or not. Regardless of the language in which they are written, if they become unfit for use they must be hidden away. [2] Why are certain of the Biblical books not read? [3] So that they may not nullify the House of Study. The case of a scroll [4] may be saved with the scroll, and the case of *Tefillin* with the *Tefillin*, even though there is money in them. Where should they be taken for safety? To an alley which is not a thoroughfare. Ben Batyra says: even to an alley which serves as a thoroughfare. [5]

---

1. On the Sabbath, by moving them from the public domain to a private place or vice versa.
2. Sacred books may not be destroyed or used for any secular purpose. A special hiding place was ordained in the synagogue as their resting place, or, more frequently, they were buried in a special crypt in the cemetery. Such a *Genizah* still exists in most major Jewish communities in the world. The *Genizah* of the Cairo synagogue was one such hiding place. Its discovery by the late Dr. Solomon Schechter proved to be of enormous value. A veritable treasure of ancient manuscripts was unearthed, including large sections of the Apocryphal Book of Ben Sira.
3. The Torah and most of the Prophets are read in the synagogue during Sabbath and holy-day services. The third section of the Bible, *Ketuvim*—the Writings—is not read for the most part. Further, some of these books are traditionally not read privately on Sabbath afternoons, the time when Torah was read and taught in the synagogue. To learn living law—Halakhah—as contained in Talmud and commentaries was considered more valuable than the study of relatively minor—i.e., non-Halakhic—Biblical works.
4. Torah scrolls were kept in metal or wooden cases in ancient times, and as late as two or three hundred years ago. The fabric mantle is relatively new.
5. An alley with three closed sides—a dead end—was safe. One with only two sides, with both ends open, though it was still considered private property, was not considered sufficiently safe. The view of the Sages was accepted as law.

Shabbat 16:6

If a non-Jew [1] comes to put out the fire, they may not say to him: "Put it out," or, "Don't put it out," since they are not responsible for this Sabbath observance.[2] But if a minor came to put it out, they may not permit him to do so, since they are responsible for his observance of Sabbath.[3]

---

1. Literally, "one who worships idols." This phrase, like *oved kok-havim*—"one who worships stars"—is often used in the Mishnah to denote a non-Jew. Later Halakhah distinguished between pagan non-Jews and monotheistic non-Jews (Christians and Moslems).
2. Sabbath observance is not one of the seven Noahidic laws non-Jews are required to observe. But a Jew may not request or require work of a non-Jew on Sabbath, except under special conditions. See the next Mishnah.
3. The passage refers to a Jewish minor, for whose actions adults must take legal and moral responsibility.

Shabbat 16:8

If a non-Jew lights a lamp on Sabbath, a Jew may make use of the light. But if he lights it for the sake of the Jew, it is forbidden. If a non-Jew fills a trough with water for his cattle, a Jew may water his own cattle afterwards. But if the non-Jew does it for the Jew, it is forbidden. If a non-Jew sets up a gangplank by which to go down from a ship, a Jew may go down after him. But if he does it for the Jew, it is forbidden. Rabban Gamaliel and some elders were once traveling on a ship, and a non-Jew set up a gangplank by which to go down from it. Rabban Gamaliel and the elders did go down by it.[1]

---

1. These examples amplify the principle enunciated in the last Mishnah: A Jew may not request or require a non-Jew to violate the Sabbath. But if the non-Jew voluntarily performs an act in violation of the Sabbath for his own benefit, a Jew may benefit

from it.

The whole concept of the *Shabbos goy* ("Sabbath Gentile") is based on this distinction. Before the invention of electronic devices which automatically turn off electric lights on the Sabbath, it was a widespread practice among Orthodox Jews to have a non-Jew turn lights off for them. Non-Jews have also been used to keep coal furnaces going on Sabbath and to perform similar minor chores— all in violation of the Sabbath. A legal fiction is used by the rabbinate to justify this practice. The Jew may not ask the non-Jew to perform the service nor may he compensate the non-Jew for performing such services. The non-Jew "volunteers for his own reasons," and the Jew benefits. Later, a gift of gratitude is given to the non-Jew for the coincidental fact that this "volunteer" service was of benefit to the Jew on Sabbath.

Shabbat 18:3

One does not deliver the young of cattle on a Festival day, but help may be given to the mother.[1] But one does deliver a woman on Sabbath, and one may summon a midwife for her from any place.[2] The Sabbath may be profaned for the mother's sake by tying up the umbilical cord.[3] R. Jose says: They may also cut it.[4] They may do everything necessary for a circumcision on Sabbath.[5]

---

1. The commentators make a distinction between actual delivery and, for example, holding the newborn foal or calf so that it does not fall or choke.
2. The travel limit of Sabbath does not apply. See pp. 92 ff.
3. They may light a fire to heat water, or do anything necessary to help the mother or the child. In rabbinic law, all rights and immunities which pertain to serious illness are invoked. Human life and danger to life supersede the Sabbath.
4. R. Jose's view was accepted as law. This legal decision is a good example of the primacy of human values over all else. As has been noted, the general tendency in Halakhah regarding Sabbath is rigorous. But for new life and for the mother, liberality prevails. Even though there may be no danger in waiting until after Sabbath to cut the umbilical cord, the Rabbis ruled that it should be cut, the

baby cleaned, and both baby and mother made comfortable.
5. Including, of course, the circumcision itself, the mitzvah which supersedes the Sabbath and even Yom Kippur.

Shabbat 19:5

A child may be circumcised on the eighth, ninth, tenth, eleventh, or twelfth day after birth, but neither before nor afterward. Why? Normally, he should be circumcised on the eighth day. But if the child is born precisely at twilight, he is circumcised on what might be considered the ninth day.[1] If he is born precisely at twilight on Friday, the child is circumcised on what might be considered the tenth day.[2] If a Festival days falls after Sabbath,[3] the child is circumcised on the eleventh day, and if the two days of Rosh Hashanah fall after Sabbath, the child is circumcised on the twelfth day. If a child is sick, he is not circumcised until he becomes well.[4]

---

1. That is, the ninth day, if the day just ending at the time of birth is counted.
2. If Friday is counted, the circumcision would take place on Sunday. A circumcision takes place on Sabbath only if the birth is clearly a Sabbath birth. When there is doubt, as here, the circumcision is delayed.
3. Beginning Saturday night, which happens routinely. Circumcision supersedes holy days as it supersedes Sabbath—only if there is no doubt about the timing of the eighth day.
4. After the child is medically certified as well, seven days go by and the ceremony is held on the eighth day. In our day, hospital procedures and crowding have brought on a tendency to arrange for circumcision to take place on the fifth day and even earlier. Quite aside from medical questions, Jewish religious authorities in both the Orthodox and Conservative movements—and some Reform rabbis as well—continue to oppose this practice on traditional and Halakhic grounds.

ERUVIN—SABBATH TRAVEL REGULATIONS

Introduction

The whole complex of regulations about travel on Sabbath as well as the moving of objects stems from a single verse in Exodus (16: 29):

> See that the Lord has given you the Sabbath; therefore He gives you on the sixth day the bread of two days; abide every man in his place, let no man go out of his place on the seventh day.

The fundamental rabbinic regulation is simple. The Torah verse was interpreted to mean that no one could travel on Sabbath more than two thousand cubits from his domicile. Certain objects could be carried no more than four cubits from one's private domain.

There was much rabbinic disagreement about these regulations. Fundamental conflicts arose, not merely minor differences over details of procedure. The Samaritans did not accept the whole idea of *Eruv*, which means "mixture, combination, fusion," and *Shittuf*, meaning "partnership." The Sadducees also ignored these regulations, as did the Karaite movement in the eighth century.

These are legal fictions whereby a bundle or basket of food is placed the proper distance from the home of the individual on Friday, or in a jointly-owned courtyard or alley. Depositing the food makes of the place an extension of the individual's domicile or domain. Another two-thousand-cubit Sabbath walk is then possible.

The first two chapters of the book deal with difficult technical problems of defining courtyard, alley, domain, and the like. Being of little contemporary interest, they are omitted here. The remainder of the book is typified by the following selections.

Eruvin 3:1

Any food may be used for an *Eruv* or a *Shittuf* except water or salt.[1] Any food may be bought with second-tithe money except water or salt.[2] If a man vows to abstain from food, he is still allowed water or salt. An *Eruv* for a Nazirite [3] may be prepared with wine,[4] and for an Israelite [5] with *Terumah*. Symmachos says: with common produce only.[6] An *Eruv* may be prepared for a priest in a field containing a grave.[7] R. Judah says: even in a cemetery, since he can go with some sort of screen and eat.[8]

---

1. Those two substances are not considered food. The Mishnah then digresses for two brief sentences about water and salt.
2. See pp. 64 ff.
3. For the laws of the Nazirite, see Numbers 6:1–21.
4. Though the Nazirite himself may not drink it.
5. Israelite here means an individual who is not a priest or a Levite. In arranging for the calling up of men for the honor of saying Torah blessings (*aliyot*), priest, Levite, and Israelite are always differentiated, and in order: a Kohen ("priest") receives the first *aliyah*, a Levite the second.
6. Symmachos' view was not accepted as law.
7. Though a priest may not enter an area containing a grave because of ritual uncleanliness. In such a field, the priest would have to be wary of touching an exposed bone, for example.
8. A screen between the *Eruv* and the graves would protect the priest from ritual contamination.

Eruvin 4:5

If a man falls asleep on a journey and does not know that night (the beginning of Sabbath) has fallen, he may move two thousand cubits in any direction, according to R. Johanan b. Nuri.[1] But the Sages say: He may move only four cubits.[2] R. Eliezer says: with

himself considered in the middle of them.[3] R. Judah concedes that
when once he has chosen a direction he may not change it.[4]

---

1. He has not planned to be away from home on Sabbath, and has
not arranged for an *Eruv*. If he is inside a city when he awakens, he
has no problem: His lodging arrangement makes him a temporary
resident of the city and its boundaries constitute his Sabbath travel
limit.
2. Because two thousand cubits would imply that he has somehow
acquired Sabbath limit rights. But this requires a conscious action.
3. That is, he may move only two cubits in any direction.
4. R. Joḥanan b. Nuri's view was accepted as law, apparently because
of the unusual circumstances. The Rabbis did not wish to force a
man to spend the Sabbath out in the middle of nowhere, possibly
without food or shelter.

Eruvin 8:2

What is the minimum quantity of the *Shittuf*, the collective *Eruv*
for a group of Jews who share a courtyard? Enough food for two
meals for each person,[1] but weekday meals rather than Sabbath
meals, according to R. Meir. R. Judah says: Sabbath meals, and
not weekday meals. Each intended to give the more lenient ruling.[2]

---

1. There is a sizable difference between Sabbath and weekday food
consumption. First, three meals have to be eaten on the Sabbath.
On weekdays, two meals are considered sufficient. Then, the amount
of food available at each meal is greater on the Sabbath. In addition,
there are real differences between the types of food consumed.
    Why two meals for each person? Three meals are required on
Sabbath. But, reason the practical Rabbis, since no one would go
visiting until after morning prayers on the Sabbath, the first meal
would have been eaten on Friday after the evening prayers. Nothing
is eaten before morning prayers are said.
2. R. Meir is talking about the total quantity of food intake on the
Sabbath, translated into bread quantities. R. Judah is talking of
bread intake alone on the Sabbath, when less bread is eaten because
more of other foods are available.

PESAHIM—PASSOVER

Introduction

Why is the name of this book in the plural? Because there are, in fact, two Passovers. A "Second Passover" was instituted, to be celebrated a month after Pesaḥ, for those who could not celebrate the festival on schedule (see Numbers 9:6–12). For accuracy, therefore, the title of the book was made plural, though the overwhelming bulk of the Mishnah's concern is with the first or Great Passover.

The importance of the Passover observance was indicated by Maimonides. He stated that this book is included in *Sefer Mo'ed* directly after the two books dealing with Shabbat because the mitzvah of observing Pesaḥ follows only the mitzvah of Shabbat in the hierarchy of holy days.

Three major Halakhic questions concern the Mishnah: first, the prohibition against leaven and all its implications; second, the eating of matzah itself; and third, the Paschal offering and the Seder service. Large parts of the Haggadah were already known and in use at the time of the writing of the Mishnah (see Chapter 10).

The festival underwent a long evolution both within the Biblical period and thereafter. As is typical of Judaism, as new layers of meaning were added, the old ones remained intact. On the pastoral festival of the spring lambs was superimposed the agricultural feast of the early grain harvest; both in turn were incorporated into the history of Israel with the Exodus story. And always, the ethical principle of human freedom was the major theme of the entire festival.

Biblical Sources for Pesaḥim

And when your children ask you, "What do you mean by this rite?" you shall say, "It is the passover sacrifice to the Lord, because He passed over the houses of the Israelites in Egypt when He smote the Egyptians, but saved our houses." (Exodus 12:26–27)

SEE ALSO

> Exodus 12:1–25, 28–29, 43–50; 13:3–10; 23:15, 18, 25
> Leviticus 23:5–8
> Numbers 9:1–14; 28:16–25
> Deuteronomy 16:1–8
> Joshua 5:10–11
> II Kings 23:21–23
> Ezekiel 45:21–24
> Ezra 6:19–22
> II Chronicles 30:1–5, 13–22; 35:1–19

Pesaḥim 1:1

At the beginning of the evening of the fourteenth [1] of *Nisan* a search for leavened food is conducted by the light of a candle.[2] A place into which *ḥametz* [3] is never brought need not be searched. Then why has it been said: They must search two rows in a wine vault? Into such a place *ḥametz* might be brought.[4]

---

1. Any given day begins with sunset. Therefore, Passover evening is not the "evening of the fourteenth of *Nisan*," but the night before.
2. Two reasons are given in later rabbinic writings for searching at night with a candle. First, the occasion is a family affair. Second, candlelight is esthetically pleasant, especially for the young. More typically, several Bible verses are invoked to prove that a candle must be used. (See Exodus 12:19, then Genesis 44:12, then Proverbs 20:27. The first two "prove" that one must search to find, and the last that searching must be done by a candle.)

3. *Ḥametz* includes any substance forbidden for use on Passover.
4. A servant could go down to the wine cellar to select a bottle while eating a piece of bread, for example.

Pesaḥim 2:1

As long as it is permitted to eat *ḥametz,* a man may feed it to cattle, wild animals, and birds, or may sell it to a non-Jew.[1] In general, it is permitted to derive benefit from it. But when the time is passed, it is forbidden to derive benefit from it. An oven or stove may not be lit with it. R. Judah says: Removal of *ḥametz* may be done only by burning. The Sages say: It may be crumbled up and scattered to the wind or thrown into the sea.[2]

1. The practice of selling *ḥametz* to a non-Jew in order to avoid destroying it has become a universal legal fiction in Jewish life. It is under the direct supervision of the traditional rabbinate. Immediately after Passover, the *ḥametz* is bought back from the non-Jew. Physically, it need not even leave the home after the "sale," but must only be isolated from Passover foods.

   Legal fictions are necessary in every system of law. For example, in contemporary law, for many purposes a corporation is considered a *person,* with constitutional and even citizenship rights and obligations. It has even been ruled that a corporation is protected like a person under the provisions of the Fourteenth Amendment to the Constitution of the United States.
2. Even though burning has become the traditional method of destroying the symbolic bits of *ḥametz* gathered around the house, the law is according to the Sages.

Pesaḥim 2:5

A man fulfills his obligation during Passover by eating these things in unleavened form: wheat, barley, spelt, oats, and rye.[1]

1. This one sentence is the basic ruling from which the entire complex of Passover food prohibitions projects. All other grains are

usable in unleavened form, but matzah may be made only from these. Any food which could conceivably be leavened or is leavenable is prohibited, along with any food which might have contacted leavened material. These facts account for the need for special Passover labels on everything from soda to sugar, certifying that the products have been prepared and packaged under rabbinic supervision to ensure that they do not contain forbidden elements and have had no contact with them.

Pesaḥim 4:1

Where it is the custom [1] to work until noon on the eve of Passover, one may do so. Where it is the custom not to work that morning, one may not do so.[2] If a man moves from a place where they do work to a place where they do not, or from a place where they do not to a place where they do, the more stringent custom of the place he has left and the place to which he has moved is applicable to him. But no man should act contrary to local custom lest it lead to conflict.[3]

---

1. This phrase dominates the first five *Mishnayot* of this chapter. Not all the regulations are relevant to Passover, but they were placed together here because of stylistic similarity.
2. In earlier days no one worked all day, and the afternoon was used to prepare for the Festival. But in some places, even the morning was taken off to burn the *hametz* collected the evening before, to prepare the Paschal lamb for roasting, and the like.
3. If he plans to remain in his new home, he accepts the local custom even if it is more stringent. If he plans to return to his former home, he maintains that town's custom, even if it is more stringent. The concept of local custom is an important one in Halakhah. Customs, in general, were taken seriously. "Custom cancels the Halakhah," says the Jerusalem Talmud (*Yevamot* 12:1). Many significant variations in ritual practice from community to community, which increased in number and importance over the centuries, still exist.

Pesaḥim 4:4

Where it is the custom to eat roast meat on the nights of Passover, one may do so. Where it is not the custom, one may not do so.[1] Where it is the custom to light candles on the night of Yom Kippur, one may do so. Where it is the custom not to kindle, one may not do so.[2] But candles may be lit in synagogues, houses of study, dark alleys, and near sick people.

---

1. The places which prohibited eating roast meat did so lest the appearance be given that the Paschal sacrifice was being consumed away from Jerusalem, which was forbidden during the Second Temple era. In addition, the Paschal lamb had to be completely consumed on the first night.
2. This regulation does not refer to the ritual lighting of candles at the beginning of the Sabbath or festivals, but to the maintaining of at least one lit candle in the home throughout the Sabbath, a requirement of Halakhah, as a symbol of joy. This is not required on Yom Kippur. The reason for permitting or prohibiting the lighting of this candle on Yom Kippur is of interest. It was permitted in some towns in order to prevent a man and wife from violating the Yom Kippur prohibition against sexual intercourse. (Halakhah prohibits intercourse when there is a light burning.) The obligatory Sabbath candle is not, obviously, lit in the bedroom. It was prohibited in other towns lest a man look at his wife in the romantic light of the candle, become sexually aroused, and violate Halakhah by having intercourse on Yom Kippur.

Pesaḥim 5:7

When the first group left, the second group entered to slaughter the Passover offering, and when the second group left the third group entered.[1] The ritual was performed in the same way with the second and third groups as it was with the first. The Levites chanted the Hallel.[2] If they finished it, they sang it a second time, and if necessary, began to sing it a third time. It never happened that they finished it the third time. R. Judah says: During the turn of the third group, the Levites never got as far as "I love the Lord because He has heard," [3] since the number of people in that group was small.

---

1. The whole pilgrim group was divided into three sections, as was taught in *Pesaḥim* 5:5, which is not included here. All descriptions of activity in the Temple in Jerusalem refer to the Second Temple period. The Samaritans erected their own central shrine on Mount Gerizim and sacrifice their Paschal lamb there to this day.
2. Psalms 113–118, still sung in the synagogue on Passover, Shavuot, and Sukkot. Part of the Hallel is sung on each New Moon and on Ḥanukkah as well.
3. Psalms 116:1. Since the whole Hallel is not long, this indicates that the number of pilgrims was not great. Since no population statistics are available for ancient times, every bit of data is significant.

Pesaḥim 7:2

The Passover offering may not be roasted on a metal spit or on a grill.[1]

---

1. A spit or grill absorbs, maintains, and radiates heat, and therefore the meat would not be entirely fire-roasted, as is required by the Torah. Nevertheless, Rabban Gamaliel did so, according to the story which takes up the rest of this Mishnah, because he believed that derivative heat was equal to direct fire-heat. The Halakhah eventually accepted Rabban Gamaliel's view, and metal spits or perforated grills were permitted, though wooden ones were preferred.

Pesaḥim 8:1

When a woman is living with her husband and he slaughters enough Passover offering for her, and her father also slaughters enough for her, she shall eat with her husband. If she goes to celebrate the first Festival [1] in her father's house, and both her father and her husband slaughtered enough for her, she may eat in whichever home she prefers.[2] An orphan for whom many guardians have slaughtered may eat in whichever place he prefers. A [non-Jewish] slave belonging jointly to two owners may not eat from the Passover offering of both. A man who is half-slave and half-free [3] may not eat of the offering of his master.

---

1. That is, the first Passover after the marriage, which was once a widespread custom.
2. That is, wherever she feels more comfortable. Distances were short and she could stay with her father, as custom required, yet still eat the festival meal at her own home with her husband if she wished. This regulation postdates the destruction of the Temple in 70 c.e.
3. A Hebrew slave whose papers of freedom had been written and sealed, but had not yet taken effect. On Passover night, he was like a free man and expected to offer his own sacrifice.

Pesaḥim 9:3

How does the First Passover differ from the Second? [1] To the first apply the prohibitions: "It shall not be seen" and "It shall not be found" (Exodus 13:7, 12:19), while at the Second Passover a man may have both unleavened bread and *hametz* in his house. During the eating of the First [offering], the Hallel must be sung (see Isaiah 30:29), but during the Second, it need not be sung. Both require the Hallel to be sung while the sacrifice is being prepared. Both are eaten roasted with unleavened bread and bitter herbs, and both override the Sabbath.[2]

---

1. See Numbers 9:6–12 and II Chronicles 30:1–27.
2. A detailed discussion of this matter appears in Mishnah 6:1–2, not included here. Slaughter outside the Temple was forbidden on the Sabbath, but Passover can begin on the Sabbath and the Paschal sacrifice did not take place only in the Temple (except during the Second Temple period). Because the sacrifice could take place only on the specified date, it had to override the Sabbath.

Pesaḥim 10:1

On the eve of Passover, a man must not eat from the time of the *Minḥah* offering [1] until nightfall.[2] Even the poorest in Israel must not eat unless they lean,[3] and they must be given [4] at least four cups of wine to drink,[5] even if it is from the *Tamḥui*.[6]

---

1. About 3:00 P.M.
2. So that he may derive maximum pleasure from the Seder meal.
3. To symbolize their status as free people. During the year, the poor ate while sitting on hard benches or standing. Only the rich had divans. But at the Seder everyone ate in a reclining position.
4. By the public official who distributed food daily to the poor. These *Gaba'im* were perhaps the first social workers in human history. Relief was distributed in a highly organized, dignified manner even before the first century C.E.
5. Four words are used in Exodus (6:6ff.) to describe the Exodus. The Jerusalem Talmud adds reasons for the practice, all in the same vein.
6. The *Tamḥui* is a bowl into which are put foods contributed for the poor and distributed immediately. It remained an integral part of the welfare system of Jewish communities for centuries.

    To provide a fine Seder for every Jew is a great mitzvah. To this day in every Jewish community of any size in the world organized efforts are made each year to continue this mitzvah.

Pesaḥim 10:3

After the Kiddush [1] they set it before him,[2] and he eats lettuce dipped in salt water or vinegar before he eats vegetables together with the cake of matzah.[3] There have been set before him matzah, lettuce, *haroset,* and two cooked things,[4] even though *haroset* is not a mitzvah.[5] And in the Temple, they also set the Passover offering before him.

---

1. Described in a previous Mishnah, not included here.
2. There is disagreement about this phrase. It appears to mean that a

small table was brought to the leader of the Seder containing all the necessary ritual items. Other commentators state that the items were brought one at a time.

3. Lettuce is classified as a bitter herb for Passover consumption. Some say it was eaten at the very beginning of the Seder to whet the appetite.
4. Items commemorating the festival sacrifice and the additional *Hagigah* sacrifice. Today the shankbone of the lamb and the roasted egg fulfill these requirements.
5. As a memorial of the mortar used by the Israelites in Egypt when they built the cities of Pithom and Ramses for Pharaoh.

Pesaḥim 10:4

The second cup is mixed.[1] The son asks his father the four questions, and if the son does not have enough knowledge his father teaches him how to ask: "Why is this night different from all other nights? On other nights we eat leavened or unleavened bread, but this night only unleavened. On all other nights we eat a variety of vegetables, but on this only bitter herbs.[2] On all other nights we may eat meat which has been roasted, stewed, or boiled, but this night only roast meat.[3] On all other nights we dip our food only once,[4] but on this night twice."[5] The father then instructs him according to his son's level of knowledge. He begins with the disgrace and ends with the glory,[6] and he expounds from "A wandering Aramean was my father. . . ." (Deuteronomy 26:5), until he finishes the whole story.

---

1. In Palestine, as in all ancient countries, wine was "cut" with water before drinking.
2. This sentence is missing in some manuscripts, but is found in the traditional Haggadah.
3. This sentence was dropped from the Haggadah as the memory of the roast Paschal lamb faded over the centuries. The four questions relate to the well-known details in the child's experience.
4. It was the general custom to begin meals with a vegetable soaked in salt water, vinegar, or oil. This kind of appetizer is still frequently

served in Mediterranean countries, often as a highly-spiced salad of cucumbers, tomatoes, or eggplant. Because Ashkenazi Jews did not know this Eastern tradition, they changed the question in the Haggadah to: "We do not dip even once."

5. The fourth question in the Haggadah, with regard to leaning at the table, appeared after the completion of the Talmud.

6. The Haggadah tells both about Egyptian slavery and about the Israelites before Abraham, who were idol-worshippers. It ends, of course, with the Exodus to freedom and praise of God.

Pesaḥim 10:5

Rabban Gamaliel used to say: Whoever has not spoken of these three things at Passover has not fulfilled his obligations: Pesaḥ, matzah, and *maror*. Pesaḥ, because God passed over the houses of our fathers in Egypt. Matzah, because our fathers were redeemed out of Egypt. *Maror,* because the Egyptians made the lives of our fathers bitter in Egypt. In each and every generation, a man must think of himself as if he came out of Egypt, as it is written: "And you shall tell your son on that day saying, it is because of that which the Lord did for *me* when *I* came forth out of Egypt" (Exodus 13:8). Therefore we are required to give thanks, to praise, to glorify, to honor, to exalt, to extol, and to bless Him who performed all those wonders for our fathers and for us. He brought us from bondage to freedom, from sorrow to gladness, from mourning to Festival, from darkness to great light, and from slavery to redemption. Let us say before Him: Hallelujah.[1]

---

1. The Hallel follows this passage in the Haggadah. Psalms 113 begins with this word. This Mishnah passed verbatim into the Haggadah, with amplifications.

Pesaḥim 10:6

How much of the Hallel should be recited? The school of Shammai says: to "a joyful mother of children" (Psalms 113:9). The school of Hillel says: to "a flintstone into a living well." [1] And this is concluded with the *ge'ullah*. [2]

---

1. Psalms 114:8. Why the difference? Shammai's school said that Psalms 114, which is concerned with post-Exodus matters, should not be said on the first night of Passover, when the Exodus was not yet completed. Hillel's school felt that the whole Exodus story, including the completion of the salvation of Israel, must be told. The view of Hillel's school has prevailed in the Haggadah.
2. "Praised be Thou, O Lord, who redeemed Israel."

Pesaḥim 10:7

After the third cup has been mixed, the leader says the blessings after the meal. Before the fourth cup, [1] he completes the Hallel and then says the blessing over song. [2] If he wishes to drink wine between the cups he may do so. But he may not drink between the third and fourth cups. [3]

---

1. Before he says the blessing and drinks it, but after it has been mixed. The custom today is to pour the next cup as soon as possible after one has been drunk.
2. The Rabbis disagreed about the words of this blessing. Some said it was the prayer which begins: "They will praise Thee, O God, for all Thy deeds." Others said it was: "The Soul of every living thing will praise Thy name." The Haggadah includes both.
3. In order that he stay sober enough to complete the service properly.

SHEKALIM—TEMPLE TAXES

Introduction

Three kinds of head-tax were lumped under the general term *Shekalim*. The most important was the annual tax of one-half shekel paid by every Israelite each spring for the maintenance of the Temple. (The value of a shekel before 1933 used to be placed at approximately one dollar, but the value of the dollar has since declined.) Though originally considered a tax paid only once, at the time of the original census, it became a routine annual tax. The second tax was the so-called "vow of persons." As ordained in Leviticus 27:1 ff., this was a method of getting God's approval. The value of a person was given to the Temple on a schedule set up in the Torah. (The late, portly Aga Khan received his weight in gold on his birthday from his worshipping followers.) And finally, individuals could give free-will gifts of money for the maintenance of the Temple.

The text digresses rapidly from the major subject of the various taxes paid in *Shekalim*. It provides us with fascinating and valuable data about the administrative workings of the Temple. The day-to-day activities come alive.

Shekalim is the only book in *Seder Mo'ed* for which there is no Babylonian Gemara, though there is a Jerusalem Gemara.

Biblical Sources for Shekalim

The Lord spoke to Moses, saying: When you take a census of the Israelite people according to their enrollment, each shall pay the Lord a ransom for himself on being enrolled, that no plague may come upon them through their being enrolled. This is what everyone who is entered in the records shall pay: a half-shekel by the sanctuary weight—twenty *gerahs* to the shekel—a half-shekel as an offering to the Lord. Every one who is entered in the records, from the age of twenty years up, shall give the Lord's offering: The rich shall not pay more and the poor shall not pay less than half a shekel when giving the Lord's offering as expiation for your persons. You shall take the expiation money from the Israelites and assign it to the service of the Tent of Meeting; it shall serve the Israelites as a reminder before the Lord, as expiation for your persons. (Exodus 30:11–16)

SEE ALSO

II Kings 12:5–17
Nehemiah 10:32–34
II Chronicles 24:4–14

Shekalim 1:1

On the first of *Adar,* notice is given that the shekel is due,[1] and warning is issued against the sowing of *Kila'yim.* On the fifteenth of *Adar,* the Megillah is read in walled cities,[2] path and road repairs are begun,[3] pools of water are repaired,[4] other public services are undertaken,[5] including the marking of graves.[6] Officials go out to check on *Kila'yim.*

---

1. The fiscal year of the Temple began on the first of *Nisan,* and the cash was needed to purchase animals for the daily offering, etc. The notice was circulated by the Sanhedrin.
2. See Mishnah *Megillah* 1:1, p. 142.
3. These had been damaged by the winter rains. Repairs had to be finished before the Passover pilgrimages began.
4. Including cisterns, wells, and public baths, all of which were affected by the rains, which are often torrential in what is now Israel.
5. Bertinora lists some of these: settlement of civil lawsuits, punishing of persons by whipping, ritual care of lepers, and the like.
6. The sides of which were washed away by the rains, which, from a ritual standpoint, was serious. For example, a priest might walk on an unmarked grave, touch a bone, and become defiled.

Shekalim 1:5

Although it was ruled that no pledges were levied on women or slaves or minors, if any of these paid the shekel it was accepted. But if a pagan or a Samaritan [1] paid the shekel, it was not accepted. Similarly, they did not accept from pagans or Samaritans the bird-offerings of men or women who had a running sore (Leviticus 15:14, 29), or the bird-offerings of women after childbirth (*ibid.*, 12:8), or sin-offerings or guilt-offerings (*ibid.*, 4:1–12, 7:1–10). But their vow-offerings and free-will offerings could be accepted. This is the general rule: What is vowed or offered freely can be accepted from them, but what is not vowed or offered freely cannot be accepted. It was explicitly ordained thus by Ezra, for it is written: "You have nothing to do with us to build a house unto our God." [2]

---

1. The status of the Samaritans in the Talmud is low. According to tradition, some of the people of the Northern Kingdom (Samaria) were not exiled when Samaria was destroyed in 722–21 B.C.E. But they never became part of Judean life, especially in their insistence on maintaining their northern religious customs. After the return from the Babylonian Exile, they did not integrate themselves into the religious life of the returning Jews. They refused to accept Jerusalem as the sole shrine and worshipped on Mount Gerizim. Ezra considered them non-Jews. Over the centuries they drifted further and further from Judaism, while maintaining certain early rituals. A small group of Samaritans still remains in Israel.
2. Ezra 4:3. The words are spoken by Zerubavel and Yeshua.

Shekalim 5:6

In the Temple were two rooms: the Chamber of Secret Gifts, and the Chamber of Vessels. The zealous used to put their gifts secretly into the Chamber of Secret Gifts, and the poor drew support from it in secret.[1] Whenever someone offered a gift of a vessel to the

Temple he put it in the Chamber of Vessels. Every thirty days the treasurers opened the room. Any articles they found which were of use for the Temple were kept. The rest were sold, and the money went to the fund for repairing the Temple.

---

1. Throughout Halakhah, stringent measures were taken to avoid embarrassing either the recipient of philanthropy or the giver. The most important statement of this principle is to be found in Maimonides' Eight Steps of Charity.

Shekalim 6:2

Once when a priest was busy in the Second Temple he saw a block of pavement which was different from the rest. He began to tell his colleague about it, but he died before he finished. Consequently, they knew that the Ark certainly lay hidden there.[1]

---

1. The whereabouts of the Ark with the Two Tablets of the Covenant plagued the whole Jewish people throughout the Second Temple period. Bertinora suggests that Josiah might have ordered the Ark hidden, as recorded in II Chronicles 35:3, but there is no later evidence to support this suggestion. There is a great deal of speculation about it in classical Jewish literature. The people could not accept the idea that the Ark and the Tablets could have been destroyed.

YOMA—THE DAY (OF ATONEMENT)

Introduction

The Day of Atonement is the most solemn occasion in the Jewish calendar. That is why this book is called Yoma, "The Day," though many centuries ago it was entitled, Kippurim, "Atonements."

Of the eight chapters in the book, seven concentrate on the

solemn observances in the ancient Second Temple in Jerusalem. The descriptions are awe-inspiring even to the sophisticated modern.

The climax of the Temple observance of Yom Kippur was the entrance of the High Priest into the Holy of Holies, the only time that even he was permitted to enter it. The High Priest burned incense and said a brief prayer, the text of which has been lost. His prayer had to be short, as the Mishnah puts it, because the people were terrified until he re-emerged through the *Parokhet,* the curtain screening off the Holy of Holies.

The incense and its proper offering were subjects of great controversy during the Second Temple period. Sadducees and Pharisees did not agree, and the matter, though relatively unimportant, became a symbol of the conflicts between the two interpretations of Judaism. As a consequence, the High Priest had to take a vow that he would perform his duties according to Halakhah—and when he did, both he and the elders wept because of the suspicions which divided Israel.

This Mishnah book is of interest today because so much of its contents has been incorporated into the Yom Kippur ritual of the synagogue.

Biblical Sources for Yoma

Mark, the tenth day of this seventh month is the Day of Atonement. It shall be a sacred occasion for you: you shall practice self-denial, and you shall bring an offering by fire to the Lord; you shall do no work throughout that day. For it is a Day of Atonement, on which expiation is made on your behalf before the Lord your God. (Leviticus 23:27–28)

SEE ALSO

Exodus 30:10
Leviticus 16:1–34; 23:26–32
Numbers 29:7–11

Yoma 1:1

Seven days before Yom Kippur, the High Priest [1] was taken away from his home to the Palhedrin [2] Chamber, and another priest was appointed as his replacement, should anything happen to make him ineligible [that is, ritually unclean]. R. Judah says: In addition, another wife was appointed for him in case his own wife should die, for it is written: "He shall make atonement for himself and for his house" (Leviticus 16:6). "His house"—that is his wife.[3] They said to him: if so, there would be no end to the matter.[4]

---

1. The High Priest played the central role in the rituals of Yom Kippur in the Temple. This is clear both in Leviticus 16 and in the Mishnah texts which follow.
2. No one knows the precise meaning of this word or the real function of the room in the Temple. Bertinora suggests that the Palhedrin were officials of the king's court, and since the High Priest was, wrongly, a royal functionary after the days of Simon the Just (beginning in the third century B.C.E.; more properly, however, after the beginning of the Maccabean period, 165 B.C.E.) he was taken to a room in the Temple with which he was already familiar. Jung, in his note on the Soncino text, suggests that the proper Hebrew word was Parhedrin, from a Greek word meaning "counselors." Some scholars have identified the room with the Sanhedrin chamber, usually called the Chamber of Hewn Stone.
3. An unmarried High Priest could not officiate on Yom Kippur.
4. That is, the second wife might die and so a third would have to be in advance reserve; but the third might die, and an infinite number of substitutes would have to be lined up. R. Judah's view was not accepted as law.

Yoma 1:3

He was assigned elders from the court. They read to him the prescribed ritual for The Day [chiefly Leviticus 16]. They said to him: "My Lord High Priest, do read it yourself, in case you have forgotten, or in case you never learned it." [1] On the day before Yom Kippur in the morning, they stood him at the Eastern Gate and brought oxen, rams, and sheep before him,[2] so that he might gain knowledge and become versed in the service.

---

1. During the Second Temple period, since High Priests were royal political appointees, they were frequently ignorant men, sometimes illiterate. This was a source of great anguish to the Rabbis. Though the commentators do not suggest that the elders were being sarcastic or contemptuous here, one wonders.
2. Animals like those which would be used in the Yom Kippur ritual.

Yoma 1:5

The elders of the court turned him over to the elders of the priesthood, and they took him to the upper chamber of the house of Abtinas.[1] They administered an oath to him.[2] Before they left, they said to him: "My Lord High Priest, we are messengers of the court, and you are our messenger as well as a messenger of the court. We adjure you by Him who made His name dwell in this house that you change nothing of what we have told you." He went off and wept, and they went off and wept.[3]

---

1. Where the incense was prepared. There the High Priest was instructed in the ritual of offering the incense.
2. He swore that he was not a Sadducee and would not follow the Sadducean form of incense ritual.
3. He wept because they suspected him of Sadducean tendencies. They wept because it had become necessary to suspect the High Priest himself. This was no ordinary political or religious controversy; it was to have profound emotional implications for every Jew for generations.

Yoma 1:6

If he was learned, he used to expound Torah.[1] If not, the Sages used to expound before him. If he was versed in reading Torah, he read aloud. If not, they read to him. What did they read to him? Job, Ezra, and Chronicles.[2] Zechariah b. Kabutal says: I read to him many times from Daniel.

---

1. Throughout the night, so that he would not fall asleep. Were he to sleep and by chance have a seminal emission, he would be defiled and ineligible to officiate the following day.
2. The choice was dictated for at least two reasons: First, these books contain dramatic materials and would arouse feeling and so prevent drowsiness in the High Priest. Second, all three dwell on high-minded men who felt deeply about Torah, and reading them might influence the High Priest toward greater piety and less court politicking.

Yoma 3:8

He went over to his bullock [1] which was standing between the porch and the altar, its head toward the south and its face toward the west. The Priest stood on the east facing west. He set both his hands on the bullock and confessed. He said: "O God,[2] I have committed iniquities, I have transgressed, and I have sinned before Thee, I and my house. O God, forgive the iniquities and the transgressions and the sins which I have committed and transgressed and sinned before Thee, I and my house, as it is written in the Torah of Thy servant Moses: For on this day he will atone for you to cleanse you; from all your sins shall you be clean before the Lord" (Leviticus 16:30). The congregation responded: "Blessed be the Name, the glory of whose kingdom is forever and ever!"

---

1. It was "his" bullock because it would atone for his sins and those of his family. See Leviticus 16:6.

2. The Hebrew here reads *Ha'Shem,* "the Name." In fact, the High
Priest began here to use the Tetragrammaton, the ineffable four-
letter name of God spoken only by him and only on Yom Kippur
during this ceremony. The word *God* is still strenuously avoided
by traditional Jews. These letters, *YHVH,* were probably originally
pronounced "Yahveh." Early German Christians added the vowels
for *Adonai* to these consonants and came up with the name
Jehovah.

Yoma 3:9

He then moved eastward, north of the altar, with the assistant [1] on
his right and the head of the father's house [2] on his left. Two he-
goats [3] were there, and also a casket in which were two lots. They
were usually of boxwood, but Ben Gamla [4] made them of gold,
and his act was remembered as praiseworthy.

---

1. The status and role of the *segan* are not clear. Early commentators
   tended to think of him as a deputy High Priest. But, as clearly indicated in the Mishnah itself, a deputy was chosen for the Yom
   Kippur ritual in the event the High Priest became ineligible. It is
   now generally believed that the *segan* was a majordomo or chief
   marshal, in charge of supervising all Temple ritual.
2. All the priests were divided into twenty-four watches, which officiated in rotation. Each watch was subdivided into "father's houses."
   At any given time, the "head of the father's house" supervised the
   priests carrying on specific duties.
3. The goats' functions are described in the *Mishnayot* which follow.
4. Apparently Joshua b. Gamla (or Gamaliel), third from the last
   High Priest before the destruction of the Temple. His service was
   after 35 C.E. and before 65, but no more specific dates can be given.

Yoma 4:1

The High Priest shook the casket and took the two lots, one in
each hand. On one was written, "For the Lord," and on the other,
"For Azaz'el." [1] The assistant was on his right and the head of

the father's house on his left. If the lot with God's name came up in his right hand, the assistant would say to him: "My lord High Priest, raise your right hand." If it came up in his left hand, the head of the father's house would say to him: "My lord High Priest, raise your left hand." He put the lots on the respective he-goats and said: "A sin offering to the Lord." R. Ishmael says: He did not have to say "a sin offering," but only "to the Lord." [2] The people responded: "Blessed be the Name, the glory of whose kingdom is forever and ever."

---

1. The origin of the word *Azaz'el* is not clear. The Gemara interprets the word to mean "hardest of the mountains." Most medieval commentators accept that rugged definition. But many scholars, even in early medieval times, were able to recognize that *Azaz'el* had something to do with a demon. The demon is connected with the *se'irim*, a goat-shaped group of demons which haunted the desert, or with the demons involved in the fall of Satan in the Apocryphal Book of Enoch. *Azaz'el* also appears in Babylonian, Sabean, and Arabian mythologies.

In contemporary Israel, *Azaz'el* is connected with hell. In street slang, *le'Azaz'el* has the connotation of "To hell with it."

2. R. Ishmael's view was not accepted as law.

Yoma 4:2

He tied a crimson thread on the head of the scapegoat, and turned it in the direction it was to be sent. On the throat of the he-goat which was to be slaughtered, he bound a second thread.[1] He returned to his bullock, placed both his hands on it, and confessed. He said: "O God, I have committed iniquities, I have transgressed, and I have sinned before Thee, I and my house,[2] and the children of Aaron, Thy sacred ones. O God, forgive, I pray, the iniquities and the transgressions and the sins which I have committed and transgressed and sinned before Thee, I and my house, and the children of Aaron, Thy sacred ones, as it is written in the Torah of Thy servant Moses: 'For on this day he will atone for you to cleanse you; from all your sins shall you be clean before the Lord.' " The congregation responded: "Blessed be the Name, the glory of whose kingdom is forever and ever!"

---

1. The second thread went around the animal's throat so that there could be no confusion between the two goats.
2. The Rabbis made a distinction among these forms of sins: *avon,* "iniquity," was a deliberate violation of Torah; *pesha,* "transgression," was an act of rebellion against God: *ḥet,* "sin," was an unwitting violation of God's law, an error.

Yoma 6:2

He then went to the scapegoat,[1] placed both hands upon it, and confessed. He said: "O God, Thy people, the house of Israel, have committed iniquities, have transgressed, and have sinned before Thee. O God, forgive, I pray, the iniquities, the transgressions, and the sins which Thy people, the house of Israel, have committed and transgressed, and sinned before Thee, as it is written in the Torah of Thy servant Moses: 'For on this day He shall atone for you to cleanse you; from all your sins shall you be clean before the Lord.' " When the priests and the people standing in the Temple court heard the Ineffable Name out of the mouth of the High Priest, they knelt and bowed down and fell on their faces and said: "Blessed be the Name, the glory of whose kingdom is forever and ever!" [2]

---

1. The intervening *Mishnayot* deal in detail with the slaughter of the goat marked "For God."
2. This is the third and last priestly confessional. The entire ritual of the three confessionals is reproduced in the traditional service for Yom Kippur.

Yoma 6:8

The High Priest was told: "The he-goat has reached the wilderness." [1] How did they know that the he-goat had reached the wilderness? They set up sentinel-posts and from these cloths were waved. Thus they knew that the he-goat had reached the wilderness. R. Judah said: Did they not have a better sign? It was three miles from Jerusalem to Bet Ḥadodo. [2] Someone could walk a mile, return a mile, wait enough time to go another mile, and then they would know that the he-goat had reached the wilderness. R. Ishmael said: Did they not have another sign? A crimson thread was tied to the door of the Sanctuary. When the he-goat reached the wilderness, the thread turned white, as it is written: Though your sins be scarlet, they shall be white as snow. [3]

---

1. Until the scapegoat reached the wilderness, the High Priest could not begin the next phase of the ritual, described in Chapter 7.
2. Bet Ḥadodo was the beginning of the wilderness. It is assumed that it was southeast of Jerusalem in the direction of the Judean desert, which had many canyons and cliffs to fit the "cut-off place" requirement for the scapegoat.
3. Isaiah 1:18. This statement is missing in many manuscripts. A more miracle-minded generation may have introduced it into the text, or a less-superstitious-minded one may have removed it from older texts. We do not know. The red thread, though, occupies a prominent place in Jewish superstition over the centuries, and in the superstitious practices of many cultures. Horses were garlanded with a red thread; children wore coral necklaces to protect them against the Evil Eye. Foolhardy indeed was the woman in labor whose bedpost was not adorned with a red ribbon. As late as our own generation, this latter superstition has persisted.

Yoma 7:1

Then the High Priest began to read. [1] If he wished to read in the linen garments, he could do so. Otherwise, he read in his own white vestment. [2] The cantor of the synagogue [3] used to take a scroll of the Torah and give it to the head of the synagogue, and he gave it to the assistant, and the assistant handed it to the High Priest. The High Priest stood as he received it, and as he read it. He read: "After the death . . ." and ". . . On the tenth day . . ." (Leviticus 16:1–34, 23:26–32). Then he rolled up the Torah scroll, held it and said: "More is written here than I have read before you." "And on the tenth . . ." which is in the Book of Numbers (29:7–11) he recited by heart. Then he pronounced eight blessings: for the Torah,[4] for the Temple service (the *Retze*), for thanksgiving (*Modim*), for the forgiveness of sin,[5] for the Temple separately,[6] for the Israelites separately, for Jerusalem separately, for the priests separately, and then a general prayer.[7]

---

1. The Torah portion for Yom Kippur.
2. A personal cloak, ankle-length, not worn for ceremonial service.
3. There were both a synagogue and an academy of study in the Temple. The Hebrew word *ḥazzan* is today universally translated as "cantor." One of the major functions of the cantor was and is to lead the liturgical service in chant form. In this Mishnah, he appears to have had an additional duty similar to that of the sexton in the contemporary synagogue. The specific duties of all synagogue functionaries have tended to vary from time to time and from place to place.
4. The blessing Jews still say after the reading of the Torah.
5. The traditional prayer which ends, "who forgives the sins of His people Israel in mercy."
6. No one knows what the word *separately* means here. Some early editions of the Mishnah omit it.
7. The texts of these last prayers are not available to us.

Yoma 8:1

On Yom Kippur, eating, drinking, washing, anointing, putting on sandals, and sexual intercourse are forbidden. A king and a bride may wash their faces,[1] and a woman who has just delivered a child may put on sandals.[2] This was the opinion of R. Eliezer. But the Sages forbade it.[3]

---

1. The king must always look well. The bride must continually impress her groom with her beauty. Incidentally, she is a bride only the first Yom Kippur after the marriage.
2. She must not expose herself to the possibility of catching a cold.
3. R. Eliezer's view was accepted as law.

Yoma 8:4

Young children are not required to fast on Yom Kippur. But they should be trained a year or two in advance [1] so that they may become accustomed to the mitzvot.

---

1. Bertinora suggests lengthening the time between meals for healthy children. Boys began to fast at thirteen, girls at twelve. In the Gemara it is suggested that fasting begin a year before it is required.

Yoma 8:6

If ravenous hunger seizes a man, he may be given even non-kosher things to eat until his eyes are enlightened.[1] If a mad dog bites him, he may not be given the lobe of its liver to eat, but R. Mattithiah b. Ḥeresh permits it.[2] R. Mattithiah b. Ḥeresh also said: If a man has a pain in his throat,[3] they may drop medicine into his mouth on the Sabbath, since it is possible his life is in danger.[4] Whenever there is a possibility that life is in danger, this overrides the Sabbath.[5]

---

1. This was considered a mortal illness. Naturally, non-kosher things (pork, shellfish, improperly cooked items) were given him only if kosher food was not available.
2. Any day of the year, not just on Yom Kippur. The liver of the mad

dog was widely believed to have curative power. But the Rabbis did not accept it that way. R. Mattithiah's attitude was variously interpreted as his belief in the liver as a cure and his desire to take no chances, even if it was not a certain thing. The law did not follow him, however.

3. Some versions read "mouth" for "throat."

4. He might choke, or the pain spread to his stomach, becoming more dangerous.

5. This general principle was consistently upheld by the Rabbis. It should be kept in mind here that the Sabbath would include Yom Kippur, which is technically a Sabbath. In fact, it is *"Shabbat Shabbaton,"* the Sabbath of Sabbaths.

SUKKAH—BOOTH

Introduction

Sukkah means "booth." It is frequently translated "tabernacle," to connect its temporary quality with the temporary quality of the traveling desert sanctuary known in the Torah as the *Mishkan.* But the sukkah itself was and is in no way connected with corporate worship. It was a family booth, built near the home, in which the family ate its meals during the seven-day fall harvest festival.

The Mishnah deals chiefly with two aspects of the Sukkot celebration. First, it goes into great detail about the nature and construction of the sukkah itself, and the circumstances under which it is to be used. A lot of attention is also paid to the "four species" —the *lulav, etrog,* willow, and myrtle—prescribed by the Torah for use during the Festival. In connection with this second aspect of the Sukkot celebration, the Mishnah tells us something of the celebration in the Temple in Jerusalem.

But the Jerusalem celebration has none of the exciting quality of either the Passover observance or the Yom Kippur ceremonies. We almost get the impression that Sukkot in the ancient Temple was not a unified celebration at all. This impression accords with the scholarly problems alluded to previously (see p. 78) in connection with the calendar, the original status of Rosh Hashanah, Yom Kippur, and Sukkot. While the first two achieved great status in Jewish religious life, the latter remained mainly a harvest festival.

Biblical Sources for Sukkah

Mark, on the fifteenth day of the seventh month, when you have gathered in the yield of your land, you shall observe the festival of the Lord [to last] seven days: a complete rest on the first day, and a complete rest on the eighth day. On the first day you shall take the product of goodly trees, branches of palm trees, boughs of leafy trees, and willows of the brook, and you shall rejoice before the Lord your God seven days. You shall observe it as a festival of the Lord for seven days in the year; you shall observe it in the seventh month as a law for all time, throughout the generations. You shall live in booths seven days; all citizens in Israel shall live in booths, in order that future generations may know that I made the Israelite people live in booths when I brought them out of the land of Egypt, I the Lord your God. (Leviticus 23: 39–43)

SEE ALSO

> Exodus 23:16, 34:22
> Leviticus 23:33–38
> Numbers 29:12–35
> Deuteronomy 16:13–15
> Ezekiel 45:25
> Zechariah 14:16–19
> Ezra 3:4
> Nehemiah 8:14–18

Sukkah 1:1

A sukkah which is more than twenty *ammot* in height is not valid.[1] R. Judah says that it is.[2] A sukkah which is less than ten handbreadths in height, or which does not have three walls, or which has a larger area unshaded than shaded, is not valid.[3] If a sukkah is old, the school of Shammai considers it invalid, and the school of Hillel says it is valid. What is an old sukkah? One constructed thirty days before the Festival. But if it was constructed specifically for the Festival, it is valid even if made at the beginning of the year.[4]

---

1. An *ammah* is the distance from the elbow to the end of a clenched fist. Any building higher than twenty *ammot* would be considered of a permanent nature, and the sukkah had to be a temporary abode.
2. R. Judah's view was not accepted as law.
3. A building less than ten handbreadths in height would be a doll's house or a toy, not fit for human habitation, even temporarily. Less than three walls would not constitute a building at all. Neither would a booth which let the sun into more than half of its area.
4. This is not clear. It cannot refer to Rosh Hashanah, which was only fifteen days earlier. The commentators give two interpretations: First, it is an offhand expression for many months; second, it refers to any time since the previous Sukkot. The latter explanation seems more consistent with the careful approach of the Mishnaic writers.

Sukkah 2:4

If a man builds his sukkah between trees, and the trees form its side walls, it is valid.[1] Those who are on a mission of mitzvah are exempt from the mitzvah of the sukkah.[2] The sick and those who take care of them are exempt.[3] One may eat and drink casually outside the sukkah.[4]

---

1. So long as the roof is not supported by the trees, but by poles or other means.
2. For example, a man who travels to ransom a captive, or to greet his teacher at a distant place. The general rule is: A man who is performing a mitzvah is exempt from all mitzvot of lesser importance, if they conflict with the major mitzvah.
3. The illness need not be a serious one.
4. That is, a snack. Regular meals have to be eaten in the sukkah.

Sukkah 2:6

R. Eliezer said: A man is required to eat fourteen meals in the sukkah, one during the day and one each evening.[1] The Sages said: There is no prescribed number, but he must eat in the sukkah on the first evening of the Festival.[2] R. Eliezer also said: If a man has not eaten in the sukkah on the first evening of the Festival, he must fulfill the mitzvah on the last evening of the Festival. The Sages said: You cannot speak of compensating for the missed mitzvah, for it is written: "That which is crooked cannot be made straight, and that which is lacking cannot be counted." [3]

---

1. The Mishnah counts all Festivals according to the old Palestinian and contemporary Israeli reckoning: seven days for Passover and Sukkot, one for Shavuot. The additional days were added to ensure continuity of celebration between Israel and faraway Jewish communities before the beginning of the Common Era, and by the time accurate calendation was firmly fixed in Jewish life in the fourth century, the Rabbis felt that the tradition of doubling the beginning and ending of each Festival was too deeply rooted to change. Reform Jewish congregations not only reverted to the original Palestinian reckoning, but many went one step further by eliminating the second day of Rosh Hashanah, which is observed even in Israel.
2. Just as one is not required to eat matzot during Passover except on the first day. One may not eat bread throughout Passover, though one need not eat matzot. Similarly, one is not required to eat in the sukkah after the first day of the Festival, but neither is one permitted to eat a full meal elsewhere.
3. Ecclesiastes 1:15. In both cases, the view of the Sages was accepted as law.

Sukkah 2:8

Women,[1] slaves, and minors are exempt from the mitzvah of the sukkah. But a minor who does not need his mother anymore must fulfill the mitzvah of the sukkah.[2] The daughter-in-law of Shammai the Elder once had a child during Sukkot. He broke away a piece of the roof and made a sukkah-roofing over the bed for the child.[3]

---

1. Women were specifically exempted by the interpretation given Leviticus 23:42: "All the home-born in Israel. . . ." The word *ezrah* is masculine. In practical terms, a woman had to be elsewhere too frequently in connection with her manifold household tasks to be able to sit in the sukkah to eat her meals, even on the first and last days of the Festival.
2. When does a minor not "need his mother any more"? According to Bertinora, when the child awakens at night and does not cry for his mother, but either waits quietly or takes care of himself, then he no longer "needs" her in the sense intended by the Mishnah.
3. Shammai believed that every child had to "dwell" in the sukkah. But his view was not accepted as law.

Sukkah 3:12

Originally, the *lulav* was used for seven days in the Temple and for only one day elsewhere.[1] When the Temple was destroyed, R. Johanan b. Zakkai ruled that the *lulav* should be used everywhere for seven days, in memory of the Temple.[2]

---

1. In synagogues, or in family Sukkot. The Mishnah also details at which point in the Hallel service the *lulav* and *etrog* should be waved. This tradition still exists in all branches of Judaism.
2. Many ceremonial rules were instituted after the year 70 c.e., "in memory of the Temple." This whole Mishnah, incidentally, is also found in *Rosh Hashanah* 4:3.

BETZAH—AN EGG

Introduction

This is one of the few books of the Mishnah which takes its name from its first paragraph (q.v.) But it is also known as *Yom Tov,* or Festival, because it deals with acts prohibited and permitted on the first and last days of major Festivals. It does not deal with any specific holy day, but with generic laws for all Festivals. Much emphasis is given to the relationship between Festivals and the Sabbath.

The laws in this book do not concern Temple observance or communal actions. They concern the obligation of the individual to make the Festivals into days of sacred joy. To define and delineate sacred joy is the task of the Mishnah.

Biblical Source for Betzah

On the first day you shall hold a sacred convocation, and on the seventh day a sacred convocation; no work at all shall be done on them; only what every person is to eat, that alone may be prepared for you. (Exodus 12:16)

Betzah 1:1

If an egg is laid on a Festival day,[1] the school of Shammai says: It may be eaten. The school of Hillel says: It may not be eaten.[2]

---

1. "Festival day" refers to the first and last days of the Festival, to Rosh Hashanah, Yom Kippur, etc., but not to other holidays and Festivals. The question is limited to the eating of the egg on a Sabbath which falls the day after the Festival. An egg laid on Saturday may be eaten on Sunday, unless Sunday is a Festival. An egg laid on Shavuot may be eaten on another day, unless that day is Sabbath. This peculiar law is based on Exodus 16:5: all preparations for Sabbath and/or a Festival had to be completed on a non-Sabbath or non-Festival day. Since the egg was laid on a Festival day, it was not "prepared" on a non-Festival, and therefore could not be eaten on a Sabbath or Festival.
2. This is one of the infrequent occasions on which Hillel's school was stricter than Shammai's. Hillel's view was accepted as law. The rest of this chapter is devoted to disagreements between the two schools on details of Sabbath and holiday prohibitions.

Betzah 2:1

When a Festival falls on the eve of Shabbat (Friday), food may not be cooked on the Festival day for Sabbath purposes. But food may be cooked for purposes of the Festival day, and if any is left over, it may be used for Sabbath purposes. If food is prepared on the eve of the Festival for Sabbath use,[1] the school of Shammai says: It should be two dishes.[2] The school of Hillel says: one dish. But they agree that fish covered with an egg counts as two dishes. If the dish intended for Sabbath use is eaten or lost, another may not be cooked to replace it. But if any of it remains, it may be used for Sabbath.

---

1. The text is deceptively simple. The rabbinical interpretation was: Because the dish was begun before the Festival for both Festival and Sabbath use, it could be added to on the Festival in order to suffice for Sabbath too. This was called *eruve tavshilin,* a procedure comparable in cookery to the *Eruv* placed in the courtyard or two thousand *ammot* beyond the urban boundary (see pp. 92 ff.).
2. The school of Shammai did not like the idea of having a dish used for two purposes even in part for both Sabbath and Festival, and insisted that the two dishes be kept separate. The underlying purpose of the law was to ensure the genuine celebration of both Festival and Sabbath by eating foods prepared specifically for each occasion.

Betzah 5:2

Any act which is prohibited [1] on the Sabbath, whether by virtue of laws concerning rest [2] or concerning acts of choice,[3] or because of mitzvot,[4] is also prohibited on a Festival day. The following acts are prohibited by virtue of the rules concerning Sabbath rest: No one may climb a tree, ride a beast, swim, clap his hands, slap his thighs, stamp his feet.[5] These acts are prohibited by virtue of rules concerning acts of choice: No one may sit in judgment, officiate at a marriage, perform *halitzah,*[6] or contract a Levirate marriage.

These acts are prohibited by virtue of mitzvot: No one may dedicate anything, or make a vow of valuation,[7] or devote anything,[8] or set apart *Terumah* or *Ma'aserot*. Everything which is prohibited on a Festival day is certainly prohibited on Sabbath as well.[9] A Festival day differs from Sabbath only in the preparation of necessary food.

---

1. Literally, "which causes guilt," and would require court punishment or the bringing of a sin-offering.
2. Following Exodus 23:12: "On the seventh day you shall rest."
3. An act which contains an element of mitzvah, ordinarily permitted but prohibited on the Sabbath because rest has a priority status.
4. A real mitzvah, normally required, but which does not outrank the Sabbath.
5. The Babylonian Gemara explains that these three acts are prohibited lest a man be tempted to fix a musical instrument used for clapping, slapping, or stamping. The last may refer to dancing, though all forms of dancing have never been prohibited on Sabbath and Festivals, and the Ḥasidim consider dancing a vital form of Sabbath and Festival worship.
6. Deuteronomy 25:5–10. See pp. 157 ff.
7. See p. 254 f. The four preceding acts are prohibited because they normally involve writing.
8. See Leviticus 27:28; Numbers 18:14.
9. This is a classic *kal veḥomer*. Since the Festival is less rigorously observed than the Sabbath (food may be cooked on the former but not on the latter), prohibitions applicable to Festivals must certainly apply to Sabbaths.

ROSH HASHANAH—NEW YEAR OBSERVANCE

Introduction

An authoritative Jewish calendar came into being two or three centuries after the completion of the Mishnah. Thereafter, observation of the moon and human calculations were no longer necessary to determine calendation.

But during the Mishnaic period, the focal point of calendation had been the visual sighting of the new moon. Much of the material in this book deals with the details of ascertaining the new moon, and the remainder with the blowing of the Shofar both inside the Jerusalem Temple and outside Jerusalem.

Rosh Hashanah as the beginning of a ten-day period of penitence, climaxed by Yom Kippur, was not yet known to the writers of the Mishnah. They observed "memorial day for the blowing of the Shofar," but the source of the memorial is not yet clear. Only later did the idea of a memorial for Creation come into the liturgy. The Rosh Hashanah celebration as described in the Mishnah is therefore pallid when compared with present-day observance.

Biblical Sources for Rosh Hashanah

Speak to the Israelite people thus: In the seventh month, on the first day of the month, you shall observe complete rest, a sacred occasion commemorated with loud blasts. You shall not work at your occupations; and you shall bring an offering by fire to the Lord. (Leviticus 23:24–25)

SEE ALSO

Exodus 12:1–2, 23:16, 34:22
Numbers 29:1–6
Ezekiel 40:1
Psalms 81:2–5
Nehemiah 8:2–12

Rosh Hashanah 1:1

There are four New Year observances: On the first of *Nisan* is the Rosh Hashanah for kings [1] and for Pilgrimage Festivals.[2] The first of *Elul* is the Rosh Hashanah for the *Ma'aser* of cattle. R. Eliezer and R. Simon said: the first of *Tishri*.[3] The first of *Tishri* is the Rosh Hashanah for the computation of the years,[4] of *Shemitah* (cycles), of Jubilees, for the planting of trees,[5] and for the *Ma'aser* of vegetables. The first of *Shevat* is the Rosh Hashanah for fruit trees, according to the school of Shammai. The school of Hillel says: on the fifteenth.[6]

---

1. Even if a king was crowned during *Adar,* he finished the first year of his reign on the first of *Nisan,* and was then reckoned to be in the second year. Many Far Eastern cultures compute the age of individuals in the same manner, using the culture's New Year's Day as the base.
2. This is the order used in the Torah for commanding these Festivals. See Deuteronomy 16:16.
3. See Leviticus 27:32. Since most cattle foaled in the summer, according to the Rabbis, the beginning of *Elul* was a good time to differentiate between one year's increase and the next. In addition, the grain and fruit harvests had not yet begun, and the farmer had time to work out the *Ma'aser* of cattle. The view of R. Eliezer and R. Simon was not accepted as law.
4. It has become clear that there was more than one calendar system in ancient Israel. The details of these calendars, when they were in effect and how they evolved, are extraordinarily complex, and are in dispute among scholars. There appears to be no doubt, however, that the *Tishri* Rosh Hashanah, Yom Kippur, and Sukkot changed over the centuries, as indicated on p. 78. But some kind of year-end observance was closely connected in time with the fall equinox.
5. For purposes of computing the three years of *Orlah* (see pp. 69 ff.).
6. The view of Hillel was accepted as law, and is the source of the *Tu bi-Shevat* observance.

Rosh Hashanah 1:7

If a father and son saw the new moon [1] together, they may both go to testify, not because they can be considered a valid pair of witnesses, but because if one is determined ineligible, the other may be included with some other person to make a pair.[2] R. Simon said: A father and son and all close relatives are eligible to testify about the new moon.[3] R. Jose said: Once Tobiah the physician saw the new moon in Jerusalem with his son and a freed slave. The priests accepted him and his son, but declared his freed slave ineligible. When they came before the court, he and his freed slave were accepted, but his son was declared ineligible.

---

1. Most of Chapters 1 and 2 of the book are concerned with the problem of announcing the new moon, the beginning of the month, on which the entire calendar depended. Detailed regulations are included here since the first of *Tishri* is not only a new moon, but one vital to the calendar process. By the time the Mishnah was written, the calendar had already assumed its present general outline. Only details were changed before final fixation took place, though arguments about them continued until the time of Saadia Gaon (early tenth century).

2. With rare exception, two witnesses are required for any legal testimony in a Jewish court. The major exception: the death and/or burial of a man, in order to avoid *Agunah* status for his widow. In general, first-degree relatives may not constitute the two witnesses.

3. The disagreement between R. Simon and the Sages, with R. Jose supporting the position of the Sages, centers about the proper interpretation of the Torah phrase: "This month shall be *lahem*—to you, for you. . . ." (Exodus 12:2). The Sages said it meant that the testimony establishing the new moon shall be "transmitted to you." R. Simon said it meant that the testimony shall be "dependent on you"—"you" meaning any and all Israelites. The view of R. Jose and the Sages was accepted as law.

Rosh Hashanah 1:8

The following are ineligible: [1] a dice-player,[2] a usurer, pigeon-flyers,[3] those who do business in Seventh Year produce,[4] and slaves.[5] This is the general rule: Any evidence which a woman is not eligible to bring, these too are not eligible to bring.

---

1. To testify about the sighting of the new moon. But the rule was generalized to include ineligibility to testify at all in a Jewish court. Part of this Mishnah is included in *Sanhedrin* 3:3 (see p. 219).

2. All gamblers were branded by the Rabbis as thieves, on three

counts: First, because gambling steals needed money from their families; second, because time spent gambling is stolen from the study of Torah and performance of mitzvot; and third, because winnings are in a sense stolen from the loser. It is this rabbinic principle which has led synagogue organizations to oppose gambling in the synagogue.

3. The purpose of pigeon-flying was gambling on the outcome. Amateur pigeon-fanciers and homing-pigeon breeders are not included in this category.

4. Seventh Year produce which grew automatically, like fruit and berries, and which may be eaten but not sold. See p. 54.

5. This similarity is for technical purposes only, not to compare the moral status of women and slaves on the one hand and the questionable types listed in the Mishnah.

Rosh Hashanah 2:2

Originally, they kindled flares,[1] but after the sabotage of the Samaritans [2] the court ruled that messengers should go out.

---

1. Signal fires on the hilltops to announce the new moon. One watcher saw the Jerusalem fire, then lit his, and lines of fires shot out north, south, and east. We are told it was a beautiful sight, in addition to its utilitarian value.

2. The Samaritans would light fires on their Samaritan hilltops one or two nights before the proper day of the month, when the Sanhedrin still had no evidence that the new moon had appeared. That month might be a "full" one; i.e., the new moon would not appear until the end of the thirtieth day, but the premature Samaritan fires confused everyone.

Rosh Hashanah 2:7

The president of the court said: "The new moon is sanctified." And all the people responded: "It is sanctified! It is sanctified!" They sanctified it whether it appeared on time or not.[1] R. Eliezer

b. Zadok said: If it did not appear on time, it need not be sanc-tified, since Heaven has already hallowed it.[2]

---

1. The proper time was the end of the twenty-ninth day, the thirtieth night. If it did not appear then, it was proclaimed the next night whether or not it was seen by witnesses.
2. The verbal hallowing of the month is not a religious requirement. Only the Jubilee Year must be proclaimed verbally (Leviticus 25: 9–10). If the new moon did not appear on the thirtieth evening, it was automatically new moon the next night, and the court did not need to proclaim it. R. Eliezer's view was accepted as law. As Jewish law evolved over the centuries, however, every month was sanctified, not by the court, but by every Jew in a ritual called *Kiddush Levanah,* the Sanctification of the New Moon.

Rosh Hashanah 3:8

"And it came to pass when Moses held up his hand that Israel pre-vailed, and when he let down his hand Amalek prevailed" (Exodus 17:11). But could the hands of Moses encourage or hinder the battle? The verse means to teach that whenever the Israelites directed their thoughts on high and kept their hearts in subjection to their Father in heaven, they prevailed; otherwise they suffered defeat.[1]

One might ask in the same way about the verse: "Make you a fiery serpent and set it upon a standard, and it shall come to pass that everyone that is bitten, when he sees it shall live" (Num-bers 21:8). But can the serpent slay or keep alive? The verse means that whenever the Israelites directed their thoughts on high and kept their hearts in subjection to their Father in heaven, they were healed; otherwise they were not. A deaf-mute, an imbecile, or a minor cannot fulfill a religious obligation on behalf of the community. This is the general rule: Anyone upon whom a mitzvah is not incumbent cannot fulfill that mitzvah on behalf of the com-munity.[2]

---

1. This thought is the reason for placing the digression at this point. The previous Mishnah, not included here, dealt with various circum-

stances under which the accidental hearing of the Shofar constituted fulfillment of the mitzvah. The chief criterion was *kavannat halev*— the direction of the heart, the concentration of the mind and soul on the act as a mitzvah or sacred act.

2. This last thought returns the discussion, in a sense, to Rosh Hashanah and the blowing of the Shofar, though the text certainly does not say so. The commentators indicated that the text had specific reference to eligibility for blowing the Shofar. The generalization is, however, an important principle of Halakhah.

Rosh Hashanah 4:1

If Rosh Hashanah fell on the Sabbath, they blew the Shofar in the Temple, but not elsewhere.[1] After the Temple was destroyed, Rabban Joḥanan ben Zakkai ruled that the Shofar might be blown wherever there was a court.[2] R. Eliezer said: Rabban Joḥanan ben Zakkai made this ruling only for Yavneh. They answered him: It makes no difference whether it was Yavneh or any place which has a court.[3]

---

1. Blowing the Shofar was not considered work. Carrying the Shofar was, and this violation might have taken place outside the Temple. Some Rabbis thought the permission was limited to the Temple itself, but Maimonides insisted that the whole of Jerusalem was included.

2. How big a court? Some scholars said a court of twenty-three, others a full Sanhedrin of seventy-one. This is the crux of the disagreement between R. Eliezer and the Sages, since Yavneh housed the Sanhedrin after 70 C.E.

3. The view of the Sages was accepted as law. Nevertheless, over the centuries it has become prohibited to blow the Shofar on the Sabbath anywhere, including Jerusalem. This practice is still maintained in all but Reform synagogues, in some of which the Shofar is blown on the Sabbath.

Rosh Hashanah 4:9

The order of blowing the Shofar is as follows: three blasts repeated three times.[1] A *Teki'ah* is three times the length of a *Teru'ah*, and a *Teru'ah* is three times the length of a *Yevava*.[2] If the first blast is blown, then the second blast is prolonged only twice as long, and it is considered as only one blast. If a man has recited the blessings, and then is assigned a Shofar, he should blow a *Teki'ah*, a *Teru'ah*, then a *Teki'ah* three times. Just as the officiant is required to say the daily *Tefillah*, so is each congregant. Rabban Gamaliel said: The officiant fulfills the mitzvah for the congregation.[3]

---

1. That is, *Teki'ah*, *Teru'ah*, *Teki'ah*, three times repeated. This is not the contemporary order. There are different orders in different contemporary Jewish communities. The Ashkenazi order in use in the United States, in general, follows:
   Malkhuyot: Teki'ah, Shevarim-Teru'ah, Teki'ah: three times
   Zikhronot: Teki'ah, Shevarim, Teki'ah: three times
   Shofarot: Teki'ah, Teru'ah, Teki'ah: three times, ending with a *Teki'ah Gedolah*, a long one.
   The Mishnah makes no reference to a Shofar call at the end of the Yom Kippur ritual. Today, Ashkenazim blow one *Teki'ah Gedolah;* Sephardim blow four calls: *Teki'ah, Shevarim, Teru'ah, Teki'ah.*
2. *Yevava* is apparently an Aramaic word, the meaning of which is not clear. Some scholars have called it the equivalent of a *Teru'ah*, others of the *Shevarim*. The *Shevarim* equivalent is accepted here because in context it appears to make better sense.
3. What is the function of the cantor or any other *shaliaḥ tzibbur*—representative of the congregation—in prayer? The Sages contended it was to fulfill the mitzvah of prayer only for those Jews not competent to do so for themselves. Rabban Gamaliel said he fulfilled the mitzvah for everyone and the prayers of the individual, though good, were not the essence of the public worship service. Once again, the conflict between *Klal Yisrael*—the congregation of Israel—as an absolute entity, an aggregation of individuals, or a combination of the two becomes important.

TA'ANIT—FAST DAY(S)

Introduction

The Shofar was blown in ancient Israel not only on Rosh Hashanah, but as an alarm in wartime and as a warning during pestilence and drought. Whenever the Shofar was blown, the tradition of communal fasting developed. It is with these fasts that *Ta'anit* is primarily concerned. Though other stated fasts are mentioned in the book, without much detail, the greatest emphasis is on fasts connected with drought.

Because Tishah Be'av, the seventeenth of *Tammuz,* and the tenth of *Tevet* all became fast days early in the evolution of Judaism, with the Fast of Gedaliah and the Fast of Esther added in pre-Talmudic times, the concept of a fast day as a commemoration of calamity became almost commonplace. Many individual Jewish communities observed such fasts. It may be assumed that world Jewry will eventually come to some agreement about an appropriate memorial to the six million Jewish martyrs of the twentieth century. Though the observance in Israel thus far does not include fasting, it may evolve in that direction.

Biblical Sources for Ta'anit

Blow the horn in Zion, sanctify a fast, call a solemn assembly. (Joel 2:15)

SEE ALSO

> I Kings 8:35–39
> Joel 1:4, 14; 2:16–17
> Zechariah 7:2–7; 8:19
> II Chronicles 20:3–4, 9

Ta'anit 1:2

Rain should be prayed for only near the normal time for rain.[1] R. Judah said: When persons officiate [2] on the last day of the Festival, the last one alone [3] may recite the prayers for rain. On the first day of Passover, only the first one recites them, and the last one does not. Until when should rain be prayed for? R. Judah said: until Passover is over. R. Meir said: until the end of *Nisan,* for it is written: "And He causes to come down for you the rain, the former rain and the latter rain in the first month." [4]

---

1. The text refers here to the prayers for rain inserted into the liturgy routinely during the fall and late winter. The question is, when to begin in the fall and when to end in the spring.
2. Literally, "pass before the Ark," which means to take the position of officiant.
3. The person who officiates at the *Mussaf,* the additional service for Sabbaths and holy days.
4. Joel 2:23. R. Judah's view was accepted as law.

Ta'anit 1:6

If those days [1] pass and their prayers are not answered, the court orders the people to fast for three more days. They may eat and drink to the end of the day.[2] Work is forbidden, as are washing, anointing, the putting on of sandals, sexual intercourse. The bathhouses are closed. If those days pass and their prayers are not answered, the court orders the people to fast for seven more days —a total of thirteen days. These last seven days are more rigorous than the first days in that on these latter days they blow the Shofar and close their shops. On Monday they may open the shops at dusk.[3] On Thursday they may open all day because of the honor due the Sabbath.[4]

---

1. The months of *Marḥeshvan* and *Kislev,* as indicated in previous *Mishnayot,* not included here.
2. The day before the beginning of the fast. This is more rigorous

than the first phase of fasting, in which the fast does not begin until the next morning.

3. Monday, one of the traditional market days. But selling was permitted only inside the shop, not on the sidewalk, as is customary in Israel even today. There is a festive air about sidewalk displays and buying and selling which the Rabbis desired to avoid at that time.

4. The mitzvah of eating three meals on the Sabbath outweighed the semi-mourning of the fast days. Therefore, shopping on Thursday was essential.

Ta'anit 3:8

The Shofar may be sounded at any time of public distress—may it never happen!—but not because of too much rain. Once Ḥoni the Circle-Maker was asked: "Pray that rain may fall." He answered: "Go out and bring in the Passover ovens [1] that they may not be softened." [2] He prayed, but the rain did not fall. What did he do? He drew a circle and stood inside it. He said: "O Creator of the world, Thy children have turned to me, for they think I am intimate with Thee. I swear by Thy great Name that I shall not move from this place until Thou will have mercy on Thy children." Rain began to fall in drops. He said: "I haven't prayed for such rain, but for rain which will fill the cisterns, pits, and caves." It began to rain violently. He said: "Not for such rain have I prayed, but for rain of acceptability, blessing, and graciousness." Then it rained in moderation until the Israelites had to go up to the Temple Mount from Jerusalem because of the flooding. He was told: "Just as you prayed for the rains to come, pray now for them to go away." He said: "Go and see if the Stone of the Lost and Found [3] has disappeared." Simon b. Shetaḥ sent his message to him: "Had you not been Ḥoni, I should have excommunicated you. But what can I do to you? You importune God, and He does what you ask, just like a son who nags his father, and he does what he asks. Of you, it was written: 'Let your father and your mother be glad, and let her who bore you rejoice' (Proverbs 23:25)."

---

1. The oven in which the Passover lamb was roasted.
2. By the rain which would fall after his prayers.

3. There was a huge boulder in Jerusalem. When someone found
something, he took it there and announced his find. Anyone who
had lost anything went there, described his loss, and received it if
it had been found. This boulder was always supposed to remain
above water, except for an extraordinary flood.

Ta'anit 4:2

These are the reasons for the *Ma'amadot:* [1] It is written: "Command the children of Israel and say to them, My oblation, My
food for My offerings made by fire, of a sweet savor to Me, shall
you observe to offer to Me in their due season" (Numbers 28:2).
How can a man's offerings be offered if he does not stand nearby?
Therefore, the First Prophets (see I Chronicles 24) ordered the
establishment of twenty-four sections.[2] For every section there was
a *Ma'amad* in Jerusalem, made up of priests, Levites, and Israelites. When the time came for a section to go up to Jerusalem, the
priests and Levites went up to Jerusalem. The Israelites of that
section went into their own cities to read the story of Creation.[3]

---

1. Referred to in the previous Mishnah, not included here.
2. The total population was divided into these twenty-four sections.
   All the people in each section came from the same tribe, the division
   being geographical.
3. Some representative Israelites actually went to Jerusalem. The rest
   went to their local synagogues, where they fasted, prayed, and
   studied to indicate that, like their representatives in Jerusalem, they
   were devoting themselves, for this period, to sacred tasks only. The
   interplay here between the Jerusalem Temple and the local synagogue is of interest.

Ta'anit 4:8

Rabban Simon ben Gamaliel said: There were no happier days for
Israel than the fifteenth of *Av* [1] and the Day of Atonement. On
those days the daughters of Jerusalem used to go out in white gar-

ments. These were all borrowed so that none would be ashamed who did not own them. Therefore all the garments needed washing before use.[2] The daughters of Jerusalem went out to dance in the vineyards.[3] What did they say? Young man, lift up your eyes and see what maiden to choose for yourself. Don't set your eye on beauty but on family background, for "grace is deceitful and beauty is vain, but a woman that fears the Lord shall be praised." In addition, it is written: "Give her of the fruit of her hands and let her works praise her in the gates" (Proverbs 31:30–31). It is also said: "Go forth, you daughters of Zion, and behold King Solomon with the crown wherewith his mother has crowned him in that day of his espousals and in the day of the gladness of his heart!" (Song of Songs 3:11). "In the day of his espousals," this is the giving of the Torah. "And in the day of the gladness of his heart," this is the building of the Temple. May it be built speedily, and in our days! Amen.[4]

---

1. The passage is added here because the fifteenth of *Av* was mentioned in Mishnah 4:5, not included here. The fifteenth of *Av* is something of a mystery. It was obviously a popular holiday—but no one is sure where it came from. The Gemara asks, and the following answers are given: It is the day when the tribes were given permission to intermarry, nullifying the ordinance in Numbers 36: 6–7. It is also the day when the tribe of Benjamin was permitted to re-enter the congregation of Israel, as described in Judges 21. It is also the day on which the generation of the wilderness ceased to die. It is also the day when Hosea ben Elah removed the guards whom Jeroboam ben Nebat had placed on the roads to prevent the people of the northern kingdom from going on pilgrimages to Jerusalem (when the kingdoms split after the death of Solomon in the tenth century B.C.E.). It is also the day when permission was granted for the burial of those killed at Betar by the Romans at the end of the Bar Kokhba rebellion of 137 C.E. There are several other explanations of the significance of the day in the Gemara, none of them convincing or satisfying.

2. To avoid ritual uncleanliness.

3. Only on the fifteenth of *Av*. If Yom Kippur was ever celebrated with such festivity, the custom disappeared before the writing of the

Torah text.

4. On the rare occasions when the Mishnah gets eloquent or sermonic, the material is usually placed at the end of a book, as here.

MEGILLAH—THE SCROLL (OF ESTHER)

Introduction

Megillah means a rolled scroll. Five Biblical books are given this name: Esther, Ruth, Song of Songs, Lamentations, and Ecclesiastes. Each is read in the synagogue in the course of the year: Esther on Purim, Ruth on Shavuot, Song of Songs on Passover, Lamentations on Tishah Ba'av, and Ecclesiastes on Sukkot. Esther is the most popular and most deserving of the generic title, "The Megillah."

Contemporary Bible scholars maintain that the story of Purim is not historical. It became extraordinarily popular because it dealt with the foiling of a phenomenon which occurred so frequently in Jewish history—the attempted genocide of Jews. In fact, many Purims were celebrated in individual towns and areas commemorating local deliverance from peril.

The last two chapters of this book do not deal directly with Purim, but digress into regulations regarding the reading of the Torah, prophetic readings, and other synagogue regulations.

The reading of the Torah in the synagogue was, in all probability, the first activity carried on there as the institution began to evolve. Originally without system, it was then organized first into a triennial cycle and, later, an annual one—to the reading both from Torah and Prophets. Both the Sephardi and Ashkenazi arrangements of Torah readings and prophetic portions (*Haftarot*) postdate the Mishnah.

Biblical Sources for Megillah

And Mordecai wrote these things, and sent letters unto all Jews that were in all the provinces of the king Ahasuerus, both nigh and far, to enjoin them that they should keep the fourteenth day of the month of *Adar,* and the fifteenth day of the same, yearly, the days wherein the Jews had rest from their enemies, and the month which was turned unto them from sorrow to gladness, and from mourning into a good day; that they should make them days of feasting and gladness, and of sending portions one to another, and gifts to the poor. And the Jews took upon them to do as they had begun, and as Mordecai had written unto them; because Haman the son of Hammedatha, the Agagite, the enemy of all the Jews, had devised against the Jews to destroy them, and had cast *pur,* that is, the lot, to discomfit them, and to destroy them; but when he came before the king, he commanded by letters that his wicked device, which he had devised against the Jews, should return upon his own head; and that he and his sons should be hanged on the gallows. Wherefore they called these days *Purim,* after the name of *Pur.* Therefore because of all the words of this letter, and of that which they had seen concerning this matter, and that which had come unto them, the Jews ordained, and took upon them, and upon their seed, and upon all such as joined themselves unto them, so as it should not fail, that they would keep these two days according to the writing thereof, and according to the appointed time thereof, every year, and that these days should be remembered and kept throughout every generation, every family, every province, and every city; and that these days of *Purim* should not fail from among the Jews, nor the memorial of them perish from their seed. (Esther 9:20–28)

SEE ALSO

Entire Book of Esther, especially Chapter 9

Megillah 1:1

The Megillah of Esther is read on the eleventh, twelfth, thirteenth, fourteenth, or fifteenth of *Adar,* never earlier or later.[1] Cities which have been walled since the days of Joshua ben Nun read the Megillah on the fifteenth.[2] Villages and large towns read it on the fourteenth, except that villages sometimes read it earlier on a market day.[3]

---

1. The Book of Esther is read twice on Purim, evening and morning. Mishnah 1:2, not included here, explains in detail how circumstances can push the reading back to the eleventh or twelfth of *Adar,* though the normative reading dates are the fourteenth and fifteenth.
2. Why since Joshua and not since Ahasuerus? Palestine had already been destroyed, according to tradition, at the time the story of Purim is supposed to have occurred, and no cities had walls, as Shushan did. Therefore, the Rabbis went back to the days of conquest of Canaan by the tribes, under Joshua's leadership. In contemporary Israel, this practice is in fact maintained. Jerusalem, Lydda, and other old walled cities celebrate Purim a day later than Tel Aviv, Haifa, and other newer, unwalled cities. As a matter of fact, the observance of Purim has become so important in Israel that it lasts almost a week all over the country.
3. Monday and Thursday, when courts met in smaller towns, when the Torah was read in the synagogue and prayer services were held.

Megillah 1:5

A Festival day differs from the Sabbath only [1] in the preparation of necessary food.[2] The Sabbath differs from the Day of Atonement only in that for the deliberate profanation of the former, punishment can be by the hand of man, and for the deliberate profanation of the latter, only by divine destruction.[3]

---

1. This Mishnah introduces a series of comparisons like this one, which go on for the rest of the chapter, and which have nothing to

do with Purim or the Megillah. They are grouped together because of their common literary form.

2. That is, insofar as prohibited categories of labor are concerned.

3. The deliberate violator of the Sabbath can be stoned to death, theoretically, by order of a court. Violation of Yom Kippur is punishable by God. See Leviticus 23:30.

Megillah 4:1

Whoever reads the Megillah may stand or sit. Whether one person reads it or two,[1] they have fulfilled the mitzvah. Where it is the custom to say a blessing after reading, they do so; where it is not the custom, it is not done.[2] On Monday and Thursday and on Shabbat afternoon, three persons are called to the reading of the Torah.[3] One does not add to the number or subtract from it, and there is no reading of a prophetic passage. The person who begins the reading of the Torah and the person who finishes it each say a blessing.[4]

---

1. Simultaneously, according to the commentators. In a large synagogue, before the invention of microphones, they might stand at opposite ends and sing together so that everyone might hear, as the Halakhah requires.

2. Three blessings must be read before the Megillah is begun. See any traditional prayer book.

3. Three *aliyot*. In olden times, the men given the honor of being called to the Torah read from it and were not limited to the blessings, as is the general practice today. Three was the maximum number on weekdays because the men were in a hurry to get to work. Three was the minimum number because one Kohen, one Levite, and one Israelite had to be honored.

4. This Halakhah was changed later, and for many centuries now it has been universal practice for a blessing to be said before and after each *aliyah*.

Megillah 4:3

The following may not be done if less than ten [1] are present: The Shema and its blessings may not be recited,[2] one does not go in front of the Ark,[3] the *Kohanim* may not lift up their hands,[4] the

Torah and prophetic portions may not be read, they do not stop on the way back from the cemetery,[5] nor say the blessing for the mourners,[6] nor the words of consolation to them.[7] The blessing for the newlywed is not said,[8] nor is God's name mentioned in the blessings after meals.[9] The redemption value of dedicated lands is assessed by nine men and one priest, as is the redemption value of a man who consecrated himself.

---

1. Ten males over thirteen years of age who are eligible to perform mitzvot.
2. In responsive fashion in the synagogue, as was customary in olden times. The officiant would say: "Hear, O Israel, the Lord is our God," and the congregation would answer, "The Lord is one." This responsive prayer continued through the three paragraphs following the Shema itself.
3. The officiant stood directly in front of the Ark during the silent, standing *Tefillah,* and remained there to repeat the prayers aloud. It must be remembered that much of the service was led from the *Bimah,* which was not adjacent to the Ark, as in many Western synagogues today, but was in the center of the synagogue.
4. In the Priestly Blessing (Numbers 6:24–27). In some traditions, chiefly the Sephardi, this blessing is recited every Shabbat. In Ashkenazi tradition, it is recited only on major festivals.
5. A custom, dating back to pre-Talmudic times, required the mourners to sit down seven times on the way back from the cemetery. Each time, friends would say: "Rise, dear ones, return, dear ones, return" (see Babylonian *Bava Batra,* 100b).
6. No one knows exactly what this series of blessings was. The Gemara (*Ketuvot* 8b) tells of an incident in which they were recited, apparently in the courtyard of the mourner's home. More than this we do not know.
7. As the mourners left the cemetery, two lines of friends formed. The mourners walked between the lines and the friends said: "May you be comforted with all the mourners of Zion and Jerusalem." This custom is still generally practiced.
8. The *Sheva Berakhot*—Seven Blessings—sung at the wedding feast, frequently by a close relative of the bride or groom, though often by a cantor. All branches of Judaism have incorporated these blessings into the body of the marriage ritual itself. They are frequently

sung at the wedding feast in addition.

9. If a minyan is present, the sentence reads: "Praised be God of whose bounty we have eaten and by whose goodness we live." If no minyan is present: "Praised be He. . . ."

Megillah 4:4

Whoever reads the Torah may not read less than three verses for each *aliyah*. He may read only one verse at a time to the interpreter,[1] or three verses from the prophetic portion. But if those three verses are separate paragraphs, he must read them one at a time.[2] Verses may be omitted in the Prophets, but not in the Torah. How much may be omitted? Not enough to permit the interpreter to pause.[3]

---

1. The Torah and Prophets were read in Hebrew. Since most of the people, from the third century B.C.E., spoke Aramaic and not Hebrew as their mother tongue, the *Meturgeman,* or interpreter, was used to insure understanding of the reading. Many non-Orthodox congregations have returned to this approach in the past 150 years by having the Torah read both in Hebrew and in translation.
2. So that the interpreter makes no mistakes. Both the Hebrew reading and the translation of the Torah had to be perfect. The prophetic reading need not be perfect, according to Halakhah. It is of lesser sanctity. For an example of three verses, each of them a paragraph, see Isaiah 52:3–5.
3. While the reader was rolling the scroll, the translator caught up. A longer pause left the congregation in silence, which was considered a dishonor to the congregation and therefore to be prohibited.

Megillah 4:6

A minor may read the Torah and translate, but he may not recite the Shema and its blessings,[1] or go before the Ark or raise his hands in the Priestly Blessing.[2] A man whose clothes are ragged [3] may recite the Shema and its blessings and translate,[4] but he may not read the Torah or go before the Ark or lift up his hands. A blind man may recite the Shema and its blessings and translate. R. Judah says: If he has never seen the light, he may not recite the Shema and its blessings.[5]

---

1. Because the minor himself is not required to say the Shema, he may not lead the congregation in its recitation.
2. It would be a dishonor to the congregation to have God's blessing invoked by a youngster.
3. So ragged that the skin of his body shows through.
4. Because these two functions do not require him to stand in front of the congregation, to be humiliated by his raggedness. But reading the Torah, serving as cantor, and reciting the Priestly Blessing do. The emphasis here is on the man's feelings, though Bertinora adds that it would be an insult not only to the man but also to the Torah and the congregation.
5. One of the blessings before the Shema is "creator of the lights." Despite this bit of logic, R. Judah's view was not accepted. The Sages said that even a man who could not see light still benefited from the sun and moon, and could, therefore, thank God for them, even as representative of the whole congregation.

Megillah 4:10

The story of Reuben [1] is read but not translated. The story of Tamar is read and translated.[2] The first story of the golden calf is read and translated,[3] but the second is read and not translated.[4] The blessing of the priests,[5] the story of David (II Samuel 11:2 ff) [6] the story of Amnon are neither read nor translated. The chapter of the Chariot may not be used as a prophetic reading.[7] R. Judah permits it. R. Eliezer said: The chapter, "Cause Jerusalem to know," is not used as a prophetic reading.[8]

---

1. Genesis 35:22, in which Reuben had intercourse with his father's concubine.

2. Genesis 38. This chapter is translated even though Judah's behavior was far from noble, because (in Verse 26) he acknowledged his guilt.
3. Exodus 32:1–20. It was all right to read and translate this passage, to remind the people of God's covenant and the dangers of idolatry.
4. Exodus 32:25 ff., where the punishment of the people was announced.
5. Numbers 6:22–27, because only the priests themselves might impart those words.
6. II Samuel 13. Some commentators say that these two stories were not read at all in the synagogue because of their content.
7. Ezekiel 1, because of its esoteric quality. But the law permitted it.
8. Ezekiel 16, because of the virulence of the prophet's attack on Jerusalem and Israel, especially in the context in which he expressed it. Nevertheless, Halakhah permitted it. Censorship was not generally an acceptable practice in Jewish law, though it became more widely practiced in later centuries.

MO'ED KATAN—MID-FESTIVAL DAYS

Introduction

Mo'ed Katan, "the small festival," deals with the middle days of Passover and Sukkot, the period we now call *Ḥol Ha-Mo'ed,* a designation found in post-Talmudic works.

The Torah was not clear with regard to prohibiting work during these days. The Mishnah writers devoted much of the book to specific regulations regarding work during the mid-festival period. It deals, too, with restrictions on private ceremonials and occasions during this time. The general principle was: Any act of work requred to prevent some kind of a loss was permitted, so long as it was neither too difficult nor too menial.

Biblical Source for Mo'ed Katan

Those are the set times of the Lord which you shall celebrate as sacred occasions, bringing offerings by fire to the Lord—burnt offerings, meal offerings, sacrifices, and libations, on each day what is proper to it. (Leviticus 23:37)

Mo'ed Katan 1:7

During the mid-festival period, marriages are not solemnized, whether virgins or widows are involved. Nor are Levirate marriages contracted,[1] since this is a time of joy.[2] But a man may take back his divorced wife.[3] A woman may prepare her adornments during this period.[4] R. Judah says: She may not use lime since this is a painful experience for her.[5]

---

1. See pp. 156 ff.
2. *En Me'arvin simḥah besimḥah* ("occasions for rejoicing are not mixed") is a principle of Halakhah.
3. Since, according to all the commentators, this is not so happy an occasion.
4. The Mishnah has specific reference to cosmetics, including blue eyeshadow, rouge, hair preparations, and the like.
5. Lime was used as a depilatory. R. Judah's view was not accepted: Despite the pain involved, the law concluded that woman's beauty and vanity outweigh pain, and permitted the use of lime.

Mo'ed Katan 3:3

The following may be written during the mid-festival period: betrothal contracts,[1] letters of divorce, receipts,[2] wills, deeds of gift, *prozbul*[3] valuations,[4] widows' allowance deeds,[5] records of ḥalitzah,[6] and refusal,[7] deeds of arbitration,[8] decrees of the court, and official records.

---

1. Including both the betrothal papers and the marriage contract itself.
2. Upon the payment of a debt.
3. See p. 57 f.
4. By the court, where property or goods are under litigation.
5. The court's approved statement of her allowance from her late husband's estate for the maintenance of her household and children.
6. See p. 162 f.
7. A minor orphan girl could be betrothed, even as an infant, but she had the right to refuse to marry the proposed groom when she reached the age of twelve.
8. Such procedures were handled precisely as arbitration negotiations and awards are today.

ḤAGIGAH—FESTIVAL SACRIFICE

Introduction

On the first day of each of the Pilgrimage Festivals of Passover, Shavuot and Sukkot, a special *Ḥagigah,* or festive offering, was sacrificed in the Temple. Parts of Chapters 1 and 3 are devoted to the subject, while unrelated matters take up the rest of the book.

Biblical Sources for Ḥagigah

Exodus 23:14–18; 34:23–24
Deuteronomy 16:14–17

Ḥagigah 1:1

Everyone is subject to the mitzvah to "appear before the Lord"[1] except a deaf-mute, an imbecile, a minor, one of double sex, women,[2] slaves, a man who is lame or blind or ill or aged, and anyone who cannot walk to Jerusalem.[3] Who is considered a child? Anyone who cannot ride on his father's shoulders and go from Jerusalem to the Temple Mount, according to the school of Shammai. The school of Hillel says: anyone who cannot hold his father's hand and walk from Jerusalem to the Temple Mount, as it is written, "three *regalim*." [4]

---

1. Exodus 23:14–17, referring to the three Festivals.
2. Specifically exempted by the Torah in Verse 17.
3. For example, an asthma victim, for whom the climb to Jerusalem might be dangerous.
4. Going up *on foot*, not appearance alone, is the core of the mitzvah.

Ḥagigah 2:1

The subject of forbidden sexual relationships may not be expounded in the presence of three or more persons.[1] The work of creation may not be expounded in the presence of two or more.[2] The description of the chariot may not be expounded even in the presence of one,[3] unless he is a sage who already understands out of his own insights. If anyone speculates about four things, it would have been merciful had he never come into the world; namely: what is above,[4] what is below,[5] what is before,[6] and what is after.[7] If anyone gives no consideration to the glory of his Creator, it would have been merciful had he never come into the world.[8]

---

1. The most careful individual attention must be given the subject found in Leviticus 18 and 20. A group consisting of three or more persons was considered too large; error might result, with tragic implications.
2. So involved is the subject of Creation that one teacher and one student were considered a maximum group for accurate discussion. Questions like *creatio ex nihilo* could not be discussed with a larger group. In addition, Creation was the springboard for a great deal of mystical speculation, considered most dangerous by many rabbis. In later centuries, some scholars prohibited mystical studies altogether.

3. As found in Ezekiel 1. We have already seen in *Megillah* (4:10, p. 146) that this chapter was considered difficult and dangerous. It also formed the basis for much mystical speculation.
4. Above the heavens, in outer space.
5. Under the earth.
6. Before the creation of the world.
7. After the end of time.
8. This sentence is a direct reaction to the Jewish Gnostics, whose esoteric theological and philosophical "systems" were already part of the Jewish scene in Mishnaic times. For a description of Gnosticism, see the *Jewish Encyclopedia,* Volume 5, pp. 681 ff.

The Third Order

NASHIM

Women

INTRODUCTION

The third order of the Mishnah is called *Nashim*—"women"—because five of its seven books deal with regulations about marriage, divorce, Levirate marriage, and related subjects.

Included in this Seder are two unrelated books: *Nedarim,* which deals with oaths, and *Nazir,* dealing with the rules about Nazirites, who entered that state by taking a vow. Since Numbers 30:3 ff, the Torah origin of laws about vows, concerns itself with vows taken by girls and women which could be abrogated by their fathers and husbands respectively, there was some basis for including those books in *Seder Nashim.*

Two fundamental attitudes of Judaism come through in the Mishnah and in all the literature following it. First, women were not considered inferior beings, or slaves, or chattel. Woman's major—if not dominant—role in society was clearly recognized by Jewish tradition. All limitations on woman's rights in the synagogue and the home were based on realistic factors in the life of the female—chiefly her household duties and her state of ritual cleanliness.

Nevertheless, in Jewish law, women have never totally achieved equal rights. During a lifetime of marriage, the woman's property was administered by her husband. In early law, subsequently modified, distinctions were made between man and woman in standards of sexual conduct and punishments for violations of those standards. In practice over the centuries, what evolved as the normal and natural relieving of women from ritual responsibilities became prohibitions which tended to put them in a secondary position religiously.

Secondly, unlike orthodox Christianity over the centuries, Judaism approved heartily of marriage, with all its implications. The penalties for extramarital sex relations were severe, but the laws regarding sex in marriage were clear and filled with insight. The Rabbis recognized and approved of woman's sexuality more than two thousand years ago, and they protected her sexual rights.

Equally healthy was Judaism's acceptance of divorce as, in certain circumstances, a wiser reality than the continuation of a bad marriage. It can be safely surmised that the low rate of divorce among Jews over the centuries has been related directly to the laws of marriage and divorce. The traditional strength of the Jewish family has been similarly derived.

YEVAMOT—SISTERS-IN-LAW

Introduction

This book deals with Levirate marriage and the ceremony of *halitzah,* which took place when a Levirate marriage was either not desired or not possible.

Though the Torah source in Deuteronomy is quite explicit regarding *yibbum* and *halitzah,* many complicated questions remained for the Rabbis to answer. The Mishnah deals with them.

The obligation of a brother to marry his childless sister-in-law after the death of his brother is very ancient, predating Torah law itself. The story of Tamar (Genesis 38) would indicate this. In addition, in the earliest eras, the obligation was not limited to a brother but to a kinsman, as is evident in the Book of Ruth.

The evolution of family relationships was such that, in effect, a woman married into a family; nor was she free of that family until she had produced a son to perpetuate the family name.

Over the centuries, *halitzah*—the rite by which the widow releases the brother from his obligation, albeit in a way which shames him—has replaced *yibbum* in countries which adopted monogamy. On the other hand, in certain eastern areas, including North Africa, *halitzah* was not practiced at all, and *yibbum* was mandatory. Even today, difficult problems arise in Israel when a Moroccan man dies without a child and his surviving brother is already married. The Israeli rabbinate tries to force him to give the widow *halitzah;* the Moroccan-trained rabbis prohibit it.

Clearly, it cannot be said that *yibbum* is favored over *halitzah,* or vice versa. Both these peculiar alternatives have faced the Jewish people, and still do.

Biblical Sources for Yevamot

When brothers dwell together and one of them dies and leaves no son, the wife of the deceased shall not be married to a stranger, outside the family. Her husband's brother shall unite with her and take her as his wife, performing the levir's duty. The first son that she bears shall be accounted to the dead brother, that his name may not be blotted out in Israel. But if the man does not want to marry his brother's widow, his brother's widow shall appear before the elders in the gate and declare, "My husband's brother refuses to establish a name in Israel for his brother; he will not perform the duty of a levir." The elders of his town shall then summon him and talk to him. If he insists, saying, "I do not choose to marry her," his brother's widow shall go up to him in the presence of the elders, pull the sandal off his foot, spit in his face, and make this declaration: "Thus shall be done to the man who will not build up his brother's house! And he shall go in Israel by the name of 'the family of the unsandaled one.'" (Deuteronomy 25:5–10)

SEE ALSO

> Genesis 38:8 ff.
> Ruth 4:5, 8–10

Yevamot 2:2

There were two married brothers, and the first died childless. The second took his deceased brother's wife in Levirate marriage. After this, a third brother was born. Then the second brother died. The wife of the first brother is exempt from Levirate marriage with the third brother because she was "the wife of the brother who did not live at the same time as he did." [1] The wife [2] of the second brother is exempt in that she was her co-wife. If the second brother had agreed to marry her [the widow of his brother], and then died, his original wife must perform *halitzah* and may not contract Levirate marriage with the third brother.[3] R. Simon says: The third brother may contract Levirate marriage with whichever of them he wishes, or may submit to *halitzah* from whichever of them he wishes.[4]

---

1. A quotation from the previous Mishnah.
2. The original wife of the second brother, to whom he was married before he took a second wife in Levirate marriage. No laws of the Mishnah are based on a monogamous marriage system.
3. She must perform *halitzah* because she was not yet co-wife to the widow of her brother-in-law. She may not contract Levirate marriage with the third brother for the same reason that the other wife may not.
4. R. Simon's view was not accepted as law.

Yevamot 2:8

The mitzvah of Levirate marriage is incumbent on the oldest surviving brother, but if a younger brother takes the initiative and marries her, the marriage is valid. If a man was suspected of having intercourse with a slave who later became free, or with a non-Jewish woman who later became a convert, he may not marry her; [1] but if he did marry her, they may not be separated. If a man was suspected of having intercourse with a married woman and the court dissolved her marriage, even though he married her they must be separated.[2]

---

1. Lest the suspicion be considered justified, according to Rashi. R. Ḥananel suggested that suspicion might fall on her conversion to Judaism; that is, she converted only to marry, which is contrary to traditional Jewish law, current practice even among Orthodox Jews notwithstanding.
2. This is clearly implied in the Torah itself, which makes adultery a capital crime. Even though the Rabbis eliminated all capital punishment by regulations which made conviction and execution impossible, divorce was made mandatory even on suspicion of adultery, and the man certainly could not be permitted to marry the suspected adulteress, thereby "proving" the suspicion justified.

Yevamot 4:2

If a man marries his deceased brother's wife, and then she is found to have been pregnant at the time of the marriage, when she gives birth, if the child appears likely to live, he must divorce her and they must bring a sin-offering.[1] But if it appears likely that the child will not live, he may continue in their marriage.[2] If it is doubtful whether the child was a nine-month child of the former husband or the seven-month child of the latter husband, he must divorce her. The child is considered legitimate, but they must offer an unwitting guilt-offering.[3]

---

1. For their marriage was not necessary, in Levirate terms, and was, consequently, a violation of the prohibition against forbidden degrees of marriage. To avoid this unhappy situation, the widow usually waited a minimum of three months after her husband's death before contracting the Levirate marriage, by which time her pregnancy would have been certainly known to her and the marriage would not take place.
2. The sole function of the Levirate marriage is to produce a child which will live to carry on the first husband's name.
3. See Leviticus 5:17–18. Though this divorce may seem harsh, it

must be kept in mind that marriage was regarded as more than a romantic relationship.

Yevamot 4:13

Who is considered a bastard? [1] The offspring of any union of near kinsmen which is forbidden in the Torah. This was the opinion of R. Akiba. Simon of Yemen says: the offspring of any union for which the punishment is divine destruction. [2] The Halakhah accepted Simon's view. [3] R. Joshua says: the offspring of any union for which the couple are liable to death at the hands of the court. R. Simon b. Azzai said: I found a family register in Jerusalem, and in it was written: So-and-so is a bastard through a transgression of the law against adultery, confirming the words of R. Joshua. If a man's wife has died, he is permitted to marry her sister. If he divorced her and she died, he is permitted to marry her sister. If she was married again to another man and then died, he is permitted to marry her sister. If he submitted to halitzah from her and she later died, he is permitted to marry her sister. [4]

---

1. The previous Mishnah, not included here, deals with the legitimacy of the offspring of certain forbidden marriages. For example, if a man divorces his wife and she then marries someone else who either dies or divorces her, the first husband cannot remarry her (Deuteronomy 24:2–4). As we have often seen in the Mishnah, the Rabbis follow such a specific question with generalized discussion, as here.

   The word bastard (mamzer) is used in the Mishnah, as in contemporary law, in a sense more limited than common usage. It does not refer to all illegitimate children but specifically to the offspring of an adulterous relationship, and the latter are limited to cases in which one or both of the offending parties was married at the time of the offense.
2. As distinguished from those who violate a clear negative law—a prohibition—whose punishment is at the hands of the Sanhedrin, and might theoretically consist of lashes or even death.
3. It is unusual for the Mishnah itself to specify the Halakhah.

4. All these decisions stem from Leviticus 18:18: "in her lifetime."
After the woman has died, her sister is eligible as wife.

Yevamot 6:6

No man may refrain from fulfilling the mitzvah of: "Be fruitful
and multiply" (Genesis 1:28) unless he already has children. According to the school of Shammai, he must have two sons.[1] According to the school of Hillel, a son and a daughter, for it is
written, "male and female created He them" [2] (Genesis 1:27).
If he marries a woman and lives with her ten years, and she bears
no child, he is still not permitted to refrain from fulfilling the
mitzvah. If he divorces her, she may be married to another man,
and the second husband may live with her for ten years.[3] If she
has a miscarriage, the time is reckoned from the date of the miscarriage. The duty "to be fruitful and multiply" is incumbent upon
the man, but not on the woman. R. Joḥanan b. Baroka says: Of
both it is written: "And God blessed them and God said unto
them, be fruitful and multiply." [4]

---

1. As did Moses, after which, according to the Torah text, he separated from his wife. He would not have done so, reasoned Shammai's school, if he had not fulfilled the mitzvah of "be fruitful and
   multiply."
2. He must divorce her and marry another woman. Why ten years?
   Because Abraham lived with Sarah for ten childless years before
   marrying Hagar.
3. The Rabbis knew that a woman may conceive children by one
   man after appearing to be barren with another, as contemporary
   medicine has demonstrated.
4. R. Joḥanan's view was not accepted, in one of traditional Judaism's
   stranger rulings. The reason given by Bertinora is weak: The phrase
   in Genesis 1:28 is followed by: ". . . and fill the earth and conquer
   it." The Hebrew word for "conquer it" is written in the singular,
   and since the Rabbis believed that man conquers woman in intercourse, they concluded that the mitzvah of reproduction is incumbent only on the man.

Yevamot 8:3

"An Ammonite or a Moabite" (Deuteronomy 23:4) is forbidden to marry a Jew, but their women are permitted at any time.[1] An Egyptian or an Edomite, male or female, is forbidden for only three generations.[2] R. Simon declared their women permitted at any time. He said: It is an inference from the lesser to the greater. If where the men are forbidden for all time, their women are permitted at any time, how much the more that where the men are forbidden for only three generations the women should be immediately permitted. The Sages said: If this is Halakhah which you received from your teacher we accept it; but if it is an inference of your own, a counter-inference might rebut it. He answered: I declare what is Halakhah.[3] Bastards and *Netinim* [4] are forbidden, and forbidden for all time, whether they are males or females.

---

1. If they convert to Judaism.
2. Deuteronomy 23:9. Since the three generations were computed from the Exodus, the discussion was certainly moot in Mishnaic times.
3. But, in fact, R. Simon did not declare Halakhah; his view was not accepted.
4. Joshua 9:3–27. *Netinim* are the converted Gibeonites, perpetual servants in the Temple.

Yevamot 12:6

This is how the mitzvah of *ḥalitzah* is performed: When the man and his deceased brother's wife come into the court, the judges offer him proper counsel, for it is written: "Then the elders of the city shall call him and speak unto him." [1] Then she shall say: "My husband's brother refuses to raise up unto his brother a name in Israel; he will not perform the duty of a husband's

brother to me" (Deuteronomy 25:7). "I do not want to take her."
They said this in the Holy Language. "Then shall his brother's wife
come unto him in the presence of the elders and loose his shoe
from off his foot and spit before him"—enough spittle to be seen
by the judges. "And she shall answer and say, 'So shall it be
done unto the man that does not build up his brother's house'"
(Deuteronomy 25:9). Thus they used to read out the prescribed
words.[2] But when R. Hyrcanus read it out under the terebinth
at Kefar Etam,[3] and continued to the end of the section (Deuteronomy 25:10), the rule was established always to complete the
section. To say the words: "And his name shall be called in
Israel, the house of him that has the shoe loosed" (Verse 10), was
the duty of the judges and not the disciples. But R. Judah says:
It was a duty of everyone present to cry out: "The man who has
his shoe loosed! The man who has his shoe loosed! The man who
has his shoe loosed!" [4]

---

1. Deuteronomy 25:8. If, for example, there was a great disparity
   in their ages, the judges counseled him to accept *halitzah* and not
   marry the woman.
2. The elders read the words verbatim from the Torah, and the par-
   ticipants repeated them.
3. No one is sure whether Etam in Judea is meant here, or what
   later became known as Akko (Acre) on the Mediterranean coast
   north of Haifa.
4. R. Judah's view was accepted as law.

KETUVOT—MARRIAGE CONTRACTS

Introduction

The *Ketuvah* is the marriage contract. The word *Ketuvot* itself is
the plural feminine passive participle of the word *katav*, "to write."
The *Ketuvah* is the core document of the traditional Jewish marriage relationship. Its form makes clear the fact that marriage was a

contractual relationship based on the exchange of *valuta*—money or property in various forms—between the fathers of the bride and groom. But it would be a misreading of Jewish tradition to insist that the marriage relationship was entered into by a couple solely on a commercial basis. In the first place, both had to agree to the marriage; involuntary marriage was forbidden. Second, the text of the *Ketuvah* itself makes clear the mutual regard and affection expected of the bridal pair. Third, it is significant that there accrued a tremendous body of Halakhah, beginning with this book of the Mishnah, to regulate the purity, fidelity, and dignity of the marriage relationship.

The purpose of this Mishnah text is to elaborate and make firm all the implications of the marriage relationship, as it was established under the terms of the *Ketuvah*. There is a wide range of subject matter, from property rights to sexual rights, from definition of marital responsibility to penalties for violation of the terms of the *Ketuvah*.

The text of the *Ketuvah* discussed in the Mishnah has not changed substantially within the traditional Jewish community. Even though the *Ketuvot* were written both in Hebrew and in Aramaic, only the latter is used today. In America and other Western countries, the *Ketuvah* is frequently a symbolic document. No question is asked about the virginity of the bride. There is no exchange of money between the father of the groom and the father of the bride, only the giving of a ring by the groom himself to the bride. The *nedan,* or dowry, has well-nigh disappeared. But the form of the *Ketuvah* document remains unchanged.

Some years ago, the Rabbinical Assembly of America, the professional body of Conservative rabbis, sponsored a new *Ketuvah* document. It made only one major change in the traditional form: It binds the bride and groom to seek counsel from trained persons before applying for a divorce.

Biblical Sources for Ketuvot

Exodus 22:15–16
Deuteronomy 22:13–21, 28–9

Ketuvot 1:1

A virgin should be married on Wednesday and a widow on Thursday.[1] For the court sits twice a week in towns, on Mondays and on Thursdays, and if the groom wants to lodge a virginity suit he may go in the morning [Thursday] to the court.[2]

---

1. The man who marries a widow should stay away from work three days; the groom of a virgin has a seven-day honeymoon. Since the honeymoon is brief for the former groom, one of the days might as well be Shabbat, when he would not work anyhow. Unromantic, but practical!
2. Before the groom's anger at being deceived dies down. Later his growing love for his wife might make him forget that if the *Ketuvah* said she was a virgin and in fact she was not, Halakhah requires him to divorce her. See Deuteronomy 22:21.

Ketuvot 1:6

A man married a woman and "found not in her the signs of virginity" (Deuteronomy 22:14). She said: "After you did betroth me, I was raped and your field was laid waste." [1] He said: "Not so, but it happened before I betrothed you and my arrangement was made in error." [2] Rabban Gamaliel and R. Eliezer said: She may be believed. But R. Joshua said: We may not rely on her words. She must be presumed to have had intercourse before she was betrothed and to have deceived her husband unless she can bring proof for her words.[3]

---

1. As by a rainstorm or other "act of God." This means that though her virginity is no longer intact, her husband has no legal recourse

and cannot change her *Ketuvah*, written before the *Erusin*, or betrothal.

2. And, consequently, the *Ketuvah* is entirely void.
3. The view of Rabban Gamaliel and R. Eliezer was accepted as law. Why destroy a potentially good marriage when so much doubt exists about the bride's condition and R. Joshua's requirement of proof is impossible to fulfill?

Ketuvot 4:2

If a man arranges a betrothal for his daughter and she is divorced,[1] or if he arranges a betrothal for her and she is left a widow, her *Ketuvah* is his.[2] If he gives her in marriage and she is divorced, or if he gives her in marriage and she is left a widow, her *Ketuvah* is hers.[3] R. Judah said: In the former case, it is the father's.[4] The Sages said to him: After her father has given her in marriage, he has no claim on her.

---

1. Even though the girl is not fully married by the betrothal document and rite, it is sufficiently binding an act as to require divorce to break it.
2. Because betrothal does not remove her from her father's jurisdiction. Marriage does. Whenever the Mishnah speaks of her *Ketuvah*, it means the amount of money specified therein to be transferred from the groom's family to the bride's.
3. There were two separate documents for betrothal and marriage. Which is in force when a divorce or death takes place? In the first example, betrothal; in the second, marriage. Therefore the change in rights from the bride's father to the widow herself.
4. Since the betrothal document was written before marriage, does it not remain in force afterwards? Should not the father receive the value of the betrothal document, since the girl was still under his jurisdiction when it was written? The view of the Sages, which answered the question negatively, was accepted. So long as the girl was married at all, the betrothal document was superseded by the marriage document, and only the latter was in force, so that the money went to her.

Ketuvot 5:5

These are the duties which a wife must perform for her husband: grinding flour and baking bread, washing clothes and cooking food, nursing her child, making his bed and working in wool. If she brings one servant with her, she need not grind or bake or wash; if two, she need not cook or nurse her child; if three, she need not make his bed or work in wool; if four, she may sit all day in an easy chair.[1] R. Eliezer said: Even if she brings him a hundred servants he should compel her to work in wool, for idleness leads to immorality.[2] Rabban Simon b. Gamaliel said: Even if a man puts his wife under a vow to do no work he should divorce her and give her her *Ketuvah,* for idleness leads to boredom.[3]

---

1. Bertinora adds, however, that even this most ladylike of ladies must mix her husband's wine, help him to wash his hands, face, and feet when he returns from work, and make his bed ready for the night. These duties must be performed only by a wife, not by a maid.
2. The commentators perceptively note that an idle woman will inevitably become involved in activities and games of chance at which flirtation is carried on.
3. Boredom is a sin in a world where so much waits to be done. A woman has obligations to others, but cannot recognize them if her domestic existence is so selfishly organized. In addition, a bored woman cannot be an adequate wife intellectually, sexually, or in any other manner.

Ketuvot 5:6

If a man takes a vow not to have intercourse with his wife, the school of Shammai says: she may consent for two weeks.[1] The school of Hillel says: for one week only.[2] Students may remain away for thirty days without the permission of their wives while they study Torah; laborers, for one week.[3] "The marital duty"

(Exodus 21:10) required in the Torah is: every day for the un-occupied; twice a week for laborers, once a week for donkey-drivers; [4] once every thirty days for camel-drivers, and once every six months for sailors.[5] The foregoing are according to R. Eliezer.

---

1. One of the most progressive principles of Halakhah has been that women, as well as men, have sexual rights. See Exodus 21:10, which, the Rabbis ruled, referred not only to a servant but to all women. Even today, the idea that women need and enjoy sex relationships as much as men is not generally recognized.

2. The two-week and one-week suggestions are derived from the implications of the length of time intercourse was prohibited after the birth of a daughter and after the menstrual period. In both cases, the commentators pointed out, a man can have feelings of anger against his wife: for bearing a girl if he wanted a boy, and for menstruating instead of having conceived if he was anxious for a child. Certainly, they went on, any man who takes a vow against intercourse must be angry with his wife. If he takes a vow for more than two weeks, however, the court can force him to divorce his wife and return her dowry money to her. This was how Halakhah protected women's sex rights.

3. The Hebrew word here, each time a week is mentioned, is Shabbat, both because it meant the end of a week and also because intercourse is a mitzvah on Friday night in order to make the Sabbath joy complete. The Sages disagreed with R. Eliezer's schedule. They insisted, in the Gemara, that scholars could stay away from their wives for years, as witness the famous case of R. Akiba.

4. The driver went out to villages to cart grain and came home only twice a week.

5. It is interesting to note that if a man wished to change his work to one which brought him home less frequently, his wife could prevent him from doing so—unless he elected to become a scholar.

Ketuvot 7:9

If physical defects appeared in the husband [after marriage] the court may not compel him to divorce his wife.[1] R. Simon b. Gamaliel said: This applies only to minor defects, but for major defects they can compel him to divorce her.[2]

---

1. Though only a man can initiate a *get,* or Jewish divorce document, the courts could, under a variety of circumstances, force him to divorce his wife. He could be severely punished for failure to comply. This ruling destroyed the notion that Jewish women had no divorce rights.
2. The view of R. Simon b. Gamaliel was not accepted as law.

Ketuvot 7:10

The following may be compelled to divorce their wives: a man who has boils,[1] or who has a goiter, or who collects dog dung,[2] or who is a coppersmith or a tanner,[3] whether these disabilities existed before they married or arose after they married. Of all these, R. Meir said: Although the husband may have made it a condition that she marry him despite his defect, she may say: "I thought I could endure it, but I cannot." But the Sages said: She must endure him in spite of herself, except for the man afflicted with boils, because she can aggravate his condition.[4] It once happened in Sidon that a tanner died whose brother was a tanner too. The Sages said: She may say: "Your brother I could endure, but you I cannot endure." [5]

---

1. Bertinora includes a leper in this category too.
2. A substance necessary at that time for the tanning of leather.
3. For olfactory reasons.
4. His skin condition was made worse by sexual activity.
5. The view of the Sages was accepted as law. Therefore, she forced him to undergo *ḥalitzah* and not Levirate marriage.

Ketuvot 11:2

A widow, whether her husband died after betrothal or after marriage, may sell property from her husband's estate without the consent of the court. R. Simon said: If she became a widow after marriage, then she may sell without the consent of the court. But if she became a widow after the betrothal, then she may sell only with the consent of the court, since she is not entitled to maintenance,[1] and anyone not entitled to maintenance may not sell without the consent of the court.[2]

---

1. Out of the estate of her husband. She is entitled only to the property specifically allotted to her in her *Ketuvah*.
2. The court disposed of estate cases in a manner not entirely dissimilar to the procedure of courts today. The situation described in this Mishnah could come up only while the widow was waiting for the court to settle her husband's estate, during which time she could not be permitted to starve.

Ketuvot 11:3

If a widow sells her *Ketuvah* or any part of it,[1] or if she pledges it or any part of it as collateral on a loan, or if she gives it away, or gives away part of it, she may not sell the remainder without the consent of the court. The Sages said: She may sell it four or five times,[2] and she may sell it for her maintenance without the court. She writes, when entering the deed, "I sold it for maintenance." But a divorcee may not sell without the consent of the court.[3]

---

1. As one sells any asset. As in the previous Mishnah, this refers to the time during which she waits for the settlement of her husband's estate.
2. In four or five installments, one after the other, as it were. It might also be interpreted to mean that she can sell it, buy it back, then sell it again, and again.

NEDARIM **171**

3. There is a qualitative distinction between widows and divorcees in all of Jewish law. There is a stigma attached to being a divorcee, and the law is not so considerate of one.

NEDARIM—VOWS

Introduction

Nedarim are vows. Each *neder* (singular) must be distinguished from a promise or an oath, generally translated as *shevu'ah*. The *nedarim* are vows of abstinence of one form or another, and were originally connected with the Temple in Jerusalem. One vowed to bring a particular sacrifice if a happy event occurred, or to abstain from some pleasurable act or habit for a period of time, the penalty being a sacrifice if the vow was not kept.

Frequently, anger was a factor in *nedarim*. A partner would vow not to talk to his business associate. A man would vow not to have intercourse with his wife for a period of time. A father would vow to punish his child unless the child obeyed.

The book of *Nedarim* is included in *Seder Nashim* because the last two chapters deal with vows of wives and children. As Maimonides put it in his introduction to the Mishnah, as soon as a woman becomes a wife, her husband has the right to annul her vows. The implications of this right must therefore be discussed as one of the books dealing with marital relations.

In general, the Rabbis frowned on the indiscriminate making of vows. They did their best to discourage them and put limitations on them, even insisting that the vow is an unworthy religious exercise. Since this kind of inner, individual test appears to be necessary in people of all ages and all cultures, so the Mishnah tries, at least, to regulate the practice.

The first chapters deal primarily with the form of vows and with which ones are binding or not binding. The word *korban* ("sacrifice") appears frequently and is a continuing link between the idea of a vow and the Temple sacrifices. *"Korban,* if I do this," or *"Korban,* if I let you do that," constituted a vow formula. Inevitably, the Mishnah asks about variations on the word. Most frequently, the word *konam* appears; while meaning "to make free," it actually made a vow binding and often replaced *korban* in the formula.

Biblical Sources for Nedarim

If a man makes a vow to the Lord or takes an oath imposing an obligation on himself, he shall not break his pledge; he must carry out all that has crossed his lips. (Numbers 30:3)

SEE ALSO

Numbers 30:2, 4–17

Nedarim 3:1

The Sages declared four kinds of vows to be not binding: vows of incitement,[1] vows of exaggeration, vows made in error, and vows which cannot be fulfilled because of outside pressure.[2] What are vows of incitement? A man wants to sell something and says: *"Konam* if I accept less than a *sela."* Another man says: *"Konam* if I pay more than a shekel." [3] Then both agree on a price of three *dinars.* R. Eliezer b. Jacob said: When a man would force another to vow to eat with him, a man may say: "Let no vow which I vow hereafter be binding," provided he is aware of what he is saying at the moment of the vow.[4]

---

1. Vows made for the purpose of arousing another to respond. Examples of this and other types of invalid vows are given in the text.
2. This matter had important practical implications. If a man said, for example, *"Konam* this piece of land if . . ." he might have to forfeit his land.
3. A *shekel* was one-half of a *sela.* There were four *dinarim* in a *sela.* Consequently, there were two *dinarim* in a *shekel.*

4. He may do so on Rosh Hashanah, for example, for the whole year. He does not have to say at the time of the vow that it is "pre-cancelled," as it were, but he has to be conscious of that fact. Why vow at all, then? Involuntary vows, forced vows, vows made under duress from a non-Jew are frequent. This law, which the Sages upheld, is in a real sense the Halakhic forerunner of the Kol Nidre, which originated seven centuries later, and whose final form evolved even later.

Nedarim 3:3

What are vows which cannot be fulfilled because of outside pressure? If someone makes him vow to come and eat with him and he then becomes ill, or his son takes sick, or a flood hinders him, this would be a vow which cannot be fulfilled because of outside pressure.

Nedarim 10:4

Among scholars, before a daughter left him, it was the custom for her father to say to her: "Let every vow which you vowed in my house be revoked." Thus, too, the husband used to say, before she entered his control: [1] "Let every vow which you vowed before you came under my control be revoked." For after she came under his control, he could not revoke any vows she had made before marriage.

---

1. That is, before the marriage ceremony, which was, in a sense, the act of transferring control over the woman's acts from her father to her husband.

NAZIR—THE NAZIRITE-VOW

Introduction

It is appropriate that *Nazir* appear after *Nedarim* in the order of books of the Mishnah. The vow of the Nazirite was one form of *Neder,* with particular characteristics. The sacrifice penalty for its violation was the same as that required for violating any vow.

But the Nazirite vow became a most popular one over a period of several centuries, requiring a whole tractate of the Mishnah to incorporate the regulations adopted with regard to it.

The concept of the *Nazir* evolved over the centuries. Samson is said to have been a *Nazir,* dedicated as such by his mother before his birth. Yet Samson violated two of the three major requirements of Naziriteship (he drank intoxicants and had contact with the dead), and he was prepared to violate the third as well (the cutting of the hair). Absalom is traditionally considered to have been a Nazirite, though he "polled his head" every year. Samuel was consecrated by his mother as a Nazirite before he was born.

These Nazirites had one characteristic in common: Theirs was a lifelong vow, and was not taken voluntarily by them.

The laws of the *Nazir* contained in Numbers 6 do not contemplate this kind of Nazirite vow. They give details of a temporary form of Naziriteship, entered into by the individual for any purpose he wished, making him "holy unto the Lord" for a period of time. These vows were generally for thirty days, but could be renewed.

After the destruction of the Second Temple in 70 C.E., with the sanction of a sacrifice removed, the Nazirite vow fell into disuse and even into disrepute. By the time of the great rabbinic commentators, so little was thought of the *Nazir* that no commentaries were written, either by the great Geonim or by Rashi. As a result, the commentaries which do exist are fragmentary, unenriched by the continuum of living Halakhah.

This neglect of the Nazirite idea was caused by more than the destruction of the Temple, however. From the status of "sacred as the High Priest," the Nazirite had sunk to a point where Rabbis wrote of him as a sinner who indulged in unnatural practices by his ascetic vows. In a sense, this was a healthy decline; it underscored the fundamental earthiness of Judaism.

Because the Mishnah was written relatively early, it still took the *Nazir* seriously, and the book deals almost exclusively with him and the nature of his status during the tenure of his vows. There is almost no Aggadah or irrelevant material in the book.

Biblical Sources for Nazir

Numbers 6:1–21
Judges 13:2–5; 16:17
Amos 2:11–12

Nazir 1:3

A Nazirite vow which is undertaken without a fixed duration is binding for thirty days.[1] If he says, "I shall be a Nazirite for one long term," or "I shall be a Nazirite for one short term," or even "from now until the end of the world," he must remain a Nazirite for thirty days. If he says: "I shall be a Nazirite for one day more," or "I shall be a Nazirite for one hour more," "I shall be a Nazirite for one term and a half," he must remain a Nazirite for two terms. If he says: "I shall be a Nazirite for thirty days and one hour," he must remain a Nazirite for thirty-one days, since Nazirite vows are not taken in hour terms.[2]

---

1. Numbers 6:5 says: *Kodesh yihyeh*, "he shall be sanctified." The Hebrew word *yihyeh* has a numerical value of thirty: *yod* equals ten, *hay* equals five. This method of making legal decisions on the basis of the mathematical total of the letters of a word or phrase is one aspect of a technique known as Gematria, from the same Greek

root as *geometry*. Though it is not used constantly in normal Halakhic discussion, it is not infrequent either. Thirty days, incidentally, was not only the standard Nazirite term but also the minimum.
2. Numbers 6:8 speaks of the "days of his Naziriteship." Here the person specified his term, but since the hours could not be counted, a day had to be added. He could have specified thirty-two, seventy-four, or any other number of days he wished.

Nazir 6:1

Three things are forbidden the Nazirite: ritual uncleanliness,[1] cutting the hair (Numbers 6:5), and anything which comes from the vine.[2] Different products of the vine can be included together,[3] and he is not guilty unless he takes an olive's bulk of what comes from the grapes.

---

1. Defilement resulting from contact with the dead. See Numbers 6:6–7.
2. Numbers 6:4. No reason is given by the commentators for the fact that the Mishnah lists the forbidden things in reverse order from the Torah.
3. For purposes of counting the olive's bulk, not just wine but grapes, pits, and mash were included as well.

Nazir 9:1

Non-Jews may not take a Nazirite vow.[1] Women and slaves [2] may take a Nazirite vow. Greater stringency applies to women than to slaves, since a slave can be compelled to break the vow, but a wife cannot be.[3] On the other hand, greater stringency applies to slaves than to women, since a man may revoke his wife's vows but he cannot revoke those of his slaves.[4] If he revokes his wife's vow, he revokes it for all time. But if he revokes that of his slave and the slave is set free, he must complete the Nazirite term.[5] If he escapes from his master, R. Meir said he may not drink wine. But R. Jose said: He may drink.[6]

---

1. Numbers 6:2 specifies "children of Israel."
2. Non-Jewish slaves, who can be circumcised, ritually bathed, and then undertake certain mitzvot forbidden to other non-Jews. Jewish slaves were not really slaves at all, but indentured servants whose term of service was a maximum of six years.
3. The master controls the slave and can force him to pick up a dead body, or to drink wine, or to cut his hair. A man cannot force his wife to break a vow; he can only revoke it under certain circumstances. See p. 173.
4. He can revoke his wife's vow the day she makes it, if he knows about it and if it does not violate the limitations indicated in *Nedarim.* He cannot do so with a slave.
5. "Revoked" here is misused; the Mishnah means that the master forced the slave to break the vow. Violation does not remove the obligation to fulfill it when the slave is free to do so.
6. The dispute between R. Meir and R. Jose is not decided Halakhically, since the matter required no legal decision. Each had a reason for his point of view, however, which the Gemara details. R. Meir wants him to be unhappy away from the master and wish to return to him. R. Jose does not want him to become weak and decimated for lack of wine.

SOTAH—THE SUSPECTED ADULTERESS

Introduction

A *sotah* is a married woman suspected by her husband of adultery. Both Biblical and Talmudic laws regarding her are unique. This is the only instance in Jewish law of trial by ordeal. Permitting the deity to proclaim the innocence or guilt of an accused by magical means was widespread in the ancient and medieval worlds. The Code of Hammurabi provided, in the case of a suspected adulteress, for her to be thrown into the "holy river." If she drowned, she was guilty; if she could swim, she was innocent! In medieval Christianity, ordeals were frequent and unpleasant. Suspected witches were cross-bound (right toe to left thumb, left toe to right thumb) and tossed into a river or pond. If they sank, they were guilty. Suspected thieves were identified by suspending a Bible or Book of Psalms from a key. The man toward whom the book turned was the thief.

A common medieval ordeal attempted to identify a murderer. Suspects were made to approach the bier of the murdered person and as the really guilty man came near, the corpse was supposed to begin bleeding through the wounds.

All manner of "poison" ordeals have been practiced in various cultures, ancient and modern. It should be noted that in this kind of ordeal—and the "bitter waters" of the *sotah* ordeal fall into this category—the results were easy to rig. If the person administering the ordeal wanted the suspect to be found guilty, more "bitterness" could be mixed into the potion; if innocence were desired, less or none.

Over the centuries, the form of the *sotah* ordeal changed. Details in the Mishnah are not the same as those in the Torah. The differences are interesting but not crucial. The fundamental ordeal was the same. It should be noted, though, that the whole ceremony was dropped, on the instructions of R. Johanan b. Zakkai, just before the destruction of the Temple in the first century C.E. Adultery had increased to the point where the ordeal no longer served any purpose.

The regulations concerning the *sotah* are confined to the first six chapters. By a logical process centering around the requirement that Hebrew be used for certain ceremonies while others can be carried on in any language, the text proceeds to discuss the rules of war conscription, communal sacrifice or expiation for an unsolved murder, and related matters.

The Gemara to *Sotah* is full of Aggadah, ranging from fascinating folk stories to illuminating ethical maxims. This is to be expected in a text which had little Halakhic basis and rapidly lost even that.

Biblical Sources for Sotah

Numbers 5:11–31
Deuteronomy 20:1–9; 21:1–9; 24:5

Sotah 1:1

If a man wants to warn his wife,[1] R. Eliezer said: He must warn
her before two witnesses, and he may then make her drink,[2]
on the evidence of one witness or on his own evidence.[3] R. Joshua
said: He must warn her before two witnesses, and he may make
her drink only on the evidence of two witnesses.[4]

---

1. Literally, "express his jealousy"; that is, he has reason to suspect
   her of wanting to commit adultery with a specific man and wants
   her to know that he may take her to the priest for the ordeal.
2. If he does not warn her previously, he cannot force her to undergo
   the ordeal.
3. Evidence that she met privately with the man after being warned.
   Were the pair caught in the act of intercourse, there would be no
   need for an ordeal. The laws of adultery would have to apply: death
   for both wife and paramour.
4. Halakhah, always careful of individual rights, agreed with R.
   Joshua. Two witnesses were needed, thus cutting down the possibility of bringing a woman to an ordeal on the basis of whim or
   momentary anger.

Sotah 1:4

They used to bring her up to the great court in Jerusalem, and
admonished her as they did witnesses in capital cases.[1] They said
to her: My daughter, much sin is caused by wine, much by frivol-
ity, much by childishness, much by evil neighbors.[2] Do behave for
the sake of His great name, written in holiness, so that it may not

be blotted out through the bitter water (see Numbers 5:23). They then told her things which neither she nor all her family were wont to hear.[3]

---

1. In the hope she would confess her guilt, if guilty, and be spared the ordeal.
2. Therefore, it is easy to fall into sin, and she should not feel alone and beyond help.
3. Stories of people who confessed serious sin and managed to achieve forgiveness—like Judah (Genesis 38:26) or Reuben (Genesis 35:22).

Sotah 1:5

If she says, "I am guilty," [1] she waives payment of her *Ketuvah* [2] and is divorced. But if she said, "I am innocent," [3] they took her up to the Eastern Gate which is near the Nicanor Gate,[4] where suspected adulteresses were given bitter water to drink, where women were made clean again after childbirth (see Leviticus 12:1 ff.) and lepers were purified.[5] A priest took hold of her garments—either tearing them or ripping them off altogether—until her bosom was uncovered.[6] In addition, he loosened her hair. R. Judah said: If her bosom was beautiful, he did not uncover it; if her hair was beautiful, he did not loosen it.[7]

---

1. Literally, "unclean."
2. She wrote a release which said, in effect, that she had no right to collect the money due her under her *Ketuvah* because of her guilt. Why was she not liable to capital punishment? Primarily because of the absence of two eyewitnesses to the act of adultery. Incidentally, it can be assumed that no woman was ever put to death for adultery. As will be seen (see p. 220 f.), capital punishment was legal but so hedged about with restrictions that it was not practiced in the rabbinic period.
3. Literally, "pure."
4. In the Second Temple period, the Eastern Gate and the Nicanor Gate were the same, between the Courts of the Israelites and the

Women.
5. Neither the woman nor the leper was permitted inside the Court of Women or the Court of the Israelites until after the purification.
6. Literally, her heart, but clearly her bosom was meant, in light of the next sentence. Why was this done? As an interpretation of the phrase in Numbers 5:18: *U'fara et rosh ha'isha. Rosh:* "her head"; therefore, "her hair was loosened." *Ha'isha:* "the woman," symbolized by her bosom. This act apparently did not contravene stringent Halakhic rules about modesty.
7. Lest the priests become prejudiced in her favor. Another interpretation: to avoid agitating the younger priests. In rabbinic literature woman's hair is a major symbol of sexuality. R. Judah's view was not accepted as law.

Sotah 3:4

She is barely finished drinking when her face turns green, her eyes bulge, her veins swell, and they say: "Take her away! Take her away! Let the Temple Court not be made unclean!" But if she had any merit,[1] her punishment was temporarily suspended. There is a degree of merit which may suspend her punishment for one year, another for two years, and yet another for three years. Therefore, Ben Azzai said: A man ought to give his daughter a knowledge of Torah so that if she must drink the bitter water she may know that the acquired merit will suspend her punishment. R. Eliezer said: If any man gives his daughter a knowledge of Torah, it is as though he taught her lewdness.[2] R. Joshua said: A woman has more pleasure in one *kav* [3] with sexual pleasure than in nine *kavs* with continence.[4] He used to say: A foolish righteous man [5] and a cunning knave [6] and a hypocritically modest woman and the wounds of the Pharisees,[7] these bring destruction upon the world.

---

1. Acquired through knowledge of the Torah.
2. She might casually commit adultery, thinking that her knowledge of Torah would prevent punishment.
3. A measure of food.
4. That is, she would rather receive fewer material things from her

husband and derive pleasure from sex than be sumptuously fed and
ignored sexually. The meaning of the sentence is: It is better for
a woman not to know Torah and to remain happily faithful to
her own husband.

5. For example, a man who saw a woman drowning and would not
jump in to save her lest he see her naked or have to touch her,
as forbidden by Halakhah under non-emergency conditions.

6. Who finds ways to disobey the law with impunity.

7. There were Jews, both Pharisees and Essenes, who practiced
flagellation. The text here refers to those who used such physical
punishment on themselves to prove how pious they were.

Sotah 7:1

The following may be said in any language: [1] the exhortation to the
suspected adulteress,[2] the avowal with regard to the Second Tithe
(Deuteronomy 26:13–15), the recitation of the Shema, the *Tefillah,*[3] the blessings after meals,[4] the oath of witnesses, and the oath
with regard to a deposit.[5]

---

1. Other formulas had to be said in Hebrew. See the next Mishnah.
2. The words spoken by the priests before the confession or the ordeal.
See Numbers 5:19–22.
3. When praying with a congregation. When praying alone, the
Tefillah had to be said in Hebrew. Why? According to R. Joḥanan,
as quoted by R. Yomtov Lipmann Heller, when a Jew prays with a
congregation, his petitions go straight to God, who understands all
languages. When he prays alone, he needs the intervention of angels
to persuade God to listen to his prayer. Consequently, he must
pray in Hebrew.
4. See *Mishnah Shevu'ot* 4:3.
5. Leviticus 5:21–25.

Sotah 7:2

The following must be said in the Holy Language: the affirmation
with the First Fruits,[1] the formula for *ḥalitzah,*[2] the blessings and
the curses, the Priestly Blessing, the blessings of the High Priest,

the words of the king, the formula when the neck of the heifer is to be broken, and the words of the Anointed for Battle when he speaks to the people.[3]

---

1. Deuteronomy 26:3–10, a beautiful paragraph which has found its way into the Passover Haggadah.
2. See *Yevamot* 12:6, p. 162 f.
3. Each of these is explained in detail in subsequent *Mishnayot*.

Sotah 7:6

How was the blessing of the priests carried out?[1] In the provinces, it was spoken as three separate blessings,[2] but in the Temple as a single blessing.[3] In the Temple they pronounced the Name as written, but in the provinces with a substitute word.[4] In the provinces the priests raised their hands shoulder-high, but in the Temple above their heads, except for the High Priest, who raised his hand only as high as his forehead band.[5] R. Judah said: The High Priest raised his hand above his forehead piece, for it is written: And Aaron lifted up his hands toward the people and blessed them.[6]

---

1. Numbers 6:23–27. Because the words *ko tevarkhu*—"thus shall you bless"—are so specific, Hebrew, the language in which the instructions were given, must be used.
2. The priests would stop after each of the three phrases in the blessings so that the congregation could respond, "Amen."
3. In the Temple it was not customary for the people to answer, "Amen."
4. The Tetragrammaton could be spoken only in the Temple (see Exodus 20:21). In the provinces they used the word *Adonay*.
5. The *Shekhinah*—"the presence of God"—rested over the Temple when the Tetragrammaton was spoken. Therefore, the priests' hands had to be raised higher than in the provinces. The High Priest had the Tetragrammaton written on the forehead piece he wore, and consequently he was not to raise his hands any higher.
6. R. Judah's view was not accepted as law.

Sotah 8:7

What has been said [1] applies to an optional war,[2] but in a religious war [3] all must go, even the bridegroom and the bride.[4] R. Judah said: What has been said applies to a religious war, but in an obligatory war all must go, even the bridegroom and the bride.[5]

---

1. Previous paragraphs, enlarging on the fact that the priest appointed to accompany troops to battle charged them only in Hebrew, dealt with the procedure for determining who must go to battle and who can be exempted, in accordance with Deuteronomy 20:2-9.
2. A war to enlarge the boundaries of the Holy Land. It must be remembered that at no time in history did the ancient Israelites conquer all the territory promised to the twelve tribes. Individual Canaanite cities held out, usually at peace with the Israelites. When there was trouble or a king became ambitious, the Israelites would go out aggressively to subdue another city or area—under divine command, they felt, as part of the ongoing process of conquering the Land.
3. A defensive battle against an invader. The word mitzvah is used only in connection with a defensive war.
4. See Joel 2:16.
5. Rabbi Judah tried to make a distinction between a defensive war, waged at God's command, as in olden days, and the latter-day wars against the might of Rome, when the total population was involved. His view was not accepted.

Sotah 9:9

When murderers increased in number, the ritual of breaking the heifer's neck ceased.[1] When Eleazer b. Dinai came [he was also called Teḥinah b. Parishah], they changed his name to Son of the Murderer.[2] When adulterers increased in number, the *sotah* ritual ceased. R. Joḥanan b. Zakkai brought it to an end, citing: "I will not punish your daughters when they commit harlotry, nor your daughters-in-law when they commit adultery, for they themselves consort with whores" (Hosea 4:14).[3] When Jose b. Joezer of Zeredah and Jose b. Joḥanan of Jerusalem [4] died, the "ripe clusters" [5] ceased, as it is written: "There is no cluster to eat, my soul desires the first ripe fig." [6]

---

1. The rest of the book is devoted to the abrogation of many rituals and the reasons therefor.
2. He was a leading Zealot in the wars against Rome. He ceased to be a popular hero when he began to kill Jews who disagreed with his militant views.
3. The moral level sank so low that men who suspected their wives of adultery were themselves dissolute, and the ceremony became a mockery. Another interpretation has it that women flaunted their adulteries openly, so that they were no longer "suspected" of being adulteresses. In addition, of course, the *sotah* ceremony was tied to the Temple and ceased with the Destruction in 70 c.e.
4. The first of the famous *zuggot* ("pairs") mentioned in *Pirke Avot,* who flourished about the time of the Maccabean Wars, 168–165 B.C.E.
5. The "ripe clusters" were the scholars who had everything: knowledge, good deeds, piety, etc.
6. Based on Micah 7:1–2.

GITTIN—DIVORCES

Introduction

The origin of the word *get* is obscure. It is used to designate only two kinds of documents: those required for divorce and the freeing of slaves. When used without qualification, the word invariably refers to the document given by a man to the wife he wishes to divorce. There is no exception to the divorce procedure: the man (or his agent) must give a *get* to the woman. The woman was not completely without rights, however. Under certain circumstances, she could use the power of the *Bet Din* to force her husband to give her a *get*. Despite this right, there appears to be a disparity of status between men and women with regard to divorce which no rabbinic rationalizations can remove.

Halakhah never clearly established any limitations on the grounds for divorce (see Mishnah 9:10, p. 189). The crux of all rabbinic arguments on the subject is the phrase in Deuteronomy 24:1, *ervat davar*—"some unseemly" or "abominable" or "unchaste" thing. Despite this vagueness, divorce never became a casual or even an accepted phenomenon in the Jewish community. Marriage was the normal status for Jews, and they worked at maintaining it.

This Mishnah concentrates not on the institution of divorce but on the details of the *get,* and the procedures for writing and delivering it.

Biblical Sources for Gittin

A man takes a wife and possesses her. She fails to please him because he finds something obnoxious about her, and he writes her a bill of divorcement, hands it to her, and sends her away from his house; she leaves his household and becomes the wife of another man; then the second man rejects her, writes her a bill of divorcement, hands it to her, and sends her away from his house; or the man who married her last dies, then the husband who divorced her first shall not take her to wife again, since she has been defiled— for that would be abhorrent to the Lord. You must not bring sin upon the land which the Lord your God is giving you as a heritage. (Deuteronomy 24:1–4)

SEE ALSO

> Isaiah 50:1
> Jeremiah 3:1, 6:8
> Malachi 2:13–16

Gittin 1:1

If a man brings a *get* [1] from overseas,[2] he must say: It was written in my presence, and it was signed in my presence.[3] Rabban Gamaliel said: even if he brought it from Rekem or Hagar.[4] R. Eliezer said: even from Kefar Ludim to Lydda.[5] But the Sages said: He must say, "it was written in my presence and it was signed in my presence," only if he brings it from overseas. If he carried it from one province to another overseas, he must say: It was written in my presence and it was signed in my presence. Rabban Simon b. Gamaliel said: even if he carried it from one jurisdiction to another within the same city.[6]

---

1. As a *shaliaḥ*, an authorized messenger of the husband. An important rabbinic decision made the messenger a valid substitute for the principal in many transactions.
2. The Sages decided that all lands outside Israel were "overseas," whether or not water separated them from the homeland.
3. For two reasons:

    a. Lest the husband later return from overseas and insist that the *get* was a forgery.

    b. Lest the court in the wife's town suspect that the Jews overseas were ignorant of Torah and that the *get* might not have been drafted under legal circumstances.

    They could question this *shaliaḥ* in detail, since the *get* had been drafted in his presence. This is one of the few situations in which the evidence of one witness is accepted as binding.
4. Rekem was beyond the eastern border of Palestine in Mishnaic times. Hagar is unknown, but the commentators believed it to be southeast of Palestine.
5. Lydda is today a thriving town in contemporary Israel, known chiefly because of its airport. Kefar Ludim was outside Palestine in Mishnaic times, though the distance from Lydda was not great.
6. The purpose of all these details was to protect both the husband and wife from accusations of fraud. The Mishnah demonstrates that though divorce could be easily obtained, in practice it was

taken seriously and not initiated or carried out casually or whimsically. This tradition continues to our own day. The writing of a *get* is a major matter for traditional rabbis.

The rest of this chapter and Chapter 2 of *Gittin*, not included here, go into more details about the *shaliah* and his responsibilities.

Gittin 2:5

Anyone may write a *get*, even a deaf-mute, an imbecile, or a minor. A woman may write her own *get*, and a man may write his own receipt, since the validity of the document depends only upon those who sign it.[1] Anyone may carry a *get*[2] except a deaf-mute, an imbecile, a minor, a blind man, or a non-Jew.[3]

---

1. The writer is not responsible. So long as the two witnesses consider the form valid enough to sign, the *get* is legal if the two witnesses are valid witnesses.
2. As the *shaliah* ("messenger").
3. Because they are not valid witnesses in a Jewish court. Nor could the deaf-mute, the imbecile, and the blind man state in court that: "This was written and signed in my presence."

Gittin 5:1

Compensation for damages is paid out of the best land;[1] a creditor out of medium-value land;[2] and a wife's *Ketuvah* out of the poorest land.[3] R. Meir said: a wife's *Ketuvah* is paid out of medium-value land too.[4]

---

1. Following Exodus 22:4.
2. See Deuteronomy 24:11. A man's natural instinct would be to "bring out" his least valuable possession in payment. To prevent the cessation of necessary loans, the Sages upgraded payment to land of average value.
3. Marriage will continue, no matter what; therefore, the poorest possessions can be used. In addition, according to Bertinora, this

decision mirrors the rabbinic belief that women are more anxious to marry than men, willing to give more than they get.

4. R. Meir's view was not accepted as law.

Gittin 9:3

The essential words of the *get* are: Behold, you are free to marry any man. R. Judah said: let this be from me your writ of divorce and letter of dismissal and deed of liberation, that you may marry any man you wish.[1] The essential words of a document of emancipation are: Behold, you are a free woman; behold you belong to yourself.[2]

---

1. R. Judah's view was accepted as law. What difference does it make? If there were minor textual errors in non-essentials, the court could still declare the *get* valid. But if the essential words were faulty, the *get* could not be valid.
2. This refers to the emancipation of a Hebrew slave. With suitable changes of gender, the same formula applied to male slaves.

Gittin 9:10

The school of Shammai said: A man may not divorce his wife unless he has discovered something unchaste about her, for it is written: Because he has found some unseemly thing in her (Deuteronomy 24:1). But the school of Hillel said: He may divorce her even if she spoiled a dish for him, for it is written: because he has found some unseemly thing in her.[1] R. Akiba said: even if he found another woman fairer than she, for it is written: . . . and it shall be if she find no favor in his eyes. . . .[2]

---

1. There is a complete difference in emphasis, though the same Torah source is used.
2. Also from Deuteronomy 24:1. Both Hillel and R. Akiba had, in this situation, profound and astonishingly contemporary understanding of the marital relationship. The view of the school of Hillel was accepted as law.

KIDDUSHIN—MARRIAGE

Introduction

It is surprising that there is no Torah law dealing with the institution of marriage as such. As indicated below, the only Torah passage of legal nature which mentions marriage does so in connection with divorce.

The only possible explanation lies in the probability that marriage was such an early institution among the Hebrews that it was taken for granted, both in substance and in form. There was no need for God to command the people regarding the details of the marriage process; everyone knew them. Though this explanation is far from satisfying, it is the best that can be adduced. There are many Torah laws about kinds of marriage—forbidden marriages, Levirate marriage—which were arguable and where divine decision was necessary. Marriage itself and the formalities of entering into it were not.

Something of this tradition remained in Mishnaic times as well. As a result, *Kiddushin* is a fascinating mélange of subject matter, most of it having nothing to do with the marriage ceremony itself.

The book begins with laws of betrothal. The clear differentiation of betrothal forms from marriage forms was not effected in the Mishnah. It became clear only in medieval times, when two different ceremonies took place: *erusin* ("betrothal") and *kiddushin* or *nissu'in* ("marriage"). But in modern times these have been merged and most Reform rabbis, at least, have removed the *erusin* formula from the marriage ceremony altogether.

The Mishnah dwells at length on the process of betrothal. Since it used the concept of *kinyan* ("acquisition") the text moves from the acquisition of a bride to acquisition of slaves, cattle, property. And since one of the major functions of marriage is the procreation of children, the text proceeds to the duties of parents to children. Then there is a digression into a discussion of laws which may be observed only in Israel and those which must be observed everywhere.

The second half of the text deals primarily with betrothal and marriage: the conditions of betrothal, betrothal by proxy, the types and kinds of commodities to be used in fulfilling the contract, marriages between persons of different classes in society—priests, Levites, etc. More than a sixth of the material is Aggadic.

The placement of *Kiddushin* at the end of *Seder Nashim* does not pass unnoticed in rabbinic literature. Why should the book about marriage follow the one on divorces? Maimonides suggested that the order was determined by Deuteronomy 24:2: "And she departs out of his house and goes and becomes another man's wife." She had to depart before she could become another man's wife; *Gittin* had to precede *Kiddushin*.

Another commentator suggests that R. Judah the Nasi, in compiling the Mishnah, did not wish to end *Seder Nashim* on the unhappy subject of divorce, so he reversed the "natural" order of things.

Biblical Source for Kiddushin
Deuteronomy 24:1–4

Kiddushin 1:1

A woman is acquired by three means [1] and she acquires her freedom by two means. She is acquired by money, contract, or intercourse. [2] If by money, the school of Shammai said: by a *dinar* or something worth a *dinar*. [3] The school of Hillel said: by a *perutah* or something worth a *perutah*. How much is a *perutah*? The eighth part of an Italian *issar*. [4] She acquires her freedom by a *get* or by the death of her husband. A deceased brother's wife is acquired by intercourse, and she acquires her freedom by *halitzah* or by the death of her deceased husband's brother.

---

1. By any one of the three.
2. The Rabbis had to accept intercourse as a means of marriage be-

cause the Torah text made it unavoidable. But they did not approve. Sexual consummation of the marriage, in their view, should follow public sanctification of the union. Bertinora added this note: The text does not read "a man acquires a woman," but deliberately says, "a woman is acquired," to teach us that a woman can be married only with her knowledge and consent. This is a fundamental principle of Jewish marriage.

3. A *dinar* was one-fourth of a *selah*.
4. An *issar* was one-twenty-fourth of a *dinar*.

Kiddushin 1:2

A Hebrew slave is acquired by money or by contract.[1] He acquires his freedom by serving six years (Exodus 21:1–2) or by the arrival of the Jubilee Year (Leviticus 25:40–41) or by redeeming himself at his monetary value. The Hebrew woman slave has an advantage over him in that she acquires her freedom also by showing signs of puberty.[2] The slave who has his ear pierced (Exodus 21:5–6) is acquired by the act of piercing, and he acquires his freedom by the arrival of the Jubilee Year or by the death of his master.[3]

---

1. Romanticists may resent the immediate switch from marriage to slavery, but in rabbinic law the two institutions had much in common—legally speaking. Six *Mishnayot* in this chapter concern themselves with the acquisition of all manner of commodities.
2. She had to be at least twelve years and one day of age, and have not less than two pubic hairs.
3. A slave still serving his six-year term does not go free if the master dies. He serves the heirs until his term is complete.

Kiddushin 1:7

All the obligations of a father toward his son are incumbent on men but not on women.[1] All obligations of a son toward his father are incumbent both on men and on women.[2] The observance of all positive commandments which have a time limit is incumbent on men but not on women.[3] The observance of all positive commandments which do not have a time limit is incumbent both on men and on women.[4] The observance of all negative commandments, whether or not they have a time limit, is incumbent both on men and on women, except: "You shall not mar the corners of your beard"; "You shall not round the corners of your head"; and "You shall not become defiled because of the dead" (Leviticus 19:27–28).

---

1. Like having him circumcised, teaching him Torah, having him learn a trade, teaching him to swim, etc.
2. On daughters as well as on sons.
3. Morning prayer, hearing the Shofar, eating in the Sukkah, etc. A woman's schedule cannot be made subject to the fulfillment of mitzvot at a specific time.
4. Charity, kissing the mezuzah, etc.

Kiddushin 1:9

Any mitzvah which depends on the Land of Israel is limited to that Land.[1] Any mitzvah which does not depend on the Land of Israel may be observed in the Land or elsewhere, except the laws of Orlah-fruit[2] and of Diverse Kinds.[3] R. Eliezer said: the law of new produce, too.[4]

---

1. For example, laws regarding Terumah ("tithes"); in fact, most of the agricultural laws and, of course, all laws involving the Temple and relationships with it.
2. See p. 69 f.
3. See pp. 48 ff.
4. Leviticus 23:14. R. Eliezer's view was accepted as law.

Kiddushin 4:7

R. Eliezer b. Jacob said: If an Israelite marries a convert to Judaism, his daughter is eligible to marry even a priest.[1] If a convert marries the daughter of an Israelite, his daughter is eligible to marry a priest. But if a convert marries a convert, his daughter is not so eligible.[2] A proselyte has equal status with freed slaves, even through ten generations, until such time as his mother is an Israelite.[3] R. Jose said: Even if a convert marries a convert, his daughter is eligible to marry a priest.[4]

---

1. This chapter has dealt, in sections not included here, with various kinds of impediments to marriage eligibility.
2. Because there is no Israelite ancestor.
3. That is, until some male marries a non-converted woman, a born Israelite.
4. If they marry, the marriage is valid. But the priest is urged not to marry such a woman. Within this limitation, R. Jose's view was accepted as law.

Kiddushin 4:13

An unmarried man may not be an elementary school teacher.[1] Nor may a woman be an elementary school teacher.[2] R. Eliezer said: Even a man whose wife is not with him may not be an elementary school teacher.[3]

---

1. The text is not clear here. It can be interpreted to mean that a bachelor may not train teachers of young children. Rashi suggested that it means that an unmarried man shall not go into training to become a teacher of young children. But the intent of the prohibition is clear. Small children are brought to school by mothers, sisters, maidservants. An unmarried man could be led to sin as a result of such daily meetings.
2. Whether or not the woman is married. For children are also

brought to class by fathers and older brothers.

3. That is, a widower or a divorced person, or one whose wife is not living with him for any reason. But his view was not accepted as law.

The Fourth Order

NEZIKIN

Civil and Criminal Law

BAVA KAMA

BAVA METZI'A

BAVA BATRA

SANHEDRIN

MAKKOT

SHEVU'OT

EDUYOT

AVODAH ZARAH

HORAYOT

INTRODUCTION

Nezikin literally means "damages." Its name derives from the first three books, which were considered one large book of thirty chapters. Because of its size a division was made, and each part was given the title "gate" or "section": first, middle, and last.

Seder Nezikin has also been called *Seder Yeshu'ot,* "the Order of Salvations." This is an apt commentary on the nature of Halakhah: the sanctification of the mundane in order that salvation may be achieved on earth.

The books of the Order comprise all matters of civil and criminal law which were dealt with by *Bate Din,* courts of law, and the Sanhedrin itself. The three *Bavot* deal with civil law. *Sanhedrin* and *Makkot* deal with criminal statutes. The rest of the Order elaborates on both, with one major exception: *Avot.*

Avot is variously translated. If the word is used with the connotation given later in *Seder Tohorot,* it deals with prototypes of law, *avot*—"fathers"—the general concepts and principles, which underlie all of Halakhah. More usually the word refers to the Rabbis of the Mishnaic period who formulated and outlined the various maxims contained in the book *Avot*—the fathers of the great Halakhic text. Because *Avot* has no Halakhah in it at all, it has not been included here. It deserves its own setting and a much more detailed commentary than is provided here.

There is little Torah law covering the areas of concern of this Order. The economy of ancient Israel was essentially simple until after the Biblical period. Urban life, expanded commerce, new crafts and products, more complex economic processes all came into being during the Greek and Roman periods of the Second

Temple. As a result, much of the legislation in this Order is either new or derived from very general Torah justification.

Because the civil and criminal statutes deal with real situations and decisions of law courts, they have a relative permanence about them. They were affected, to some degree, by Greek and Roman law and, later, by Persian law as it was applied in Babylon. There may be some value in comparisons between these statutes and contemporary law in the same areas. These have been included to some extent in the commentary.

BAVA KAMA—THE FIRST GATE

Introduction

"The First Gate " of the three books constituting the Mishnah's major regulations in civil law limits its concern to two general areas: compensation for damages to person or property, and the implications of misappropriation of property. The tone of the book is businesslike. It does not moralize about torts or thefts; it legislates.

The subject matter varies: the classification of damages inflicted by man or beast; damages caused by pits, land obstructions, and other objects; techniques of assessing damages; restitution in cases of theft; battery and assault.

This latter inclusion in the book makes it clear that Halakhah did not always distinguish clearly between civil and criminal statutes, as does contemporary law.

Biblical Sources for Bava Kama

Exodus 21:18–25, 28–37; 22:3–8
Leviticus 5:20–26; 24:18–20
Numbers 5:5–8
Deuteronomy 19:21

Bava Kama 1:1

The four primary categories of damage listed in the Torah are: the ox,[1] the pit, the *mav'eh*,[2] and fire. There is some distinctive feature of the ox which is not like that of the *mav'eh*, and vice versa. Neither of these is exactly like fire, since they are alive. Nor are any of these exactly like the pit; their normal way is to be mobile and do damage, while the pit does not do so.[3] The feature common to them is their habit of causing injury so that you must keep them under control. When they do damage, the offender must make restitution with the best of his estate.

---

1. "Ox" here refers only to the ox which gores a man or another beast. The Torah differentiates between a first offender and a habitual gorer. This differentiation is also made regarding other damaging actions of beasts and men as well, as will be seen.
2. There is a disagreement in the Gemara about the meaning of *mav'eh*. Some Rabbis said it referred to men who damage standing crops in the field. Others insisted it referred to beasts which did damage with their teeth. The latter view appears to have prevailed.
3. Because every word of the Torah has unique significance, the Mishnah had to prove that each of these categories of damage-doers is exclusive in some way—or the Torah would not have listed all four of them. This is elaborated in subsequent *Mishnayot*, not included here.

Bava Kama 2:6

Man is always *mu'ad*,[1] whether he acts inadvertently or with premeditation, whether awake or asleep.[2] If a man blinds another person or damages his possessions, he must pay full recompense.[3]

---

1. An attested danger. See Exodus 21:29.
2. If two men share a bed at an inn and one jams the other in the eye with his elbow in the middle of the night, full compensation

must be made. Bertinora adds the following: If A went to bed first and was joined by B, A is not guilty if he injures B; B is guilty if he injures A. For A was not aware that B was there.

3. Common law today is very different. A sharp distinction is made between a willful tort or negligence on the one hand, and accidental damages on the other. This case would involve neither willful damage nor negligence.

Bava Kama 5:4

If an ox was charging another ox and struck a pregnant woman, causing her to miscarry, its owner is not liable for the value of the embryo.[1] But if a man, while striking out at another man, hit a woman and she miscarried, he must pay the value of the embryo. How is the compensation for the embryo fixed? The estimated value of the woman before she miscarried is compared with her value afterward.[2] Rabban Simon b. Gamaliel said: If this is so, a woman increases in value after giving birth.[3] Therefore, it is the value of the embryo which must be estimated, and that amount paid to the husband. If her husband is dead, his heirs receive the money. But if she is a freed slave or a proselyte no payment is due.[4]

---

1. Exodus 21:22–26 refers only to a man who causes a woman to miscarry, not to an animal. These Biblical verses constitute the famous *Lex Talionis,* the "eye for an eye" concept. Note how casually and finally the Mishnah interpreted the Torah text to mean compensation in money. Whether or not it was always so intended in the Torah itself, this is an example of ethical evolution in law.

2. Were she to be sold as a slave. The difference was to be paid to her husband.

3. And, consequently, nothing would be paid to the husband. She is more valuable because she has gone through the dangers of delivery safely. Also, she can do more kinds of work when not pregnant.

4. A freed slave who was married to a freed slave who died, and a proselyte whose husband died and was a proselyte as well, have no

heirs under Halakhic rulings if their children were born before her conversion. If they were born afterwards, they have full rights as Jews. Naturally, there was no suggestion that the money might be paid to the woman. She had some property rights (see Numbers 27:1–11) but these were limited. Rabban Simon b. Gamaliel's view was accepted as law.

In contemporary law, there are comparable situations. The owner of the ox might not be liable, under the concept that this act was outside the realm of foreseeability and could not be considered negligence. Where the man is concerned, there might be a question of transferred intent in willful torts.

Bava Kama 8:1

A man who injures another person becomes liable to him on five counts: [1] for damages, for pain, for healing, for loss of time, and for indignity.[2] What does "damages" mean? If he puts out his eye, cuts off his arm, or breaks his leg, the injured person is imagined a slave to be sold, a valuation is made about his worth previously and his worth now. What does "pain" mean? If he burns him with a spit or a nail, even though on his fingernail where no bruise shows, a calculation is made regarding the payment a man can require to undergo such pain.[3] "Healing?" If he hits him, he must pay his medical expenses. Should ulcerations appear on the skin as a result of the blow, he is liable. But if they are not the result of the blow, he is not liable. If the wound heals, then reopens, heals again, and reopens, he continues to be liable for medical expenses. But once the wound is completely healed, he is under no further obligation to pay for healing him. "Loss of time?" The injured person is thought of as a watchman of cucumber patches,[4] since he has already been compensated for his hand or foot.[5] "For indignity?" Everything is determined by the status of the offender and offended.[6] If someone offends a naked man [7] or a blind man or a sleeping man,[8] he is liable. But if the offender was asleep, he is not liable.[9] If a man falls off a roof and causes injury and indignity, he is liable for the damages but not for the indignity, for it is written: And she puts forth her hand and takes him by the genitals. A man is liable only when he acts with intent.[10]

---

1. Not necessarily all five, which is the maximum number which can be considered by the court.
2. Four of these five still play a role in law. There is a question regarding the contemporary relevance of "indignity."
3. The case cited involves pain but no injury. If he burns the finger itself, he is liable for both damages and pain.
4. Even a lame or a one-armed person can do this kind of work. If the injured party is that sick, he is paid for loss of his vocational time.
5. The loss of wages from his previous employment, to which he cannot return because of his injury, is included in the damages for the specific part of the body injured.
6. Some people are in a social position to be humiliated more than others, depending on who does the humiliating. This is sound psychology.
7. Even though the naked man is not humiliated just by virtue of being naked.
8. Even though the sleeping man does not know he is being subjected to indignity.
9. Deuteronomy 25:11. Conscious intent must be present.
10. Liable for indignity, that is. Other liabilities can be incurred regardless of intent, as we have seen.

Bava Kama 10:3

If a man identifies his articles or books in the possession of someone else, and it has already been reported in the city that these things were stolen, the purchaser would have to swear about the price he had paid, and would be paid accordingly. But if the theft has not been reported, his claim is worthless, for I might say that he sold them to a second person from whom yet another had purchased them legally.[1]

---

1. The Mishnah here tackles a problem which is still a major police headache: the owner of stolen goods who fails to report the theft.

The Rabbis recognized property rights but demanded responsible protection of the property. They were zealous to protect the innocent—in this case, the man who bought the goods in good faith, even though they were stolen.

Common law today operates differently: "A thief cannot pass title." The purchaser of stolen goods can recover his costs only from the person who sold the goods directly to him. The original owner does not have to pay—again—for his possessions.

BAVA METZI'A—THE MIDDLE GATE

Introduction

Bava Metzi'a continues the general subject matter of the preceding tractate, with changes of specific emphasis. Concerned primarily with partnerships and transactions, this book is the chief Talmudic source on business matters.

Lost property, including deeds; the responsibility of guardians of property; barter and its limits; usury; employer-employee relationships; tenancy; and joint ownership of houses—all are part of the discussions. There is little Aggadah: almost none in the Mishnah, and little even in the Gemara.

Biblical Sources for Bava Metzi'a

Exodus 22:6–14, 20, 24–26; 23:4–5
Leviticus 25:14, 35–37
Deuteronomy 22:1–4; 23:20–21, 25–26; 24:6, 10–15, 17–18; 25:4
Jeremiah 22:3
Ezekiel 18:7–8; 22:12, 29
Psalms 15:5
Proverbs 28:8

Bava Metzi'a 1:1

Two men hold a cloak.[1] One says: "I found it." The other says: "I found it." One says: "It's all mine." The other says: "It's all mine." Then each must take an oath claiming not less than half, and the value shall be divided between them.[2] If one said: "All of it is mine," and the other said: "Half of it is mine," the one who said "all" must swear that he claims no less than three-fourths, and the one who said "half" must take an oath that he claims no less than one-fourth. Then the former receives three-fourths of the value and the latter one-fourth.[3]

---

1. All the commentators remind us that in Mishnaic times, the *tzitzit*, the ritual fringes, were not worn on a separate garment called a *tallit* as they are today. They were attached to the corners of a man's cloak, then called a *tallit*. Two different situations may be covered here: the joint, simultaneous finding of a cloak in the public domain which cannot be identified as belonging to a specific person, or the claiming by two different men of a cloak which has been purchased.

2. Because of the disagreement on the nature of the case, there is also disagreement about the oath. Bertinora insisted that an oath—a serious matter in Halakhah, never to be taken lightly—would not be required for a cloak found on the street, but would be for a purchased article. Other authorities felt that any dispute between two men justified an oath in order to resolve the conflict and restore peace.

3. The man who says "half of it is mine" has already stated implicitly that the other half does not belong to him. In dispute, then, is only the half that both men claim, and only the half gets divided.

Contemporary common law is very different in its approach. If such a case went to court, it would be decided on an all-or-nothing basis. Even an equity court would probably not be able to fashion a remedy like this one. Theoretically, the Mishnah uses an advanced approach, but one which is difficult to handle in a large, complex society.

Bava Metzi'a 2:11

If a man goes looking for his lost property and his father's as well, his own takes precedence.[1] His own and his teacher's, his own takes precedence. His father's and his teacher's, his teacher's takes precedence. His father brought him into the world, but his teacher, who instructed him in wisdom, brings him to eternal life. But if his father is also a Sage, his father takes precedence. If his father and his teacher are both carrying a burden, he must first help his teacher lay it down, and then his father. If his father and his teacher are both taken captive, he must first redeem his teacher and then his father. But if his father is a Sage, he must first redeem his father and then his teacher.

---

1. If he could carry only one of them. This is based on Deuteronomy 15:4.

Bava Metzi'a 3:4

Two men deposited money with a third, one of them one hundred *zuzim* and the other two hundred. Later, both men said: "The two hundred *zuzim* are mine." He should give one hundred *zuzim* to each of them, and the rest must remain in escrow until Elijah comes.[1] R. Jose said: If so, what does the deceiver lose? The whole amount must remain until Elijah comes.[2]

---

1. In Talmudic literature there recurs the word *teku,* the first letters of four Hebrew words which are taken to mean: Elijah, the Tishbite, will answer all questions and problems. In specific cases, courts often had to rule anyhow, by majority vote, but many discussions of Halakhah are not concluded with finality in the Talmud.

    Why Elijah? He will come, according to tradition, to announce the impending arrival of the Messiah. Of course, all outstanding Halakhic problems must be solved before the Messiah arrives—there

will be no problems then—so Elijah will bring divinely-approved answers with him.
2. R. Jose's view was not accepted, but the commentators tell us that, in fact, the Rabbis later decided cases according to his view.

Bava Metzi'a 4:4

Fraud applies both to the buyer and to the seller.[1] Just as a layman has the right to take back a sale when overcharged so can a merchant. R. Judah said: The merchant does not have the right.[2] He who was deceived has the upper hand. He can say: "Give me back my money," [3] or, "Give me back what you overcharged me." [4]

---

1. There were two major forms of fraud in Talmudic times: the use of improper coins, and overcharging. The former is easier to discover: the coins can be weighed. The latter is more difficult.
2. Because he is supposed to be expert and should know better than to allow himself to be overcharged. Nevertheless, R. Judah's view was not accepted. In all matters of business, the Mishnah is extraordinarily careful about justice for all.
3. And the sale is void altogether.
4. Pay the difference between an honest charge and the overcharge, and the sale remains valid. Common law is identical with the Mishnah. Though the Roman principle of *caveat emptor*, which Judaism despised, has played a role in common law, it does not give license to defraud. The remedies at law are the same: rescinding of sale and/or damages for fraud.

Bava Metzi'a 4:10

Just as fraud exists in buying and selling, so wrong can be done by the spoken word. A man may not say: "How much is this?" if he has no desire to buy it. If a man is a repentant sinner, one must not say to him: "Remember your previous deeds." [1] If a man is descended from proselytes, one must not taunt him: "Remember the deeds of your ancestors," for it is written: "And a stranger you shall not wrong nor shall you oppress him" (Exodus 22:20).

1. This change of subject, and the next sentence as well, have to do with the improper use of words.

Bava Metzi'a 4:12

A merchant may buy from five threshing-floors and put the produce into a single storeroom, or from five winepresses and put the wine into a single barrel, so long as he has no intention of mixing them for fraudulent purposes.[1] R. Judah said: A shopkeeper may not give parched corn or nuts to children, for then he gets them accustomed to come only to him. But the Sages permit it. The merchant may not lower the price.[2] But the Sages say: If he does he should be remembered with gratitude.[3]

1. By mixing different qualities of grain or wine in order to charge a high price for inferior goods.
2. Below the general market price.
3. Because the poor can purchase more for their money. The law did not accept fair-trading—as, in general, contemporary law has not—and the Sages prevailed.

Bava Metzi'a 5:4

It is forbidden to put a shopkeeper in business on a half-profit basis, and to advance him money to buy produce on a half-profit basis unless he is paid a wage in addition.[1] It is forbidden to use another man's fowl to hatch eggs on a half-profit basis. Nor may calves or foals be given out to be raised on a profit-sharing basis unless pay is given for both labor and food costs.[2] But a man may undertake to raise calves and foals in return for half the profits until they are one-third grown; donkeys are kept so until they can bear a burden.³

---

1. In addition to his share of the profit. A partnership has to be a real one in which both partners share alike in work and profits as well as in losses. Otherwise, usury is involved.
2. Sharecropping was legally impossible among the Israelites. It too was a form of usury.
3. In this case, the second man accepts no responsibility for losses in case the animal dies. Therefore, he is in fact working for a wage, and usury is not involved.

Bava Metzi'a 5:7

The price of a man's produce may not be fixed until the market price is known. After the market price is known, a deal may be made,¹ for even if one man has no stock another will have it.²

---

1. Even before the produce itself reaches the market.
2. Such a law would effectively cripple the kind of speculation in food futures which our economy sanctions. Since the producer himself may not set a price on his own crop until the crop is grown, all costs known, and quality determined, there was a real moral issue in their decision. In the old common law, prices could be set on grain in the field or wool on the sheep—but no earlier.

Bava Metzi'a 5:11

The following transgress a negative injunction when money is lent at interest: the lender, the borrower, the guarantor, and the witnesses. The Sages added: the notary too. They transgress the command: You shall not give him your money at usury (Leviticus 25:37); and take you no usury of him (*ibid.*, 25:36); and you shall not be to him as a usurer (Exodus 22:24); and neither shall you lay upon him usury (*ibid.*); and you shall not put a stumbling block before the blind, but you shall fear Your God; I am the Lord (Leviticus 19:24).[1]

---

1. The lender transgresses all of these. The others transgress only the last.

Bava Metzi'a 9:2

If a man leases a field from his neighbor [1] which was irrigated or included an orchard, and the spring dried up or the trees were felled, he may not reduce the rental.[2] But if he had said: "Lease me this irrigated field," or "this field which contains an orchard," and the spring dried up or the trees were felled, then he may pay less than the agreed-upon rental.[3]

---

1. The rental to be paid by part of the crop.
2. For his intent in leasing the field was not expressed contractually in terms of the irrigation or the fruit of the trees, but presumably to grow the grain.
3. For he did express his purpose, which included the spring or the orchard. Ingenious systems were used, in Talmudic and even in Biblical days, to irrigate the fields. Some of these are being employed today in modern Israel.

   The situation described here is paralleled in contemporary common law. The problem is called the problem of "impossibility" or "commercial frustration." The resolution follows the pattern of the Mishnah.

Bava Metzi'a 9:7

If a man leases a field from another in return for ten *kors* of wheat a year, and the crop is poor, he pays him out of that crop. But if the grain is good, he may not say: "I will buy other wheat for you in the market"; he must pay him from the field's crop.[1]

---

1. Unless their contract had specified a grade of wheat in which the payment had to be made no matter what the field produced. This appears to be an obvious point accepted in contemporary common law as well, but cases still arise.

BAVA BATRA—THE LAST GATE

Introduction

Bava Batra, the last of the three "gates," deals with the right of possession, chiefly of real property. Logically, much of the legislation dealing with inheritance and estates is included in the book.

Partnerships, rights of ownership, contracts of deed or sale, liabilty of vendor, hereditary succession—these constitute the major areas of concern.

Biblical Sources for Bava Batra

Leviticus 19:35–36
Numbers 27:8–11
Deuteronomy 21:15–17; 25:13–16

Bava Batra 1:3

If a man has fields surrounding those of another man on three sides, and he fences those three, the other is not required to share in the cost.[1] R. Jose said: If the second man undertook to fence the fourth side, he is responsible for everything.[2]

---

1. The fencing of three sides of his land does not constitute fencing, since the land is still not protected on all four sides and, conse-

quently, he does not profit from his neighbor's work.

2. That is, for the cost of fencing the fourth side of his property and half the cost of fencing the other three sides. He has, in fact, profited from his neighbor's work and must pay his share. R. Jose's view was accepted as law.

Bava Batra 1:5

Everyone who dwells in a courtyard may be compelled to share in the cost of building a gate house and a door for the courtyard. Rabban Simon b. Gamaliel said: Not all courtyards need a gate house.[1] Everyone who lives in a town may be compelled to share in the cost of building a wall around the town, with double doors and bolt. Rabban Simon b. Gamaliel said: Not every town needs a wall.[2] How long must a man live in a town to be counted as a townsman for purposes of taxation? Twelve months.[3] If he has bought a house, he is counted as a townsman immediately.[4]

---

1. That is, if the courtyard is far from a public road and there is little traffic. Nevertheless, the law follows the Sages on the general basis of majority rule. The same general principle applies today where assessments for sewers, sidewalks, paving, and similar improvements are involved.

2. Again, the Sages disagreed with Rabban Simon. But American constitutional law suggests that he had a point (Article I, Section 8:17): Congress may authorize the purchase of land only for "needful buildings." This doctrine has been expanded to mean that the right of eminent domain can be exercised only for legitimate public purposes.

3. The commentators tell us that in many localities the time was set at thirty days.

4. The responsibility of property owners to bear a greater share of certain kinds of taxes than non-owners of property is almost a universal phenomenon and has been for many centuries. All too often, of course, it has been linked with greater privileges, including franchise.

Bava Batra 2:3

No one may open a bakery or a dyer's shop under another man's warehouse, nor may he maintain a cow barn near by.[1] In fact, these have been permitted under a winery, though not a barn.[2] If a man wishes to open a shop in a courtyard, his neighbor can prevent him by saying: I cannot sleep through the noise of all the people coming and going. A man can make articles in the courtyard so long as he goes to the market to sell them, and no one can prevent it by saying: I cannot sleep through the noise of the hammer or the noise of the millstones, or even because of the noise of the children.[3]

---

1. The smoke and heat from the former and the odors from the latter could harm the stored goods, especially foods.
2. Wine is not hurt by heat or smoke, at least not in Israel. The commentators add that in countries where it is thought that wine is hurt by heat or smoke, the bakery and the dye-works cannot be opened.
3. Children studying Torah in the home of a teacher who lived in the courtyard—but only Torah. If the teacher is holding classes in mathematics or some other subject, the protest is legitimate. There is a strong parallel in the common-law principle of nuisance.

Bava Batra 5:1

When a man sells a ship, he automatically sells the mast, the sails, the anchor, and the steering gear. But he has not sold the slaves, the packing bags, or the ship's stores. But if he said to the purchaser: "It and all that is in it," then all these are sold too.[1] If a man sells a wagon, he does not automatically sell the mules; if he sells the mules, he does not sell the wagon. If he sells a yoke, he does not sell the oxen, and if he sells the oxen, he does not sell the yoke. R. Judah said: The price proves what the sale includes. Thus, if someone said to him: "Sell me your yoke for two hundred *zuz*," it is obvious that no yoke costs two hundred *zuz*. But the Sages ruled: The price is no proof.[2]

---

1. At first glance, one might think that the purpose of this ruling was to prevent fraudulent contracts. The commentators deny this and concentrate instead on accidental, mistaken misunderstandings in the writing of contracts. In contemporary law, there are many such cases.
2. R. Judah's view was not accepted; the Sages tended to prefer the explicit to the manifest and their view was accepted as law.

Bava Batra 5:10

A wholesaler must clean his measures every thirty days,[1] and the small producer-seller once every twelve months.[2] Rabban Simon b. Gamaliel said: The rules are reversed. In addition, a shopkeeper must clean his measures twice a week, must polish his weights once a week, and clean off his scales after every weighing.[3]

---

1. To scrape off dried liquids or bits of solids which cling to the sides and bottom of the measure and decrease the amount which it can hold.
2. Because his volume of sales is smaller and takes place all at once— when the produce is ready—so that no accumulation occurs at other times.
3. This is a rather remarkable rule, since equivalent legislation was not accomplished in most states of the United States until well into the twentieth century, and then only after bitter legislative battles.

Bava Batra 8:3

The daughters of Zelophehad [1] received three portions of the inheritance of land: the portion of their father, who came out of Egypt,[2] his share of the property of Hepher, along with his brothers ³ which, since he (Zelophehad) was the first-born, consisted of a double portion.

---

1. See Numbers 27:1–7. The decision to permit these women to inherit property was remarkable in its time. The rights of women to own real property is still not established in many parts of the world, and was realized in England only a generation ago.
2. The Promised Land was divided according to the people who came out of Egypt, and passed to their heirs as they died off in the wilderness.
3. Zelophehad's father, who also left Egypt and died in the desert. The daughters had precedence over their uncles in receiving their grandfather's inheritance. This is detailed in Mishnah 8:2, not included here.

SANHEDRIN—THE HIGH COURT

Introduction

The Sanhedrin is probably the source of more scholarly speculation and controversy than any other institution in the history of Judaism and the Jewish community.

There are only a few areas of scholarly agreement with regard to the Sanhedrin. The word comes from Greek, and the Sanhedrin functioned during the last part of the Second Temple period—though there is disagreement about its origin and even more about its end.

The large areas of controversy include the following: Was there one Sanhedrin, or two, or more? Were they a hierarchy of courts, coexistent for varying areas of jurisdiction or in competition one with the other? Was the president of the Sanhedrin—if there was one Sanhedrin—the High Priest, the king, the *Nasi,* or someone else, or more than one of these persons in rotation? What did the *Av Bet Din* have to do with the Sanhedrin? Or the *Mufla?* What were the relationships of Pharisees, Sadducees, priests, and nobility to the Sanhedrin?

Authoritative answers to these and other related questions are not forthcoming. The growing mass of scholarly research is not yet conclusive. Contradictions in the classical literature prevent authoritative or final decisions. The Mishnah and Josephus are in conflict; the Gemara adds to the difficulties. Then there is always the antagonistic view of the New Testament.

The Mishnah text is superficially clear and simple. It speaks of a Sanhedrin which met in the Hall of Gazit in the Temple at Jerusalem, and which was the Supreme Court in a system that included two lower court systems: courts of three and courts of twenty-three judges. The Sanhedrin itself had seventy-one judges.

The preoccupation of the Sanhedrin was criminal law, especially cases involving possible capital punishment. This is an oversimplification of the scope of the Sanhedrin, but the Mishnah's text is limited to this area of concern, as is *Makkot,* the next book in the Order.

The Mishnah traces this judicial system to Moses and regards it as having existed over the centuries. There is no evidence in prior literature to support this claim. Torah law does not give any clues, nor does the rest of the Bible. The first clear record we have dates from the middle of the first century B.C.E.

These controversies are for scholarly investigators to pursue. We must accept the fact that Jewish tradition saw a certain body called Sanhedrin as *the* supreme court and regarded its decisions as final. The restoration of national life, that great dream which did so much to keep Jews and Judaism alive over the centuries, included the restoration of the Sanhedrin with its old authority. It is in this context, regardless of all the debatable aspects which surround it, that we approach the Mishnah's regulations about the Sanhedrin.

Biblical Sources for Sanhedrin

Exodus 23:2
Leviticus 21:10–12
Numbers 35:30
Deuteronomy 13:13–18; 16:18–20; 17:6–13; 21:18–23

Sanhedrin 1:5

A tribe,[1] a false prophet (see Deuteronomy 18:20), or a High Priest can be tried only by a court of seventy-one. A voluntary [2] war can be decreed only by a court of seventy-one. Additions to the city of Jerusalem or to the Temple area can be sanctioned only by a court of seventy-one. Sanhedrins for the tribes may be authorized only by a court of seventy-one.[3] A city can be declared an Apostate City (see Deuteronomy 13:13 ff.) only by decision of a court of seventy-one. No frontier city may be condemned as apostate, nor three cities at once, but only one or two.[4]

---

1. For practising idol-worship, or as a result of an inter-tribal quarrel over boundaries, for example.
2. Defensive wars and the conquest of the seven nations resident in Canaan at the time of Joshua were *milḥamot mitzvah*, and participation was not voluntary. Wars "to enlarge the boundaries" were voluntary.
3. A court of twenty-three judges was permitted each tribe and major city.
4. For security reasons, lest an enemy learn that the frontier was abandoned and invade. Then, as now, border towns were established in Israel with military security in mind.

Sanhedrin 1:6

The Great Sanhedrin consisted of seventy-one members; the small Sanhedrin of twenty-three. How do we know that the Great Sanhedrin should have seventy-one? It is written: "Gather unto Me seventy men of the elders of Israel" (Numbers 11:16) and that plus Moses at their head totals seventy-one. R. Judah said: The total was seventy.[1] How do we know that the smaller Sanhedrin had twenty-three? It is written: "The congregation shall judge" (Numbers 35:24), and "The congregation shall deliver" (*ibid.,* 35:25):[2] One congregation judges and another delivers, making a total of twenty. But how do we know that a congregation consists of ten? It is written: "How long shall I bear with this evil congregation" (ibid., 14:27).³ Excluding Joshua and Caleb from the twelve original spies leaves ten. Where do we derive justification for the other three? By the implications of: "You shall not follow after the majority to do evil" (Exodus 23:2). I infer that I may follow them for good. If so, why is it written: to turn aside . . . after the majority (ibid.)? It means that the verdict of conviction is not the same as the verdict of acquittal. For acquittal, a majority of one is enough; for conviction, a majority of two is required. Since a court cannot be equally divisible, another is added, making a total of twenty-three.

---

1. Including Moses. R. Judah's view was not accepted as law. The Sanhedrin, in Talmudic and later literature, was always said to have consisted of seventy men plus the Nasi.
2. Deliver means "acquit."
3. This statement is the primary basis of the regulations that a minyan ("congregation") for prayer must consist of not less than ten men.

Sanhedrin 3:3

The following are not eligible to be witnesses or judges: one who gambles with dice,¹ a usurer, pigeon racers, and traders in Seventh Year produce. R. Simon said: At first they called them "gatherers" of Seventh Year produce. But when oppressors multiplied, they changed this to "traders" in Seventh Year produce.² R. Judah said: When is this so? If they have no other occupation, but if they have some other means of livelihood, they are eligible.³

---

1. We are not quite sure how this ancient game reached Palestine. Egyptians played, as did early Greeks. The Rabbis used this form of gambling as the symbol of all gambling, and they opposed every form firmly. See p. 130.
2. Originally, Torah law prohibited both the gathering of produce in the Seventh Year and its sale (see p. 53 f.). When the oppressive foreign government (Rome) began to tax even such produce still

in the field, the law was altered to permit the individual owner to gather fruit for his own use. To eat the fruit in the field was always permissible.

3. Rabbi Judah's ruling applied to all four groups. The Rabbis split in interpreting this paragraph, and no one line came down through Halakhic literature. The Gemara gives many details in its lengthy comments. Bertinora held that R. Judah's view was accepted as law.

Sanhedrin 4:1

The form of investigation is the same in non-capital and in capital cases,[1] as it is written: "You shall have one manner of law" (Leviticus 24:22). What are the differences between non-capital and capital cases? [2] Non-capital suits are decided by three and capital cases by twenty-three judges. Non-capital cases may be opened by either defense or prosecution; capital cases must be opened for acquittal and not for condemnation. Non-capital suits may be decided by a majority of one, either for acquittal or conviction; capital cases may be decided by a majority of one for acquittal, but for conviction only by a majority of two. In non-capital cases, a verdict may be reversed from conviction to acquittal, or from acquittal to conviction.[3] But in capital cases, a verdict can be reversed only from conviction to acquittal. In non-capital cases, everyone may argue for or against the defendant; in capital cases everyone may argue for acquittal, but not for conviction.[4] In non-capital cases, a judge who argues in favor of conviction may later argue for acquittal and one who had argued for acquittal may later argue for conviction. In capital cases, a judge who had argued in favor of conviction may later argue in favor of acquittal, but one who had argued in favor of acquittal may not argue in favor of conviction. Non-capital suits are tried by day and concluded at night. But capital suits must be tried by day and concluded by day.[5] In non-capital cases the verdict, acquittal or conviction, may be reached on the same day. In capital cases a verdict of acquittal can be reached the same day, but a conviction must be decreed only on the next day. Consequently, no trial may be held on Friday or on the eve of a Festival.[6]

---

1. There is a difference between the two Hebrew words used for investigation. *Derishah* involves the asking of obvious factual questions. *Ḥakirah* requires the asking of subtle, roundabout questions to check the accuracy of the witness' memory or integrity.
2. There now follows one of the classic passages indicating the reluctance of Halakhah to execute a criminal. When these passages are added together, they amount to an attempt to negate capital punishment.
3. If, after a decision has been announced, errors are discovered or new evidence is found, the verdict can be changed. Under certain circumstances, our appeals system operates in a related fashion.
4. All the judges can examine witnesses or submit arguments or interrogate one another. But even students, who sat behind the judges, were permitted to join in the arguments for acquittal in capital cases.
5. In case some new bit of evidence can be turned up during the night.
6. Lest the accused have to live through an unhappy Sabbath or Festival with his fate hanging in the balance.

There is one real similarity to contemporary law. The Supreme Court of the United States has made a clear distinction between capital and non-capital cases in the strictness of due process required. Mr. Justice Frankfurter, who tended to avoid Federal interference in state jurisdiction, especially in criminal matters, specifically excepted capital cases.

Sanhedrin 4:5

How are witnesses inspired with awe in capital cases? They are brought in and admonished as follows: In case you may want to say what is only conjecture or hearsay or second-hand evidence, even from a person you consider trustworthy; or in the event you do not know that we shall test you by cross-examination and inquiry—then know that capital cases are not like non-capital cases. In non-capital cases a man can make monetary restitution and be forgiven,[1] but in capital cases his blood and the blood of his descendants to the end of time are the witness' responsibility. For thus we find in the case of Cain, who killed his brother, that it is written: "The bloods of your brother cry unto me" (Genesis 4:10); not "the blood of your brother," but the bloods of your brother"— that is, his blood and the blood of his potential descendants. Another interpretation of "bloods of your brother": His blood is spilled on trees and stones. For this reason only one Adam was created, to teach you that whenever a single soul is destroyed in Israel, Scripture imputes guilt to the destroyer as though he had destroyed a complete world. Whoever preserves a single soul in Israel is given merit by Scripture as if he had saved a whole world.[2] Furthermore only one Adam was created for the sake of peace among men, so that no one could say to his fellow, "My father was greater than yours," and so that the *Minim* [3] might not say, "There are many ruling powers in heaven."

---

1. If financial loss is caused through false testimony of a witness.
2. This emphasis on the individual is one of the spiritual hallmarks of Judaism. This dictum leads the Mishnah into a series of statements, each of which is worthy of a full sermon and is often the subject of modern preaching.
3. The allusion is not clear, but it may well have been to Gnostics. The sense is that if two Adams had been created people might have argued that each was created by a different divinity.

Sanhedrin 7:1

Four forms of death penalty were available to the court: stoning, burning, death by the sword, and strangulation.[1] R. Simon listed them in this order: burning, stoning, strangulation, and death by the sword.[2]

---

1. In descending order of severity. All these four forms are Biblical in origin. Stoning and burning are specifically mentioned in the Bible, and there is allusion to death by the sword for mass apostasy. Strangulation meant hanging, in fact, not garrotting or manual strangulation. Burning consisted of pouring molten lead into the

victim's mouth. But the entire systematized approach to capital punishment was Mishnaic in origin, as were the regulations which made it virtually impossible for any criminal to be executed.

2. The law did not agree with his order. This paragraph has followed a full chapter of details and differences of opinions about the stoning procedure. The reason for so many differences: lack of precedents or experience.

Sanhedrin 8:5

A stubborn and rebellious son is tried because of his potential for evil.[1] Let him die innocent rather than die guilty. For the death of the wicked benefits themselves as well as the world, just as the death of the righteous injures themselves as well as the world.[2]

---

1. The present conduct pattern of the child has not included a capital crime. But he appears to be beyond emotional cure, so it is deemed better to execute him in order to prevent a capital crime. This was a drastic notion indeed, but we learn in the Gemara (*Sanhedrin* 71a) that there never was a stubborn and rebellious son in the Biblical sense (Deuteronomy 21:18 ff) and one was never expected to appear in the future. This was, therefore, only theoretical law.
2. A whole series of maxims contrasting the righteous and the wicked follows, each related to the world at large.

Sanhedrin 10:1 [1]

All Israelites will have a share in the world-to-come. For it is written, "Your people also shall be all righteous, they shall inherit the land forever, the branch of My planting, the work of My hands, that I may be glorified" (Isaiah 60:21). But the following do not have a share in the world-to-come: anyone who says that resurrection is not of Torah origin; [2] anyone who says that the Torah was not divinely revealed; [3] and an *apikoros*.[4] R. Akiba said: in addition, anyone who reads the "outside" books,[5] and anyone who whispers a mystical charm over a wound and says, "I will bring none of these diseases upon you which I brought upon the Egyptians; for I am the Lord who heals you" (Exodus 15:26).[6] Abba Saul said: also anyone who pronounces the Divine Name as it is spelled.[7]

---

1. The Jerusalem Talmud placed this whole chapter after Chapter 11 of the Mishnah, which also deals with capital punishment, on the theory that the purpose of this chapter is to emphasize that even criminals executed after conviction can achieve eternal life. Some Mishnah editions also do so. The first part of this Mishnah is also found, as a rule, before the first chapter of *Pirke Avot*.

2. The doctrine of the resurrection was denied altogether by both the Sadducees and the Samaritans, partly on the ground that it was not Biblical in origin. The Gemara adduces a number of Biblical verses to "prove" the Biblical origins of the doctrine (*Sanhedrin* 90b).

3. But that Moses wrote it himself.

4. Epicurean philosophy infiltrated Palestine, especially among the wealthy, and was condemned by the Rabbis because it conflicted so completely with the Jewish concept of responsibility for the world, of acceptance of the "yoke of heaven." No form of hedonism mixes well with Judaism. The work *apikoros* came to mean any licentious person, then any Jew who scoffed at Halakhah, any unbeliever.

5. There is disagreement about what is meant here. Some scholars have felt that the sentence referred specifically to the "external books," the Apocrypha, and prohibited teaching them in public, which would imply sanctity equal to that of Scripture. (A number of these books were known and were not prohibited reading.) Other scholars felt that Gnostic literature was meant here. Still others took the verse to mean Greek philosophical writings in general.

6. Apparently this had become a cure-all incantation.

7. The Tetragrammaton, YHVH, is referred to. The prohibition against pronouncing it developed during the Second Temple period. The only exceptions to the prohibition: the High Priest in the Holy of Holies on Yom Kippur (see p. 113 f.), and possibly the priests in the Temple in Jerusalem pronouncing the Priestly Blessing.

MAKKOT—PUNISHMENT BY FLOGGING

Introduction

Makkot follows *Sanhedrin* not only in chronology; it is the direct successor in terms of subject matter. While *Sanhedrin* dealt with major crimes and their adjudication, *Makkot* concerns itself with those violations of law the punishment for which was flogging. The major Torah source of the book is Deuteronomy 25:1 ff.

Chapter 2 of *Makkot* deviates from crimes involving flogging to those for which the punishment is banishment into exile.

Makkot is another of the businesslike books of the Mishnah. It has no Aggadah and no digressions from its allotted subject matter. The term *Rabbi* used alone refers to Judah HaNasi.

Biblical Sources for Makkot

When there is a dispute between men and they go to law, and a decision is rendered declaring the one in the right and the other in the wrong; if the guilty one is to be flogged, the magistrate shall have him lie down and be given lashes in his presence, by count, as his guilt warrants. He may be given up to forty lashes, but not more, lest being flogged further, to excess, your brother be degraded before your eyes. (Deuteronomy 25:1–3)

SEE ALSO

> Exodus 20:13
> Numbers 35:9–28, 32
> Deuteronomy 5:17; 19:1–13, 15–21
> Joshua 20:1–9

Makkot 2:1

The following are banished: [1] he who kills accidentally. For example, if he is pushing a roller on the roof and it falls over and kills someone. Or, if he is lowering a barrel and it falls down and kills someone. Or, if he is descending a ladder and falls and kills someone. Such are banished. But if, while he is pulling the roller up to the roof it falls back on someone and kills him; or while he is raising a barrel the rope breaks and the barrel falls and kills someone; or while he is going up a ladder he falls down and kills someone—then he is not banished. This is the general rule: When death is caused during a downward movement, banishment occurs. But if death is caused not as the result of a downward movement, banishment does not occur. [2] If an axe-head slips from its handle and kills someone, Rabbi says he may not be banished; the Sages say he may be. [3] If a piece of log being split flies up and kills someone, Rabbi says he may be banished; The Sages say he may not be. [4]

---

1. To one of the six cities of refuge. See Numbers 35:9 ff. The question in this Mishnah is: When is death accidental, so that the innocent killer may take refuge, and when is he responsible, so that the blood avenger has a right to attack him? The whole concept of the blood avenger gradually disappeared from Halakhah, so that these regulations are all theoretical.

   Contemporary law makes an equally sharp distinction between premeditated and unpremeditated killing. Unlike the ancient Jewish law, however, contemporary law will try an accidental killer in order to protect him from further prosecution or from civil damage suits. In a sense, this protection is comparable to the city of refuge.

2. It is presumed that the downward movement permitted less control in the hands of the killer, whereas for upward movement he should have taken every precaution, including inspecting the rope, etc.

3. The view of the Sages was followed, despite Rabbi's cogent idea that the individual should have inspected the axe-head before swinging the axe.

4. The view of the Sages was accepted as law.

Makkot 2:4

Where are they banished? To the three cities located on the east side of the Jordan and to the three cities located in Canaan. As it is written: "You shall establish three cities beyond the Jordan and three cities in the land of Canaan. They shall be cities of refuge" (Numbers 35:14).[1] Not until three cities were selected in the Land of Israel did the three cities beyond the Jordan receive fugitives. As it is written: "Six cities for refuge shall they be unto you" (*ibid.*, 35:13),[2] which means that all had to receive fugitives simultaneously.

---

1. Moses is supposed to have established the three cities on the east side of the Jordan.
2. See Joshua 20:1 ff, for the establishment of the three cities of refuge in Canaan. See also Deuteronomy 19:1–13 for a different version of the law. In addition, the forty-eight cities given to the Levites for their habitation became known as cities of refuge, if the inhabitants were willing in any given case. The altar of the sanctuary was also a refuge, if the killer was innocent—both when there were local shrines and when the Jerusalem sanctuary became the sole shrine. It is doubtful whether any of these laws operated to any extent even during the early part of the Mishnaic period.

Makkot 3:10

How many lashes are given? Forty minus one, for it is written: "by number forty" (Deuteronomy 25:2–3),[1] which means, a number near forty.[2] R. Judah said: He is given the full forty lashes. And where is the additional lash applied? Between the shoulders.[3]

---

1. Connecting the two verses in this manner is an ingenious rabbinic device to justify lowering the number from forty. See below.
2. The Septuagint translates it so.
3. R. Judah's view was not accepted as law. Thirty-nine lashes were

the maximum. Tradition has it that the fortieth lash was never inflicted because it would imply that the man was totally guilty, a
concept which Jewish thought found unacceptable.

SHEVU'OT—OATHS

Introduction

Two books of the Mishnah deal with oaths: *Nedarim* (see p. 171
ff.) and *Shevu'ot*. The distinction between them is not absolute,
according to our logical categories. But Halakhically, the difference
was great. The vow (*neder*) to do something or to refrain from
doing something, when violated, required the individual to bring a
penitential sacrifice to the Temple. The oath (*shevu'a*), whether
taken on the initiative of the individual—that something was true
or untrue, that he had done something or had not, that someone
else had done something or not— or on the orders of a *Bet Din,*
was frequently punishable by lashing when found to be untrue.
Though the Mishnah distinguishes many kinds of oaths from the
several types mentioned in the Torah, they tend to concentrate
around evidence given in a courtroom or in connection with a case
at law. Consequently, the *shevu'a* was a basic statement, to be
taken seriously if organized society was to function at all.

Nedarim is included in *Seder Nashim,* as already indicated.
Shevu'ot is included in *Seder Nezikin* because most of the oaths
discussed have to do either with fiscal matters in particular or with
court cases in general.

The oath was administered only in certain types of civil cases:
where there is a partial admission of claim by the defendant; where
the claimant has only one witness instead of the required two; and
in cases where guardians deny liability for things which were left in
their care. In all these cases only the defendant took an oath. But
the Rabbis were flexible in this matter, and there is considerable
evidence in the Gemara that they did not hesitate to use discretion
in requiring plaintiffs to take oaths as well.

Biblical Sources for Shevu'ot

Exodus 20:7
Leviticus 5:1–13, 20–26; 19:12
Numbers 30:3

Shevu'ot 3:8

What is a vain oath? If someone swears that something well known is not so. For example, if he says of a pillar of stone that it is gold; or of a man that he is a woman; or of a woman that she is a man. If he swears about something which is impossible; for example, if he says, "I have seen a camel flying in the air," or, "I saw a snake as thick as the beam of an olive press." If a man says to witnesses: "Come and testify for me," and they say: "We swear that we will not testify." [1] If a man swears to annul a mitzvah; for example, not to make a Sukkah, or not to carry a *lulav,* or not to put on *tefillin.* These are vain oaths, for which one is liable, for willful transgression, to flogging; but for unwitting transgression, one is not liable.

---

1. This is a violation of a Torah mitzvah. See Leviticus 5:1.

Shevu'ot 4:3

What is an oath of testimony? If a man says to two persons: "Come and testify for me," and they reply: "We swear we know no testimony about you"; or they say: "We know no testimony about you," and he says: "I adjure you," and they say, "Amen," they are liable.[1] If he adjures them five times outside the court-room,[2] then they come to the court and admit that they have testimony to offer, they are exempt.[3] But if they deny before the court, they are liable for each.[4] If he adjures them five times before the court and they deny knowledge, they are liable only once. R. Simon said: What is the reason? because they cannot afterwards admit having knowledge.[5]

---

1. If it later becomes known that they did in fact have testimony to offer, they are liable to an offering for having sworn falsely.
2. And each time they deny knowing anything about which to testify.
3. A denial made to others outside the courtroom does not bring liability. This was decided in the first Mishnah in this chapter, not included here.
4. Because in fact they swore falsely a total of six times.
5. Because theoretically they could not swear five times in a courtroom. There is a principle of rabbinic law that a witness can testify only once to any given fact. See the Gemara, *B. Sanhedrin* 44b.

Shėvu'ot 7:1

All those who take oaths enjoined in the Torah do so in order not to pay.[1] But the following take an oath in order to receive payment: the hired laborer, one who has been robbed,[2] one who has been injured,[3] one whose opponent is suspected of swearing falsely,[4] and a store-owner with his account-book.[5] The hired laborer—in what way? If he says to his employer: "Give me the wages you owe me," the employer replies: "I've already paid you," and the laborer says: "But I have not received it," he takes an oath and receives payment.[6] R. Judah says: not unless the claim was partially admitted. If, for example, the laborer says: "Give me my wages of fifty *denars* which you owe me," and the employer says: "You've already received one gold *denar*.[7]

---

1. Normally the defendant alone takes an oath, then does not have to satisfy the claim of the plaintiff.
2. When the robber has been caught and testified against by competent witnesses, the victim must swear that specific articles were taken in order to get them back.
3. Accidentally, and is entitled to money damages. He must swear that

he did not injure himself. The commentators note that if the injury was on a part of the body inaccessible to him, he does not have to take the oath.

4. Then the opponent who is to collect swears that the other is liable.

5. In dealings with suppliers, not customers. When the employees of a supplier deliver goods to the store-owner and he claims payment, if the shopkeeper claims the payment has already been made and cites his books, the supplier can swear he did not receive the money and can have his employees swear that they did not receive the money. He can then collect.

6. For the employer may have many hired hands, and may have neglected to pay one.

7. One gold *denar* equals twenty-five silver *denars*. But R. Judah's view was not accepted as law.

EDUYOT—TESTIMONIES

Introduction

This book of the Mishnah is the most peculiar in the entire Talmud. It is the only book of Halakhic content which is not organized in any way by subject matter. Most of its statements are repeated elsewhere in the Mishnah, usually in verbatim form. As a result, it has neither Babylonian nor Palestinian Gemara following it.

The name of the book gives a clue to its contents: testimonies, statements made by scholars in assemblies of scholars about Halakhic matters, as they learned them from their teachers and masters. In the Gemara to *Berakhot* (28a), we are told that this collection of rabbinic statements was first issued at Yavneh, the small coastal town where Joḥanan ben Zakkai established his academy to save rabbinic study when the Romans destroyed Jewish national life in 70 C.E. The occasion was the chaos caused by the deposition of Rabban Gamaliel from his post as head of the Sanhedrin. There may be some truth in this tradition, but it is only partial—for statements of Rabbis who lived both before the generation of Gamaliel and after him are included in its contents.

If we accept the idea that the Mishnah as we have it is but the last of a series of documents written down over a period of one to two centuries, as indicated in the Introduction, then we can accept *Eduyot* as one such collection, made at Yavneh beginning in the last quarter of the first century and continuing into the second century. When R. Judah HaNasi supervised the editing of the Mishnah, this document was naturally included. And since the Mishnah in general was being organized by subject, the individual Halakhot were also set down where they belonged.

Because of the diversity of subject matter, no Biblical sources are listed for this book. We limit ourselves here to those statements not appearing elsewhere in this volume.

Eduyot 1:4 [1]

Why do they record the opinions of Shammai and Hillel which did not prevail? In order to teach future generations that a man should not persist in his opinion, for even "the fathers of the world" did not have all their opinions prevail.

---

1. This Mishnah is preceded by three cases in which both Hillel and Shammai expressed opinions, both of which were unacceptable to the Sages, with the views of the Sages becoming the Halakhah.

Eduyot 1:5

Why are the opinions of an individual recorded in opposition to the majority, since the Halakhah must follow the opinion of the majority? So that, if a court should prefer the individual's opinion, it may rely on him,[1] since a court cannot annul the opinion of an earlier court unless it is greater in wisdom and in number.[2] If it exceeds in wisdom but not in number, or in number but not in wisdom, it cannot annul the earlier opinion, but only if it exceeds both in wisdom and in number.

---

1. That is, the minority opinion is on record as a possible precedent, according to R. Abraham ibn Daud. This procedure still persists in contemporary jurisprudence. The Supreme Court of the United States has often accepted dissenting opinions in earlier cases as the basis for majority opinions in later cases.
2. The wisdom of the Nasi of the Sanhedrin or of the presiding judge in a smaller court is referred to. In addition, a court of twenty-three could overrule a court of three, and the full Sanhedrin could overrule a court of twenty-three. According to Maimonides, the new decision became Halakhah only if it was accepted by a majority of all scholars then alive. There is almost no evidence that his statement was ever in practical use.

AVODAH ZARAH—IDOLATRY

Introduction

From the time the Israelites conquered most of the Holy Land, toward the close of the thirteenth century before the Common Era, the most serious problem they faced in the battle for monotheism and Torah was paganism. First it appeared in the fertility cults of Baal, Astarte, and the whole pantheon of Babylon and Israel's other neighbors. The Persian deities followed, then those of the Greeks and Romans, each in turn beckoning to the people to abandon God and Torah.

The Torah contains many statutes and warnings against idolatry. Deuteronomy is one long sermon against idolatry.

Despite the relatively better organization of the people after the Babylonian Exile and the beginnings of the rabbinic period, rival religions remained a problem. This Mishnah reflects the continuing seriousness of the situation.

The response of the community to idol-worship and idol-worshippers is not the subject. These are treated primarily in *Sanhedrin* and *Makkot*. We are concerned here primarily with regulations regarding vessels used in idolatrous rites, social relationships with idol-worshippers, and similar subjects.

The Rabbis tended to define idolatry narrowly. They made it clear that all non-religious systems were not idolatrous. There was controversy over the status of Christianity in its early beginnings, but eventually it was accepted as a non-idolatrous faith, as was Islam when it came on the world scene in the seventh century.

Some of the regulations against idolatry may seem harsh to relatively tolerant twentieth-century persons, but it must be remembered that at stake was ethnic and religious survival against overwhelming odds. The Jews feared assimilation and attempted to counter it.

Biblical Sources for Avodah Zarah

You shall make no covenant with them and their gods. They shall not remain in your land—lest they make you sin against Me by serving their gods—for this would be a snare to you. (Exodus 23: 32–33)

SEE ALSO

Exodus 23:13, 24; 34:12–16
Deuteronomy 7:1–5, 25–26

Avodah Zarah 1:1

For three days before festivals of idolators, it is forbidden to do business with them—to lend them articles or borrow from them, to lend or receive money from them, to repay a debt or receive payment on a debt from them.[1] R. Judah said: Payment may be taken from them, since this can only pinch them.[2] The Sages said to him: Even though it may pinch them now, they will rejoice later.[3]

---

11. Since the profit accruing to the pagan from such transactions may be used for idol-worship. In addition, a beneficial transaction would

make him happy and move him to rejoice before his idol.

2. Consequently, they will not rush off to thank their pagan gods.
3. Because their minds will be free of concern over the debt, and then they will want to give thanks. R. Judah's view was not accepted as law. In matters of idolatry, the Sages were rarely lenient.

Avodah Zarah 2:1

Cattle should not be kept in the barns of heathen-owned inns, out of suspicion that they may practice sodomy with them. A woman should not be alone with them, out of suspicion that they may violate her. A man should not be alone with them, out of suspicion that they may murder him. An Israelite woman should not act as midwife to a heathen woman, since she would be helping give life to an idol-worshipper. But a pagan woman may assist an Israelite woman.[1] An Israelite woman may not nurse the child of a heathen, but a heathen woman may nurse the child of an Israelite, in the latter's home.[2]

---

1. But not alone, since bodily harm might be done to mother or child.
2. Not in the pagan home, to prevent harm to the child and also to prevent his secret induction into some pagan rite. Jewish history records more than one case of this kind, not only with pagan groups, but with Christianity and Islam as well. The entire Jewish community was outraged in 1858, when Papal guards abducted Edgar Mortara from his parents' home, after he had been secretly baptized by his nurse. Despite all pressure, the child was never returned to his parents and later became a priest.

Avodah Zarah 5:1

If a pagan hires an Israelite laborer to help him with libation wine, his wages are forbidden.[1] But if he hires him to help with some other work, and incidentally says to him, "Move this jar of libation wine from here to there," his wage is permitted. If a pagan hired the donkey of an Israelite to carry libation wine, its hire is forbidden. But if he had hired it to ride upon, even if the pagan rests a flagon of libation wine on it at the same time, the hire is permitted.

---

1. That is, forbidden to be used by the Jew in any way. The phrase *Assur behanna'a* is frequently used to indicate total prohibition, with no benefit of any kind to be derived. Many foodstuffs grown or produced by pagans fall into this category. On the other hand, others may be sold by a Jew even though he may not use or eat them himself. Much of Chapter 2 of *Avodah Zarah* deals with these problems of foodstuffs.

HORAYOT—ERRONEOUS DECISIONS

Introduction

Horayot is one of the shortest books of the Mishnah. In various editions, it was placed seventh, eighth, or tenth and last in the *Seder Nezikin*. Its position at the end of the Seder is explained by Maimonides as a reminder to us that even the greatest of scholars (as found in *Avot,* which traditionally precedes it), can err in their decisions.

Sins committed in error required penance—less than deliberate sins, naturally, but penance nonetheless. *Horayot* deals with such errors and the required penance.

Biblical Sources for Horayot

If you unwittingly fail to observe any of the commandments which the Lord has declared to Moses—anything that the Lord has enjoined upon you through Moses—from the day that the Lord gave the commandment and on through the generations:

If this was done unwittingly, through the inadvertence of the community, the whole community shall present one bull of the herd as a burnt offering of pleasing odor to the Lord, with its proper meal offering, and one he-goat as a sin-offering. The priest shall make expiation for the whole Israelite community and they shall be forgiven; for it was an error, and for their error they have brought their offering, an offering by fire to the Lord and their sin-offering before the Lord. The whole Israelite community and the stranger residing among them shall be forgiven, for it happened to the entire people through error.

In case it is an individual who has sinned unwittingly, he shall offer a she-goat in its first year as a sin-offering. The priest shall make expiation before the Lord on behalf of the person who erred, for he sinned unwittingly, making such expiation for him that he may be forgiven. For the citizen among the Israelites and the stranger who resides among them—you shall have one ritual for anyone who acts in error. (Numbers 15:22–29)

SEE ALSO
>   Leviticus 4:1–5, 13–23

Horayot 1:1

If a *Bet Din* ruled that any mitzvah of the Torah could be transgressed, and an individual proceeded and acted in error following their ruling, whether they acted and he acted with them, or whether he acted after them, or even if they did not act and he did, he is exempt,[1] because he relied on a ruling of the court. If a *Bet Din* ruled erroneously and a member of the court knew that they had erred, or a disciple who was capable of deciding matters of Torah knew they had erred and still went and acted on their ruling, whether they acted and he acted with them, or they acted thereafter, or whether they did not act at all but he did so, he is liable since he did not have to depend on the ruling of the court.[2] This is the general rule: Anyone who can rely on himself is liable, but anyone who must depend on the court is exempt.

---

1. From the penitential sacrifice.
2. But knew himself that they were wrong. In a sense, this is a

dangerous doctrine, since it makes the individual the final authority over constituted authority. But it is soundly Jewish.

Horayot 1:3

Should a *Bet Din* rule that an entire principle of Torah should be uprooted, if they said for example, "There is no law about the menstruating woman in the Torah," or, "There is no law about the Sabbath in the Torah, or, "There is no law about idolatry in the Torah," they are exempt.[1] If, on the other hand, they ruled that part of a principle should be annulled and part sustained, they are liable. How is this so? If they said: The law of the menstruating woman does occur in the Torah, but if a man has intercourse with a woman who is waiting one day,[2] he is exempt. Or if a court ruled that there is law about Sabbath in the Torah, but if a man carries something from the private domain to the public domain he is not liable,[3] or if a court ruled that the law of idolatry does occur in the Torah, but if a man bows to an idol he is not guilty, the court is liable. For it is written, "If something be hidden" (Leviticus 4:13)—something, but not the whole principle.

---

1. From the communal sacrifice (Leviticus 4:13 ff.), since the decision was a palpably foolish one and no Jew should have obeyed it. If an individual did carry it out, he was liable for a sacrifice.
2. That is, she bled during the time no menstrual blood could have been expected. One day of waiting was required before normal marital relations could be resumed. According to Halakhah, the man is liable for a sacrifice, and the court's ruling was in error.
3. Obviously contrary to Halakhah. See p. 86.

The Fifth Order

KODASHIM

Sacred Things

INTRODUCTION

Kodashim, the Fifth Order of the Mishnah, refers primarily to the sacrifices which were brought to the Temple in Jerusalem. But it also includes the contrarily named book *Ḥullin,* "secular things," which deals chiefly with the dietary laws and ritual slaughter of food animals. But the word *secular* actually has the wrong connotation because in Judaism there is nothing secular. The Mishnah makes a distinction between cultic sanctity and non-cultic sanctity; no other differentiation is meaningful in Judaism.

Kodashim is placed before the last Order, i.e. *Tohorot* (ritual cleanliness of all varieties), because its laws precede those in Leviticus, according to Maimonides. Within the Order, the books appear in descending size: the longest first and the shortest last. There are eleven books in all.

There is no Palestinian Gemara for this Order, though a full Babylonian Gemara is available to us. No good historic reason can be given for this. Surely the scholars in Palestine studied the cultic laws as avidly as did their brothers in Babylon. Apparently the Palestine Gemara was lost and has not yet been found; a stir of excitement was created, however, in 1907–8, when a scholar named Friedlander claimed to have unearthed parts of the Palestine Gemara and published them. They proved to be a forgery.

Rabbinic scholars have always placed great emphasis on the study of this Order, and for two reasons. First, continuing study of the Temple sacrificial cult and the details of its administration would continue to show confidence in the restoration of the Temple, and would serve as a living reminder to God for that restoration to become a reality. Second, the study would constitute a substitute for the sacrifices themselves. This thought is akin to the idea that the repetition of Torah passages dealing with specific sacrifices serves as a substitute for the sacrifices, as is expressed in the traditional prayer book.

The origin of the practice of animal, vegetable, and other sacrifices is shrouded in antiquity. It certainly predates the ancient Israelites, and it continues in many societies to our own day. It seems to be an existential response to the human condition, with all its anxieties and limitations. To give of ourselves to the Divine must somehow help to make us more worthy in His sight. This concept has not changed materially over the centuries, though the techniques of sacrifice have.

Jewish sacrifice during the Temple Era was marked by two unique characteristics. First, a sacrifice could be made only on a ritual basis: there were obligatory and stated sacrifices, or voluntary ones. The latter could atone only for sins committed against God. Sins against fellow-men could not be atoned for by sacrifice alone but by restitution, the seeking of forgiveness, and the like. Secondly, only acts committed inadvertently could be atoned for by sacrifice. Premeditated sins were not atoned for by offerings. We have already dealt with various forms of restitution for such sinful acts.

All laws regarding sacrifices fall into the category of *Ḥukkim,* those laws for which no reason is given in the Torah itself or can be assigned by rabbinic tradition. Maimonides distinguished in this regard between obligatory and voluntary sacrifices. The latter were true *Ḥukkim;* there was no reason for them, and, he suspected, they were a response to the idolatrous propensities of ancient Israel. The obligatory sacrifices, however, served as a discipline, as a reminder of God's presence and His demands. Maimonides maintained, however, that the details of both types of sacrifice fell into the category of *Ḥukkim,* to be obeyed just because God commanded them that way.

ZEVAḤIM—ANIMAL SACRIFICES

Introduction

This book deals with seven kinds of sacrifices of animals and birds which were brought, first to the portable *Mishkan,* the sanctuary in the wilderness, then to the various "official" local shrines in the Land of Israel, and finally to the Temple in Jerusalem. These seven types were:

1. *Olah*—a wholly burned animal or bird, offered on various occasions ranging from the routine daily and Sabbath sacrifices to fulfillment of vows, from the purification sacrifice of the mother after delivery of a child to the High Priest's offering on the Day of Atonement.

2. *Ḥattat*—a sin-offering to atone for accidental or unpremeditated offenses of a ritual character.

3. *Asham*—a repentance-offering to atone for accidental or unpremeditated offenses of a social character, after restitution had been made.

These first three types of sacrifice were of greater sanctity than those which follow. The Mishnah distinguishes between them for many purposes.

4. *Shelamim*—the exact translation of this word is unclear; they have been called "peace" offerings, "well-being" sacrifices, and related names, because the word *shalem* is closely related to *shalom.* These are offerings of thanksgiving on various occasions, some required and some voluntary.

5. *Bekhor*—the sacrifice of the first-born, specifically ordained in Numbers 18:17–18.

6. *Ma'aser Behemah*—the animal tithe, as ordained in Leviticus 27:32.

7. *Pesaḥ*—the Paschal sacrifice, which had laws all its own, most of them dealt with in Mishnah *Pesaḥim.*

This is a businesslike book dealing with all the details of proper sacrificial animals, sacrificial procedures, and the like. Of particular interest may be the sections dealing with the historic evolution of some sacrificial forms between the time of the desert wandering and the final establishment of the central sanctuary in Jerusalem.

Biblical Sources for Zevaḥim
Leviticus 1:1–9, 14–17; 3:1–5; 4:27–31; 7:1–8

Zevaḥim 5:4

The burnt offering, which is of highest sanctity, was slaughtered on the north side, its blood was received in a vessel there. Its blood was applied twice, which really meant four times.[1] Then it had to be flayed, cut into pieces, and completely consumed by fire.

---

1. The blood was tossed in a way which permitted it to spread to all four sides of the altar. This procedure was different from that followed in making the sin-offering, for example, when the four sides were individually sprinkled. These are the kinds of differences which make us wonder about the "why" of sacrificial details. Rabbinic literature never enlightens us, but joins Maimonides in urging us to accept these laws without asking for reasons.

Zevaḥim 14:4

Before the tabernacle was erected in the wilderness, individual altars were permitted, and the ritual was officiated at by the first-born. Thereafter, individual altars were forbidden and only the priests officiated. The most sanctified sacrifices [1] were eaten only inside the curtains of the tabernacle. The sacrifices of lesser sanctity were eaten anywhere within the Israelite camp.[2]

---

1. Details of which sacrifices were of greater and of lesser sanctity are given in Chapter 5 of the Mishnah book.

2. After the settlement in the Land of Israel, the three areas of sanctity were transformed. The immediate tabernacle area became the Temple; the Levitical area was the Temple Mount; the "camp of the Israelites" area became the whole city of Jerusalem. All the pertinent laws were so adapted, including those dealing with lepers and persons with other afflictions, along with the permitted areas for eating various kinds of sacrifices.

Zevaḥim 14:6

When they came to Shiloh [1] individual altars were forbidden. The sanctuary there had no roof, but it consisted of a stone building with curtained ceiling, and this was the "resting place." [2] The most sanctified sacrifices were consumed inside the curtains, and the lesser sacrifices and Second Tithes [3] were consumed in any place within sight of Shiloh.

---

1. This is one of several *Mishnayot* dealing with changes in the sacrificial laws which occurred in the evolution of the history of the Jewish people after the wandering in the desert. Only a history-conscious people would include in a law book such references to procedures done away with centuries earlier. For the beginnings of the sanctuary at Shiloh, see Joshua 18:1 ff.
2. See Deuteronomy 12:9 ff. for the Torah source of this change in law.
3. Second Tithes were required only after the conquest and division of the Land of Israel. Therefore, there was no reference to them in previous discussions of the locale of sacrifice consumption.

Zevaḥim 14:7

When they came back to Nob and Gibeon, individual altars were again permitted.[1] The most sanctified sacrifices were consumed inside the curtains and the lesser sacrifices in all the cities of Israel.

---

1. After Shiloh was destroyed. See I Samuel 21:2–7.

Zevaḥim 14:8

When they came to Jerusalem, individual altars were forbidden and never again permitted. This was the "inheritance." [1] The most sanctified sacrifices were consumed inside the curtains, while the lesser sacrifices were eaten, along with Second Tithes, within the wall of Jerusalem.

---

1. Another reference to the predicted change in law in Deuteronomy 12:9.

MENAḤOT—FLOUR OFFERINGS

Introduction

The word *minḥah* originally referred to any sacrificial offering to God (see Genesis 4:3). Later, the term was limited to offerings of flour and oil. When these were brought to the sanctuary, they were mixed in various ways and prepared in various forms.

The Mishnah is matter-of-fact in discussing these meal offerings. It deals with valid and invalid meal offerings; the procedure for burning the "handful" on the altar; the distribution of the rest of the offering to the priests; details of the preparation of the various kinds of cakes and loaves; the majestic *Omer* ceremonial, which began on Passover and reached its climax on Shavuot; and similar matters.

Because of the practical nature of the material, there is no Aggadic material in the Mishnah at all. Even in the Gemara to *Menaḥot,* little Aggadah appears.

Over the centuries, the Rabbis loved to study *Menaḥot* because meal offerings were small, compared to sacrifices of bullocks or even goats and lambs, and therefore less of a burden to the poor man. Rabbi Isaac is quoted in the Gemara (104b) as saying that God particularly loves the meal offering because the poor man brings it: "I account it as though he had offered his own soul to Me."

Biblical Sources for Menahot
Leviticus 2:1–13; 6:7–11; 7:9–10

Menahot 6:1

The handful [1] must be taken from the following flour offerings, then the remainder is for the priests: the offering of fine flour (Leviticus 2:2), that prepared on a griddle, the one prepared in a pan (*ibid.* 2:5–10), the cakes and the wafers; the flour offering of non-Jews,[2] the flour offering of women, the flour offering of the *Omer*,[3] the sinner's flour offering, and the flour offering of the *Sotah*.[4]

---

1. One handful of meal or of the baked product was burned on the altar. Though flour offering requirements ceased with the destruction of the Temple, this custom is still carried out by observant bakers, both industrial and domestic.
2. A free-will offering by a friendly non-Jew. No such offerings were required, of course.
3. See next Mishnah.
4. See pp. 177 ff.

Menahot 10:3

What was the procedure? [1] The messengers of the court went out on the eve of Passover and tied the unreaped grain in bunches to make it easier to reap. People from nearby towns all gathered there so that the reaping could take place ceremoniously. As soon as it was dark [2] one called out: "Has the sun set?" Everyone answered: "Yes." Again: "Has the sun set?" "Yes." "With this sickle?" "Yes." "With this sickle?" "Yes." "Into this basket?" "Yes." "Into this basket?" "Yes." On the Sabbath he called: "On this Sabbath?" They answered: "Yes." "On this Sabbath?" "Yes." "Shall I reap?" "Yes." "Shall I reap?" "Yes." He repeated each matter three times and they answered: "Yes! Yes! Yes!" Why was all this? Because of the Boethusians,[3] who insisted that the *Omer* was not to take place at the close of the first day of the Festival.

---

1. For getting the *Omer* of barley.
2. On the eve of the second day of Passover.
3. A sect which opposed Pharisaic practice. Some identify them with the Sadducees, but this fact is in doubt. They, too, believed that the *Omer* should be cut on the first Sunday after the beginning of Passover because the Torah says: "on the morrow after the Sabbath" (Leviticus 23:11). They could not accept the word Sabbath, as the Rabbis did, as meaning a major festival whose restrictions were like those of the Sabbath.

Menaḥot 13:11

It is said of the burnt offering of cattle: "a fire offering, an odor of sweet savor" (Leviticus 1:9). Of the bird offering: "a fire offering, an odor of sweet savor (1:17). And of the flour offering: "a fire offering, an odor of sweet savor" (2:2). The purpose is to teach that it does not matter whether a man offers much or little, if only he directs his mind toward heaven.[1]

---

1. Here is as clear a refutation as can be found of the notion that even in early Judaism sacraments had a sanctity in and of themselves. *Kavannah* ("inwardness") was already the chief criterion in the thought of the Rabbis. The quantity of sacrifice did not matter. What was important was the intent.

ḤULLIN—UNCONSECRATED ANIMALS

Introduction

The more accurate name for this book is *Sheḥitat Ḥullin,* the slaughter of unconsecrated animals, the title given the book in many rabbinic sources in early times. The book is concerned with the dietary regulations in general, which involve animals, fowl, fish, eggs, and milk products. The last two chapters digress into regulations about the required offering of the first fleece and the humanitarian commandment in Deuteronomy 22:6 ff., prohibiting the separation of a mother bird from her young in the nest.

The Gemara is one of the most diffuse in the entire Talmud, ranging over a wide variety of subjects. Not so the Mishnah.

There is no area in all of Halakhah in which such an enormously detailed structure of regulations has been built out of so little Torah law. The Torah's dietary regulations stressed forbidden animals. These are outlined in categories and in specific detail both in Leviticus 11 and in Deuteronomy 14.

But the Torah says nothing about slaughtering procedures, and the only statement regarding the mixing of milk and meat foods is the thrice-repeated: "You shall not boil a kid in its mother's milk." By the time of the Mishnah, however, both areas of Halakhah were well developed, and this Mishnah deals with them.

Biblical Sources for Ḥullin

Genesis 32:33
Exodus 22:30
Leviticus 17:13–14; 22:28
Deuteronomy 12:20–24; 14:21; 18:3–4; 22:6–7

Ḥullin 1:1

Anyone may slaughter—and what they slaughter is kosher—except a deaf-mute, an imbecile, and a minor, lest they impair what they slaughter. But if any of these slaughter while others watch them,[1] what they slaughter is kosher.[2] Any animal slaughtered by a non-Jew is considered carrion, and it conveys defilement by carrying.[3] If a man slaughters at night, or if a blind man slaughters, the slaughtering is kosher. If he slaughters on the Sabbath or on the Day of Atonement, although he is guilty within himself,[4] the slaughtering is kosher.

---

1. To be sure that the procedure is properly carried out.
2. The Rabbis were well aware of the value of an animal or even of a bird, and they were not anxious to declare them unfit for consumption. The Mishnah and Gemara are lenient in this area.
3. The animal cannot be eaten or profited by on the part of a Jew. This is based on Deuteronomy 12:21: "And you shall sacrifice."
4. He is theoretically liable to death by stoning for Sabbath violation, or to *Karet* (death by divine justice) for Yom Kippur violation.

Ḥullin 7:1

The prohibition of the ischiatic nerve [1] is binding both in the Land of Israel and outside it, both during the existence of the Temple and thereafter, both with regard to unconsecrated and consecrated animals. It applies both to cattle and to wild animals, both to the right thigh and to the left. But it does not apply to birds because they have no spoonlike hip. It applies to a fetus. Rabbi Judah said: It does not apply to a fetus.[2] Its fat is permitted.[3] Butchers are not trustworthy regarding the removal of the ischiatic nerve, according to R. Meir. The Sages said: They are trustworthy regarding both the nerve and the fat.[4]

---

1. See Genesis 32:33 for the Torah basis of the prohibition.
    This basis is a rare one—unconnected with Moses, Mount Sinai,

or the other dietary laws. The Jacob story falls into the category of the "etiological," giving historical validation to a previously accepted action or idea. Though many speculative reasons are suggested by scholars for this prohibition, we do not know the real one.

2. R. Judah's view was not accepted as law.

3. But there is a longstanding tradition not to use it. There is some question about the antecedent here: the ischiatic nerve or the fetus. Most scholars accept the former, but the tradition applies to both.

4. The law followed the Sages, but practice has frequently followed R. Meir. In the United States, for instance, there apparently has been universal agreement not to permit the complicated butchering of the hindquarter in order to remove the nerve in question. Instead, the whole hindquarter is considered non-kosher and is not sold to religious Jews.

Ḥullin 8:1

It is forbidden to cook all flesh in milk [1] except the flesh of fish and locusts. It is also forbidden to place flesh on the table with cheese, except the flesh of fish and locusts. If a man vows to abstain from flesh, he is permitted to eat the flesh of fish and locusts. A fowl may be placed on the table with cheese, but may not be eaten with it,[2] according to the school of Shammai. The school of Hillel said it may neither be placed upon the table with cheese nor eaten with it. R. Jose said: This is an instance where the school of Shammai adopted a more lenient ruling and the school of Hillel a more stringent one. Of what kind of table did they speak? Of a table at which men eat. But if a table on which food is set is referred to, one may place the one beside the other without hesitation.

---

1. This is a generalization of the Torah commandment: "You shall not boil a kid in its mother's milk." This command is repeated three times in the Torah (Exodus 23:19; 34:26; Deuteronomy 14:21). The Rabbis interpreted it to mean that cooking, eating, and profiting from a mixture of milk and meat were all forbidden.

2. The designation of fowl as meat is not Torah law. The Rabbis attributed it to the scribes who, beginning with Ezra, transmitted the teachings of Torah in an authoritative way until the organization of the Great Assembly. The reason usually given was to avoid

confusing the people. Fowl looks so much like meat that, seeing chicken cooked in milk, people might conclude that the law had been changed; and veal, for example, which looks almost identical, might also be cooked in milk. This is both *Mar'it Ayin*—"appearances"—and an aspect of building "a fence around the Torah."

Ḥullin 8:3

If a drop of milk falls on a piece of meat cooking in a pot and there is enough milk to flavor the piece of meat,[1] it is forbidden.[2] If the pot is stirred, it is forbidden [3] if there is enough milk to flavor all the contents of the pot.

---

1. "Enough milk to flavor" is defined by the Rabbis as one part of milk to sixty of meat. If the bulk of the piece of meat is more than sixty times that of a drop of milk, the meat remains kosher. This constitutes a quantity too small to be concerned about.
2. The one piece of meat on which the milk fell.
3. The entire contents of the pot.

BEKHOROT—FIRST-BORN

Introduction

Immediately after the Exodus from Egypt, this command was given to Moses: "Sanctify unto Me all the first-born, whatsoever opens the womb among the children of Israel, both of man and of beast, it is Mine" (Exodus 13:2).

The implications of this sentence constitute the contents of the book. In general, there are four sets of regulations:

1. The first-born of a donkey was redeemed by the offering of a lamb to the priests. If this was not possible, it was destroyed by breaking its neck.

2. The first-born of a kosher cow was given to the priest to be sacrificed and eaten. If blemished, the animal was eaten by the

priest, but no parts were sacrificed, and the sanctuary in Jerusalem was not the locale.

3. The first-born of an ox could not be used for labor. The first-born sheep could not be sheared.

4. The first-born male child was redeemed by the payment of five *shekels* to the priest (Numbers 18:15–16). This is the basis of the ceremony of *Pidyon Ha'ben,* still carried on by religious Jews today.

There was great rabbinic controversy over an apparent contradiction between Exodus 13:2 and Numbers 18:15. Were all unclean animals to be redeemed, or only donkeys? Philo, Josephus, and others maintained that all first-born had to be redeemed. Halakhah ruled otherwise.

Biblical Sources for Bekhorot

Exodus 13:2, 11–13; 22:28–9; 34:19–20
Leviticus 27:26
Numbers 3:13; 18:15–18
Deuteronomy 15:19–23

Bekhorot 2:9

If the first-born was delivered by Caesarean section and then another was born by normal delivery, R. Tarfon said: Both must be let out to pasture until they become blemished; then they may be eaten by their owner. R. Akiba said: Neither is considered a first-born—the first because it was not the first of the womb,[1] and the second because it was preceded by another.[2]

---

1. Exodus 13:12, the words of which are interpreted to mean that the first-born must be delivered from the womb via the vagina in order to be a true first-born.

2. R. Akiba's view was accepted as law, meaning that there were no restrictions at all on either animal. The law is the same for humans. In addition, if a woman has a miscarriage and later de-

livers a son, he is not a first-born, and the ceremony of *Pidyon Ha'ben,* the redemption of the first-born, is not required.

Bekhorot 4:6

If a man takes payment to act as a judge, his decisions are void;[1] if to give evidence, his evidence is void; if to sprinkle[2] or to sanctify,[3] the water is considered cavern water and the ashes are ordinary ashes. If a priest is ritually unclean and could not eat his *Terumah,*[4] he must be given food and drink and should be rubbed with oil. If he is an old man, he must be given a donkey to ride. The priest is also paid as a workman.[5]

---

1. R. Ovadya of Bertinora injects here a fiery condemnation of the judges and rabbis of Germany in his day (late fifteenth century) who took ten gold pieces for writing a divorce; he calls them thieves. The professionalization of the rabbinate came late in Jewish life and with difficulty. Though it began in the fourteenth century, the full-time, salaried rabbi was not really accepted until late in the eighteenth century.
2. The water of purification made with the ashes of the red heifer. See Numbers 19.
3. To mix the ashes of the red heifer with the water.
4. By the inspection of a first-born, or by serving as judge or as a witness.
5. A man and his family must eat. Since judging, witnessing, and the like take time, some compensation was found not to be inconsistent with the principle of non-professionalization. But the compensation was to be on the basis of the labor performed rather than the priest's higher level of living, according to the Gemara.

ARAKHIN—EVALUATIONS

Introduction

As an act of piety or devotion, a Jew could vow his "evaluation" as a gift to the Temple. The circumstances and amount of the evaluation are detailed in Leviticus 27.

"Evaluation" must be distinguished from "worth," a different concept which has to do with the market value of the individual were he to be sold as a slave. This, too, could be offered as a one-time gift to the Temple.

The first six chapters of the Mishnah deal, to an extent, with the process of evaluation. There are many digressions in the text, however. The last three chapters deal with the evaluation, sale, or dedication of houses or real estate.

Biblical Sources for Arakhin

Leviticus 25:25–34; 27:17–24, 28
Numbers 18:14

Arakhin 1:1

Everyone may evaluate or can be evaluated by others. All may vow the worth of another or be the subject of another's vow: priests, Levites, Israelites, women, and slaves.[1] Persons of unknown sex [2] and hermaphrodites may vow the worth of another, may have their worth vowed by another, and may evaluate, but they may not be evaluated by others, since the person evaluated may be only definitely male or female (see Leviticus 27:3–4). A deaf-mute, an imbecile, or a minor may have their worth or their evaluation vowed by another, but they may not vow the worth or evaluation of another, since they have no understanding. An infant less than a month old may be vowed but not evaluated.[3]

---

1. "Evaluation," as used here, is the self-valuation made for the money gift to the Temple, specified in Leviticus 27. "Worth" is an estimate of a man's price were he to be sold as a slave. A man can offer his worth to the Temple as a vowed gift. He can also vow a gift equivalent to someone else's worth, just as he can vow to pay someone else's evaluation, with the exception noted here.
2. A *tumtum* is a person born with no exterior genitalia. Consequently, in ancient times, sex could not be determined. The hermaphrodite was thought to be bisexual. Neither designation needs to exist any

longer, since the dominant sex can be determined at birth by cellular chromosome tests, and both surgery and hormones can be used to bring out the dominant sex.

3. This is also specified in the Torah law.

Arakhin 2:3

They never blew less than twenty-one Shofar blasts in the Temple, and never more than forty-eight in one day.[1] They never played on less than two harps or more than six; never on less than two flutes or more than twelve.[2] The flute was played at the altar twelve times a year: at the slaughtering of the first Passover offering;[3] at the slaughtering of the second Passover offering;[4] on the first day of Passover; on Shavuot; on the eight days of Sukkot. They did not play a bronze pipe but a reed one, since its sound was sweeter. They finished with a pipe solo, since this made the best finale.

---

1. Why this digression? As has happened before, textual form is responsible. The first Mishnah in the chapter began: "They do not give more than . . . or less than. . . ." Ranges of activities like this in matters totally unrelated to *Arakhin* were added because they took the same textual form.

2. The instrument names are approximate and may bear little resemblance to contemporary instruments. The "flute" was a simple wind instrument, much like contemporary Israel's *halil*. The "harp" was a simple stringed instrument. The important fact is that musical instruments were freely used as routine parts of the Temple service.

3. On *Nisan* 14, Passover eve.

4. On *Iyyar* 14, the Passover for those who were ritually unclean on *Nisan* 14. See Numbers 9:6 ff.

TEMURAH—EXCHANGES OF SACRIFICIAL CATTLE

Introduction

The Torah source for the primary subject matter of the book is Leviticus 27:9 ff., which prohibits exchanging animals which have been dedicated for sacrifice in the Temple. Though the practice was illegal, there were apparently many who indulged in it and were prepared to pay the price for their transgression—which was thirty-nine lashes.

A large part of the book does not deal with exchanges at all, but with the young of dedicated animals, the importation of sacrificial animals, sin-offerings, and the classes of animals which are unfit for sacrifice under certain circumstances.

Biblical Sources for Temurah

If [the vow concerns] any animal that may be brought as an offering to the Lord, any such that may be given to the Lord shall be holy. One may not exchange or substitute another for it, either good for bad, or bad for good; if one does substitute one animal for another, the thing vowed and its substitute shall both be holy. (Leviticus 27:9–10)

All tithes of the herd or flock—of all that passes under the shepherd's staff, every tenth one—shall be holy to the Lord. He must not look out for good as against bad, or make substitution for it. If he does make substitution for it, then it and its substitute shall both be holy; it cannot be redeemed. (Leviticus 27:32–33)

Temurah 1:1

Anyone can exchange, men as well as women.[1] One is not permitted to do so, but if he did, it becomes sacred [2] and he receives forty lashes.[3]

---

1. Not legally. The Torah law is clear both in Leviticus 27:9–10 and 32–33. This statement means that the implications of exchanging a dedicated beast for a previously undedicated one apply to everyone.
2. The animals are both sacred. It is not possible to desanctify an animal which remains unblemished.
3. For transgressing a negative commandment. Actually he received only thirty-nine lashes, because of the rabbinic interpretation of Deuteronomy 35:3.

Temurah 1:2

Oxen may be exchanged for small cattle, and small cattle for oxen; sheep for goats and goats for sheep; males for females and females for males; unblemished for blemished and blemished for unblemished; for it is written: "He shall not alter it nor change it, a good for a bad or a bad for a good" (Leviticus 27:10). What does "a good for a bad" mean? A blemished animal which was dedicated before it became blemished. One animal may be exchanged for two, or two for one; one instead of a hundred, or a hundred for one. R. Simon said: Only one animal may be exchanged for one animal, since it is written: "Then both it and that for which it is changed." Just as "it" means one, its exchange may only be one.

KERITOT—DIVINE PUNISHMENT

Introduction

Karet comes from the word which means "to cut off." Nowhere in the Torah is the meaning of *Karet* made clear. Recurring frequently, however, is the statement that punishment for a specific sin is to be "cut off." It is noted in three different forms by Maimonides, who distinguished among them in this way:

Venikhrat ha'ish: "the man will be cut off"—the punishment is premature death, but the individual is eligible for *Olam Haba,* "eternal life";

Venikhretah hanefesh: "the soul will be cut off"—the individual may live a full span of years, but will not be eligible for *Olam Haba;*

Venikhretah hanefesh hahi: "that soul will be cut off"—a serious sin is involved, and both early death and ineligibility for *Olam Haba* are involved. Maimonides' view did not become universally accepted, however.

It is clear that *Karet* is a divine punishment for sin, but the same sin requires other forms of atonement on earth as well. As a consequence, much of the material in the book deals not with speculation about *Karet,* but with guilt offerings, suspensive guilt offerings, and related subjects. The book is brief, as is its Gemara.

Keritot 1:1

The Torah lists thirty-six transgressions the punishment for which is *Karet:* sexual intercourse with one's mother, with one's father's wife, with a daughter-in-law, with another male or with an animal, between a woman and an animal, with a woman and her daughter, with a married woman, with one's sister, with one's father's sister or one's mother's sister, with one's wife's sister,[1] with one's brother's wife or one's father's brother's wife, with a woman during the menstrual period; blasphemy; idolatry; sacrificing a child to Molokh; communicating with the dead through the use of a medium; profaning the Sabbath; [2] eating sacrificial food when one is ritually unclean; entering the Temple in a state of ritual uncleanliness; eating the fat, the blood, the remnants, or the refuse of sacrifices; slaughtering or offering up a sacrifice outside the Temple; eating leavened bread during Passover; eating or doing work on the Day of Atonement; compounding (anointing) oil or incense; anointing oneself with anointing oil. From among the positive commandments: transgressing the laws of the Passover offering and of circumcision.[3]

---

1. While his wife is living, that is.
2. In one of the thirty-nine ways not punishable by death at the hands of the Sanhedrin. See p. 80, 82, 83.
3. If he does not do what is required of him. All these transgressions must be intentional. If they are accidental, a sin-offering must be brought, and *Karet* is not expected as punishment.

Keritot 6:3

R. Eliezer says: A man may offer a suspensive guilt-offering (Leviticus 5:17–19) on any day and at any time he wishes. Such an offering was called the guilt-offering of the righteous. It was said of Baba b. Buta that he offered a suspensive guilt-offering every day except the day after Yom Kippur. He said: By this Temple, had they permitted me, I should have brought one even then. But they said to me, wait until there can be some doubt.[1] On the other hand, the Sages held that one may bring a suspensive guilt-offering only for a specific sin, the deliberate transgression subject to *Karet* and the accidental transgression subject to a sin-offering.[2]

---

1. Yom Kippur atones for all sins, including the doubtful ones. The very next morning there would be no conceivable doubtful act to justify a suspensive guilt-offering.
2. The view of the Sages was accepted as law.

ME'ILAH—INADVERTENT SACRILEGE

Introduction

Me'ilah is a specific form of sacrilege consisting of inadvertently profiting in some way from sacred things. The law is found in Leviticus 5:15–16: "If any one commit a trespass, and sin through error, in the holy things of the Lord, then he shall bring his forfeit unto the Lord, a ram without blemish out of the flock, according to your valuation in silver by *shekels,* after the *shekel* of the sanctuary, for a guilt-offering. And he shall make restitution for that which he has done amiss in the holy thing, and shall add the fifth part thereto, and give it unto the priest; and the priest shall make atonement for him with the ram of the guilt-offering, and he shall be forgiven."

The Torah treated this act of sacrilege as a form of theft, and the penalty corresponded to the penalty for theft.

Both the Mishnah and the Gemara stay close to the subject and the brief work is totally Halakhic in character, with one exception in the Gemara.

Me'ilah 5:1

If a man derived a *perutah's* worth of benefit from Temple property, even though he did not lessen its value, he is guilty of *Me'ilah,* according to R. Akiba. But the Sages say: whatever deteriorates through use, the law of *Me'ilah* applies to it only after it has suffered deterioration. Whatever does not deteriorate through use, as soon as any use has been made of it, *Me'ilah* has been committed.[1] For example, if a woman puts a necklace around her neck or a ring on her finger, or if she drinks from a golden cup, she is guilty of *Me'ilah* as soon as she uses them. But if a man puts on a shirt or covers himself with a cloth, or if someone chops wood with an axe, he is guilty of *Me'ilah* only if these suffer deterioration. If a man plucks wool from a sin-offering while it is still alive, he is guilty of *Me'ilah* only if he diminishes its value; if after its death, he is guilty of *Me'ilah* as soon as he makes use of it.

---

1. The view of the Sages was accepted as law, ameliorating the radical implications of the Torah statement in Leviticus 5.

TAMID—DAILY SACRIFICE

Introduction

The Book of Numbers 28:3–4 prescribes the offering of two he-lambs each day in the Temple, one in the morning and one in the evening. These were wholly burnt-offerings.

The Mishnah consists of a careful, detailed description of the procedures by which this injunction was carried out during the Second Temple era. It contains no discussions, disagreements, arguments, or decisions. It is factual, concise, and crisp, and includes the following materials: the priestly watch; the daily inspection of Temple vessels and ash-removal in preparation of sacrifice; the kindling of the new fire; the slaughtering of the sacrificial lamb; the flaying and cutting up of the lamb; additional ceremonies then performed, including the incense ritual; the closing prayers and benedictions; and the psalms sung by the Levites.

It is not surprising that there is almost no Gemara in the Babylonian Talmud and none at all in the Palestinian.

Tamid 1:1

The priests kept watch at three places in the Temple: at the Chamber of Abtinas,[1] at the Chamber of the Spark, and at the Chamber of the Hearth.[2] In the Chamber of Abtinas and in the Chamber of the Hearth there were balconies where the youths kept watch. But the Hearth Chamber was vaulted.[3] It was a large room, and around it ran a raised stone pavement. There the elders of the *Bet Av*[4] slept. The keys of the Temple Court were in their possession. Each young priest slept with his mattress on the ground. They did not sleep in vestments, but took them off, folded them, put them under their heads. They covered themselves with their own clothes. If one of the novices had a seminal emission, he would go out along the passages and down the winding stair, where there were lights burning, to the bathing place. There was a fire near by, and a privy. This was its advantage: If it was locked, he knew someone was there. If it was open, he knew that no one else was using it. He went down, bathed himself, then came up and dried himself and warmed himself by the fire. He returned to his place and lay down among his brethren until the gates were opened in the morning. Then he went out of the Temple area.[5]

---

1. Where the incense was ground.
2. Where a fire burned night and day, at which the priests warmed themselves. At least half the year it gets very cold in Jerusalem at night and early in the morning, and a warming fire was an essential.
3. Therefore it could not have a balcony.
4. Priests served in rotation by "fathers' house." See p. 114.
5. He had to stay out all day, despite his ritual bath. He returned at evening to resume his duties and his priestly privileges.

Tamid 7:4

This was the music which the Levites sang in the Temple:[1] On the first day they sang: "The earth is the Lord's and the fullness thereof; the world and they that dwell therein" (Psalms 24). On the second day, they sang: "Great is the Lord and highly to be praised in the city of our God, even upon His holy mountain" (Psalms 48). On the third day: "God stands in the congregation of God, he is a judge among the gods" (Psalms 82). On the fourth day: "O Lord God, to whom vengeance belongs, Thou God to whom vengeance belongs, show Thyself" (Psalms 94). On the fifth day: "Sing we merrily unto God our strength, make a joyous noise unto the God of Jacob" (Psalms 81). On the sixth day: "The Lord is king, and has put on glorious apparel" (Psalms 93). On the Sabbath, they sang: "A Psalm, a song for the Sabbath day" (Psalms 92); "a Psalm, a song for the time that is to come," for the day that shall be all Sabbath and rest in life everlasting.[2]

---

1. Each morning and evening, when the wine was being mixed and offered.
2. Reasons for the selection of each of these Psalms are given in the Gemara, *Rosh Hashanah,* 31a.

MIDDOT—MEASUREMENTS

Introduction

The book consists almost entirely of a description of Herod's Temple, completed about the year 19 B.C.E. The important Temple area was almost the same size as Solomon's Temple and the building described in the Book of Ezekiel had been. But many additional buildings were erected by Herod, and the architectural style was greatly changed.

Because the book is purely descriptive, it is brief and there is no Gemara at all.

Biblical Source for Middot

And if they be ashamed of all that they have done, make known unto them the form of the house, and the fashion thereof, and the goings out thereof, and the comings in thereof, and all the forms thereof, and all the ordinances thereof, and all the forms thereof, and all the laws thereof, and write it in their sight; that they may keep the whole form thereof, and all the ordinances thereof, and do them. (Ezekiel 43:11)

Middot 1:2

The officer of the Temple mountain used to go around to every watchman with lighted torches. If any watchman did not rise and say to him: "Peace be to you, supervisor of the Temple mountain," it was clear that he was asleep. He would beat him with his staff. He had the right to burn his cloak. Then the others would ask: "What is the noise in the court?" "It is the cry of some Levite who is being beaten and whose cloak is being burnt because he was asleep on watch." R. Eliezer b. Jacob said: "They once found my mother's brother asleep and burnt his cloak."

Middot 2:1

The Temple mountain was five hundred cubits by five hundred.[1] The largest part of it faced south, the next largest toward the east, the third northward, and the smallest was to the west. The largest part was the most used.[2]

---

1. The present area of the Dome of the Rock, which occupies the site of the ancient Temple, is 488,500 square feet. If a cubit is reckoned at eighteen inches, which is fairly accurate to the best of our knowledge, the Mishnah's measurements are found to be amazingly accurate. The Temple area was almost five hundred cubits square.
2. Most people entered the Temple area from the south; it was most convenient.

KINNIM—BIRD OFFERINGS

Introduction

There are two kinds of bird-offerings prescribed in the Torah: free-will offerings and obligatory ones. The latter include: purification from defilement resulting from contact with the dead; persons cured of an infection, or of other diseases; women after childbirth; Nazirites who have not completed their term in purity. The pairs of doves or pigeons were substitutes for larger sacrifices in some cases, when the worshipper could not afford the more expensive offering.

The Mishnah discusses the regulations regarding these bird sacrifices in a most unusual way. The Rabbis thought up difficult hypothetical possibilities, and looked for further complications. As a result, much of the material is most far-fetched—and almost impossible to translate accurately. The medieval commentators despaired of finding out precisely what was meant in some instances, especially in the last chapter. To make their search even more difficult, there is no Gemara to consult.

Kinnim 3:6

If a woman said: "I pledge myself to bring a pair of birds if I bear a son," and she did bear a son, she must bring two pairs, one for her vow [1] and one for her obligation.[2]

---

1. To be brought immediately after the birth of the child.
2. To be brought in accordance with the explicit commandment in Leviticus 12:6.

The Sixth Order

TOHOROT

Ritual Purity

KELIM

OHOLOT

NEGA'IM

PARAH

TOHOROT

MIKVA'OT

NIDDAH

MAKSHIRIN

ZAVIM

TEVUL YOM

YADAIM

UKTZIN

INTRODUCTION

The Sixth Order of the Mishnah follows logically the subject matter of *Kodashim*. *Tohorot,* too, is closely tied to the Temple in Jerusalem. Almost all its regulations were applicable only when the Temple was in existence. (Two major exceptions: the laws regarding the woman during her menstrual period, and those involving the ritual uncleanliness of the priest who has had contact with a corpse.) As a result, the regulations, with exceptions noted, ceased to have any relevance after the destruction of the Temple.

Only *Niddah,* the book dealing with the menstruating woman, has any Gemara extant. It is not known with any certainty whether Gemara was ever written for the other books of the Order. There are occasional hints about Gemara to this book or that, but they are not in any way authoritative. Apparently, the scholars in Palestine and Babylon dedicated their yearning for a return to Palestine and the Temple to their studies of parts of *Kodashim* and did not study *Tohorot* with any systematic fervor.

This is unfortunate for many reasons, chiefly because the Torah laws with regard to ritual cleanliness—concentrated in Leviticus 11–15, for the most part—are obscure and unclear, requiring much elucidation. Because they did not receive enough rabbinic elucidation, the material remains difficult and complex.

Contemporary Jews have a problem with *Tohorot,* bound up in a primary question: why ritual cleanliness or defilement in the first place? Most reputable Jewish teachers reject out of hand the notion that the primary intent of the Torah in the promulgation of these laws was hygienic. As with the dietary laws and others, these are *Ḥukkim,* commandments for which we do not have a rational

269

human explanation. They were obeyed because God commanded them. We must, at the outset, discount any connection between cleanliness as we speak of it and ritual cleanliness as the Torah and the Mishnah treat it.

Historically considered, there appear to have been two motives for the concept of ritual cleanliness in general, and for the subsidiary *Tohorot*. To an extent, they fall into the category of anti-idolatry statutes. There are four major causes of ritual defilement: death, disease, creeping things (*sheratzim*), and sexual functions. All four were closely connected with pagan ritual practices among the Canaanite fertility cults against which Judaism contended over a period of centuries. There is a certain logic to the evolution of a system of regulations making many actions in these areas the cause of defilement.

Maimonides, in his *Guide for the Perplexed*, indicated that the primary divine motive in promulgating the laws of *Tohorot* was disciplinary:

. . . the whole intention with regard to the Sanctuary was to affect those that came to it with a feeling of awe and of fear. . . . Now if one is continually in contact with a venerable object, the impression received from it in the soul diminishes and the feeling it provokes becomes slight. The Sages, may their memory be blessed, have already drawn attention to this notion, saying that it is not desirable that the Sanctuary should be entered at every moment. . . . He, may He be exalted, forbade the unclean to enter the Sanctuary in spite of there being so many species of uncleanness so that one could—with a few exceptions—scarcely find a clean individual. You already know what the Sages literally say: "Even a clean man may not enter the Hall for the purpose of performing divine service before having immersed himself [in water]." In consequence of such actions, fear will continue and an impression leading to the humility that was aimed at will be produced (Maimonides, *Guide for the Perplexed*, ed. Pines and Strauss, III, 47, pp. 593–94).

In short, these laws were promulgated for God's own purposes, to increase *kedushah* ("sanctity") among His people.

The books of *Tohorot* deal minutely with the causes of defilement, its transmission, and the process of purification from it.

Five categories of objects are the *avot hatum'a,* the "fathers" (primary causes) of contamination: one who has contact with a human corpse; eight types of creeping things; dead animals; matter issuing from human skin eruptions; semen; menstrual blood; and the leper. There is some doubt about the accuracy of the term "leprosy" for the Biblical word *tzora'at.* Of the five categories, the primary one was the corpse; it is called *avi-avot hatum'a,* "the proto-father" of contamination. *Avot hatum'a* transmit uncleanliness to both men and objects.

Any object or person coming into contact with an *av hatum'a* becomes contaminated. It is a *velad hatum'a,* "a child of contamination." Under certain circumstances, some of these objects can transmit contamination in a tertiary degree.

Among the objects which can become ritually contaminated, in addition to human beings, are: clothing; metal objects; wooden vessels; skin vessels; bone vessels; earthenware; food; and drink—though food becomes contaminated only if it has first been "prepared" by being dampened with some liquid.

The order of the books in *Tohorot* has changed from time to time. In editions of the full Talmud, *Niddah* is placed first because it alone has Gemara. But in most separate Mishnah editions, the books are printed in descending order of size.

KELIM—VESSELS

Introduction

The word *kelim* theoretically means "vessels." But in connection with ritual cleanliness the word is routinely used to mean a large variety of articles: vessels and utensils, garments, weapons, and instruments, among others. The word can be said to refer to any inanimate object which is susceptible to secondary defilement; that is, which can become a *velad hatum'a*—"a child of contamination."

Kelim has the distinction of containing more chapters than any other book in the entire Talmud, though it is far from being the longest book. It is businesslike, rarely straying from its assigned subject, with many cogent details. It treats with relative severity types of defilement, types of objects susceptible to it, protection against defilement by insulation or covering, and related subjects. There is one important and necessary digression in Chapter 17; some paragraphs are devoted to discussing standard measurements in connection with questions like: "How much of a thing does it take to transmit defilement?" That chapter makes fascinating but frustratingly inconclusive reading.

Biblical Sources for Kelim
Leviticus 11:29–37; 15:4–6, 9–12, 19–27
Numbers 31:19–24

Kelim 1:1

The *Avot hatum'a* are: a dead creeping thing,[1] semen (Leviticus 15:16–17), one who has contracted defilement from a corpse;[2] a leper during the days of counting;[3] and purification water in insufficient quantity to be sprinkled (Numbers 19:20–22). These convey defilement to people and vessels[4] by contact and by the air-space inside earthenware vessels,[5] but they do not convey defilement by carrying.[6]

---

1. The eight types specified in Leviticus 11:29–30.
2. How much the more so the corpse itself; therefore, its designation as *avi avot hatum'a.* See Numbers 19:11, 16.
3. Seven days, during which he does not live in his dwelling, after the external symptoms of his illness have passed, and he is still considered contaminated. See Leviticus 14:8.
4. The word *vessels* throughout *Seder Tohorot* is used generically to mean any object susceptible to ritual contamination.
5. Whether or not the substance touches the inside walls of the vessel.

6. So long as there is no direct contact. For example, a dead turtle (a defiled object) carried on a stick does not transmit its ritual uncleanliness to its bearer.

Kelim 30:4

R. Jose said: Blessed are you, O *Kelim,* for though you did enter in contamination, you go forth in purity.[1]

---

1. Before all the laws of this long book were expounded, many problems of cleanliness were unsolved. While R. Jose's enthusiasm and piety are commendable, his optimism was excessive. Later Jewish literature contains many hundreds of volumes devoted solely to the implications of the same problems dealt with in this book.

OHOLOT—TENTS

Introduction

Two aspects of the transmission of defilement are discussed in great detail in this book: contact with a corpse or any part of it, and a tent in which a corpse has lain.

The book contains a few interesting digressions. There is a catalogue of the parts of the body, as the Rabbis understood anatomy (p. 276). Obstetrics and surgery are given some attention, along with the condition of blood flow at the time of death, and the digestive rate of animals. The book also includes some information about the decomposition of human flesh.

Biblical Sources for Oholot

He who touches the corpse of any human being shall be unclean for seven days. (Numbers 19:11)

This is the procedure: When a person dies in a tent, whoever enters the tent and whoever is in the tent shall be unclean seven days; and every open vessel, with no lid fastened down, shall be unclean. And in the open, anything that touches a person who was killed or who died naturally, or human bone, or grave, shall be unclean seven days. Some of the ashes from the fire of cleansing shall be taken for the unclean person, and fresh water shall be added to them in a vessel. (Numbers 19:14–17)

Whatever that unclean person touches shall be unclean; and the person who touches him shall be unclean until evening. (Numbers 19:22)

Oholot 1:3

How does contamination befall four series of things? If vessels touch a corpse and a man touches the vessels, then the man touches other vessels, all three series contract seven-day defilement.[1] The fourth, man or vessels, can contract defilement until evening. R. Akiba said: "I can cite a case where a fifth series of contamination can happen: if a metal tent-peg was pegged into a tent, the tent, the peg, the man who touches the peg, and the vessels touched by the man all contract defilement for seven days.[2] The fifth, man or vessel, contracts contamination until evening." The Sages said to him: "The tent cannot be counted." [3]

---

1. Vessels cannot transmit the status of *av hatum'a* to other vessels, but they can to a man. A man can transmit this status to other vessels—three series—and then, finally, the fourth is the "minor" defilement.
2. R. Akiba presupposed that the tent-peg was far enough away from the tent-wall to constitute a separate entity.
3. Since the tent does not contaminate the peg by contact, that contamination is automatic, and therefore the tent cannot be counted in the sequence. Because this discussion was academic and not practical, there is no rabbinic decision.

Oholot 1:6

A person cannot transmit defilement as a corpse until his soul has departed.[1] Even if his arteries are cut or he is in death agony, he is still considered alive and can require a Levirate marriage [2] or liberate someone from one; he can qualify his mother for *Terumah* [3] or disqualify her. So, too, cattle and wild animals cannot transmit defilement until their souls have gone forth.[4] If their heads have been cut off, even though they may still move convulsively, they are non-kosher, like a lizard's tail which moves convulsively.

---

1. When is death "official" in Judaism? In some religions, it is believed that the soul remains within the body for a stated time after death. (In Roman Catholic law, the soul departs the body four hours after death.) Not so in traditional Judaism. When aspiration and heartbeat stop, the soul leaves, according to tradition. As a result of medical advances, the traditional position has been necessarily changed. No specific moment of death is being posited by authoritative Jewish scholars. When no means of restoring life is effective, when basic life functions have irreversibly ceased, then death has Halakhically occurred, it would seem. The Halakhic implications of the new situation are of great interest, and new literature about many of them is appearing, dealing with organ transplants, the freezing of bodies, and many other procedures.
2. Of his childless brother's widow. She cannot remarry unless she marries him or he gives her *halitzah* (see pp. 156 ff.).
3. So long as he lives, his Israelite mother who is a widow of a priest still has priestly privileges because she has a priest son.
4. This passage does not imply that animals have souls in the spiritual sense. The phrase is used to try to pinpoint the technical moment of death.

Oholot 1:8

There are 248 parts in the human body: [1] thirty in the foot, six to every toe, ten in the ankle, two in the lower leg, five in the knee, one in the thigh, three in the hip, eleven ribs, thirty parts to each hand (six in each finger), two in the forearm, two in the elbow, one in the upper arm, and four in the shoulder. This totals 101 on one side of the body and 101 on the other. There are eighteen vertebrae in the spine, nine parts of the head, eight in the neck, six in the chest cavity,[2] and five in the genitals. Each one of these parts can transmit defilement by contact, by being carried, or by being in a tent. When? Only when they have their appropriate flesh.[3] If they do not have their appropriate flesh, they can transmit defilement by contact and by carrying, but they do not do so by being in a tent.

---

1. These 248 plus 365 days in the year total 613, the theoretical number of mitzvot contained within the Torah, according to tradition.
2. The Hebrew phrase is literally translated as "the opening of the heart." Maimonides explains the phrase thus: The movements of the chest cavity cause the lungs to breathe on the heart, opening the way for fresh air.
3. That is, flesh which, were the part attached to a living body, would be considered normal. The problem of old bones conveying defilement by contact plagues traditional Jews in many countries today, especially in Israel, where every plow may dig up bones.

NEGA'IM—LEPROSY

Introduction

Both the Torah and the Mishnah used the word *leprosy* to describe a wide variety of diseases which caused scales, eruptions, and all kinds of dermatitis, in addition to leprosy itself. All these diseases, which were thought to be leprosy, were enormously feared by the ancients. As a result, the Mishnah regulations regarding diagnosis, treatment, and purification of the victim are numerous and specific.

Halakhah recognized three kinds of "leprosy" symptoms: on the body itself, on a house, or on garments. Ten of the thirteen chapters of this book, however, concern themselves with the human body.

It cannot be emphasized too strongly that the concern of the Mishnah, like that of the Torah itself, was not medical. Their concern was *Tohorah,* or ritual cleanliness.

Biblical sources are greatly detailed. This is not surprising in view of the dread feelings which were connected with this category of ritual law.

Biblical Sources for Nega'im

In cases of a scaly affection be most careful to do exactly as the levitical priests instruct you. Take care to do as I have commanded them. (Deuteronomy 24:8)

SEE ALSO

Leviticus 13 and 14

Nega'im 1:4

R. Ḥanina, the deputy High Priest, said: There are sixteen colors of leprosy symptoms. R. Dosa b. Harkinas said: There are thirty-six colors of leprosy signs. Akabya b. Mehalaleel said: seventy-two.[1] R. Ḥanina, the deputy High Priest, said: Leprosy symptoms may not be inspected for the first time on Sunday, since the end of that week would fall on the Sabbath.[2] Nor may inspection take place on Monday, since the end of the second week would fall on Sabbath. In the case of houses, inspection does not take place on Tuesday, since the end of the third week would fall on Sabbath. R. Akiba said: They may be inspected at any time. If the time for inspection falls on the Sabbath it is postponed to Sunday. This procedure sometimes leads to leniency, sometimes to greater restrictions.[3]

---

1. The law has already been stated: four major color types. The Rabbis were vying to proliferate more and more subtypes for more careful diagnosis.
2. No inspections were permitted on the Sabbath, of course.
3. R. Akiba's view was not accepted as law. But the next two *Mishnayot* elaborate this last sentence in great detail.

Nega'im 11:1

All garments may contract the contamination of leprosy except those of non-Jews.[1] If a man bought garments from non-Jews, leprosy symptoms must be inspected as if they had just appeared. The hides of creatures of the sea cannot contract the contamination of leprosy, but if one connected them with anything that grows on land, even if it is only a thread or a cord, if the latter is of a material that is susceptible to defilement, they, too, become susceptible.

---

1. This is another strong proof against the belief that laws of cleanliness, diet, and the like were introduced into Judaism for hygienic or medical reasons. Had this been the case, certainly all garments would have been found susceptible to the contamination of leprosy, known as the most dreaded of contagious diseases. The exemption of the non-Jews' clothes proves that there was a solely ritual basis for these laws.

PARAH—THE (RED) COW

Introduction

As we have seen previously in connection with the various areas of ritual cleanliness, the Torah's laws are very specific. The process of purification is no exception. The requirements were to slaughter a red cow, burn it completely, add cedar wood and hyssop to the burning animal, then mix the ashes with pure water to serve as a solution for the purification of the ritually unclean. These requirements are found in Numbers 19:2 ff.

The function of the Mishnah is to raise problems in connection with the procedure and to solve them. What animals are eligible, how perfect must the cow be to be "unblemished," cleanliness of the vessels to be used, eligible and ineligible waters, details of the process of slaughter, sprinkling the blood, the burning, the types of cedar and hyssop to be used, the ritual condition of the priests who did the work (never the High Priest, for the ashes were prepared outside the sanctuary and he never went out), the use of the purification mixture—all these and related matters make up the Mishnah.

In typical fashion, the Mishnah is not concerned with "why?" Why the ashes? Why a red (red-brown, no doubt) heifer? Where did the ceremony come from?

The use of the color red has two explanations: Red is connected with sin (see Isaiah 1:18, for example) and the function of the purification mixture is to help atone for the sin of defilement. The *Zohar* says, on the other hand, that red is the color of judgment, a reminder to the people that only a holy people (i.e., ritually sanctified as well as sacred in action) can survive divine judgment.

Apparently the ceremony had very ancient and primitive beginnings, connected with the removal of a ritual taboo through the medium of water and ashes.

Biblical Source for Parah
Numbers 19:2 ff.

Parah 2:1

R. Eliezer said: A red cow for the sin-offering which became pregnant is still valid. But the Sages ruled it invalid.[1] R. Eliezer said: It may not be purchased from non-Jews; the Sages ruled it valid.[2] In addition, they ruled that all offerings, both communal and individual, may be brought either from the Land of Israel or from outside the Land, from new produce or from old, except for the *Omer* and the two display loaves, which must be brought only from new produce and from inside the Land.[3]

---

1. The question is: Is the embryo an integral part of the cow, or is it a separate entity? If the former, then the cow remains valid for sacrifice when pregnant; if the latter, then she is not. The view of the Sages was accepted as law.
2. R. Eliezer was concerned lest the non-Jewish owner might have used it for work, and thus made it invalid for sacrifice. But the view of the Sages was accepted as law.
3. R. Eliezer disagreed with the Sages on all these matters, but was overruled on all of them.

Parah 2:3

A cow that is born by Caesarean section, the wage of a prostitute, or the exchange price of a dog are valid.[1] R. Eliezer ruled the latter two of these valid, for it was written: "You shall not bring the hire of a harlot or the price of a dog into the house of the Lord your God" (Deuteronomy 23:19), and this—the red cow—was not brought into the Temple. All blemishes which caused consecrated animals to be invalid cause the red cow to be invalid too.

If it had been ridden on, leaned on, had its lead rope doubled over its back, if someone had crossed a river with its help,[2] or put one's cloak on it, it is invalid. But if one had only fastened it by its lead rope or had made a sandal to keep it from slipping, or spread a cloak on it because of flies, it remains valid. This is the general rule: whenever something is done for the sake of the cow, it remains valid; but if for the sake of someone else, it becomes invalid.

---

1. These characteristics invalidate any animal for any sacrifice, according to the Sages.
2. By hanging onto the tail of the cow.

TOHOROT—CLEANLINESS

Introduction

This is the only case of a book of the Mishnah bearing the same name as a whole Order. The book deals with the ritual cleanliness of foods and liquids in particular, and with men who are involved in the preparation of both and in their consumption. In addition, there is some discussion of vessels.

Within this framework, the book ranges far. It deals with kosher birds which have died, degrees of ritual contamination possible in foods, and the transmission of defilement from people to food and vice versa. It discusses the ritual cleanliness of foods which change their condition from solid to liquid and vice versa. The transmission of contamination from the private domain to public domain and vice versa comes under discussion. Much attention is given to contamination of olives and olive-presses, as well as of grapes and winepresses.

The two most interesting chapters, from a contemporary standpoint, deal with types of persons who automatically transmit defilement: the *am ha'artez* (see p. 282), the thief, and the tax-collector.

Tohorot 5:2

If a man said: "I touched something but I do not know if it was ritually pure or impure," or "I touched something but I do not know which of two I touched," [1] R. Akiba ruled him ritually unclean. But the Sages ruled him ritually clean.[2]

---

1. One of them was ritually clean and the other defiled, of course.
2. The view of the Sages was accepted as law.

Tohorot 7:2

If a man left an *am ha'aretz* [1] in his house awake and returned to find him awake, or left him asleep and found him asleep, or awake and found him asleep, the house remains ritually clean. [2] But if he left him asleep and found him awake, the house is defiled, according to R. Meir. But the Sages ruled: Only that part becomes defiled which he could touch by stretching out his hand: [3]

---

1. The words literally mean "people of the land." Both in the Torah and in rabbinic literature, the *am ha'aretz* was the untutored peasant who was careless about ritual law, especially about the laws of ritual cleanliness. In the Talmud there are many regulations limiting his status as a Jew, as in this Mishnah.
2. In each of these situations, the *am ha'aretz* could not have been alone and awake and unaware of the imminent return of the master of the house, so that he would, either by ignorance or by malice, render some part of the house ritually unclean.
3. The view of the Sages was accepted as law.

MIKVA'OT—RITUAL BATHS

Introduction

Since the use of water to purify men and women of ritual contamination is prescribed throughout this Order of the Mishnah,
inevitably the Mishnaic teachers had to discuss the form of the
immersion pool and procedure for using it.

Several requirements are clear: There had to be enough water
to cover the body entirely. The amount was fixed at forty *se'ah*
if rainwater was the source. Less could be used from a spring or
fountain. No distinction was made between salt water and fresh
water. Water drawn from a well could be added, after forty *se'ah*
of rainwater were present, under certain circumstances.

These requirements were expanded in post-Talmudic literature
into a tremendous body of detailed requirements for the building
of the *mikveh.* Even though the laws of *Tohorot,* as has been
indicated, were not followed except for the menstruating woman
and, under a few circumstances, the priestly families, the *mikveh*
was a vital facility of the community. It was even said that a
synagogue could be sold in order to procure money for a *mikveh.*

Biblical Sources for Mikva'ot

Leviticus 11:31–32, 36; 15:13, 17
Numbers 31:23

Mikva'ot 2:1

If a ritually unclean person goes down to immerse himself and it
is doubtful whether he immerses himself properly or not; or if he
immerses himself and it is doubtful if the *mikveh* contains forty

se'ah or not; [1] or if there were two *mikva'ot,* one containing forty *se'ah* and the other less, and he immerses himself in one of them but does not know which, in these cases he is considered ritually unclean. [2]

---

1. Forty *se'ah* equal approximately 100 to 120 gallons.
2. His defilement was certain, his purification is questionable, so he remains ritually unclean.

Mikva'ot 5:4

All seas are valid as a *mikveh,* for it is written: "And the *mikveh* of the waters called He seas" (Genesis 1:10), according to R. Meir. R. Judah said: The Great Sea [1] alone is valid as a *mikveh* and it was written "seas" only because there are many kinds of seas in it. [2] R. Jose said: All seas can purify as flowing waters, but they are not valid for persons who have had a running issue, and for lepers, and for the preparation of the waters of purification. [3]

---

1. The Mediterranean and, by extension, all major oceans. The verse intends to exclude inland seas.
2. Many sources contribute to its waters. One commentator naively "proved" R. Judah's statement by indicating that fish caught at Acre taste differently from fish caught at Sidon in Phoenicia.
3. For these three require *mayim hayyim,* "living waters" (Leviticus 15:13), while other forms of purification require only "water." R. Jose's view was accepted as law.

NIDDAH—THE MENSTRUATING WOMAN

Introduction

The Torah deals with two types of feminine bleeding: the menstrual period itself, and the period of *zivah,* or vaginal bleeding at some other time (Leviticus 15:19–24, 25–30 respectively). This distinction remained clear in the Mishnah. When the menstrual period was over, the woman went to the *mikveh,* was deemed ritually clean, and could resume sex relations with her husband. Post-Talmudically, Jews made the rules regarding the menstrual period more detailed until, in fact, the two types of emission were combined. Under current Orthodox regulations, after the menstrual period is finished, there begin the "seven clean days" when some vaginal bleeding might presumably take place. Whether or not there is bleeding, the seven days must pass. Only then does the woman go to the *mikveh* and resume her marital relationship.

The ten chapters of the Mishnah include some of the following concerns: the length of the period of ritual uncleanliness—when it begins and when it ends—since its beginning cannot be known exactly and the end is legally presumed to be seven days after the beginning; how to determine if a vaginal discharge is indeed menstrual bleeding; the laws of the woman who has delivered a child; how to determine when puberty begins in a woman.

Niddah 1:1-2 [1]

If a woman has regular menstrual periods, it is acceptable to count her period of ritual uncleanliness from the time she discovers the flow. If she uses testing pads [2] before and after intercourse, this serves as an examination to lessen the period of the "last twenty-four hours," [3] or the period from a previous examination to the last examination. [4] How is the ruling to be interpreted that it suffices to count her period of ritual uncleanliness from the time she discovers the flow? If she was sitting on a bed and was concerned with ritually clean objects, [5] then went elsewhere and discovered the menstrual flow, she becomes ritually unclean, while the objects remain ritually clean. Although it was ruled that she [6] conveys defilement for a period of twenty-four hours retroactively, she still counts the seven days of menstrual term from the time she discovered the flow. [7]

---

1. This Mishnah began with a disagreement between Shammai and Hillel about the determination of the beginning of the menstrual

period, from the standpoint of ritual cleanliness. Shammai was deemed too lenient for the Rabbis, and Hillel too stringent.

2. To be sure that her menstrual period had not begun. Intercourse during the menstrual period has been a serious sin in Judaism.

3. A woman with irregular menstrual periods was deemed by the Sages to have transmitted defilement for twenty-four hours before she discovered that she was menstruating.

4. This has to do with Hillel's ruling, which did not become law.

5. Like food preparation.

6. The woman who menstruated irregularly.

7. The seven days, prescribed in Leviticus 15:19, constituted her period of ritual uncleanliness.

Niddah 2:4

Women are presumed to be ritually clean for their husbands.[1] When men return from a journey, their wives are presumed to be ritually clean. The school of Shammai ruled: A woman must have two testing pads for each intercourse, or the intercourse must be performed by lamplight.[2] The school of Hillel said: Two testing pads are enough for the whole night.[3]

---

1. That is, during the two-week period each month when intercourse is permitted, the man can assume that his wife is not menstruating. He need not ask her if she is ritually clean, and she does not have to test in his presence whether or not she is menstruating.

2. There is a lot of disagreement about the meaning of this statement. Some say that it refers to one pad for testing before intercourse, and one to be used afterward. Others say one pad was to be used by the woman, one by the man. The Gemara objects strenuously to the idea of lovemaking by lamplight. The Shulḥan Arukh clearly prohibits it.

3. They may be used after each intercourse and examined in the morning, or one may be used before the first intercourse and the other after the last. The Gemara's teachers are divided on the subject of multiple acts of intercourse in one night, but the Halakhah does not prohibit them.

MAKSHIRIN—PREREQUISITES FOR NON-KASHRUT

Introduction

The title of this tractate is almost paradoxical. It is a form of the word *kasher,* the root meaning of which is "fit." Its usual meaning, therefore, is "ritually proper or fit." However, it can also mean "fit to receive ritual impurity." The subject of this tractate is those conditions which make the object "ready" or "fit" to become ritually defiled.

No natural food is ritually unclean when it is still attached to the earth, except the proscribed animals, birds, and fish. No such food can be susceptible to defilement unless it has been in direct contact with certain liquids. These liquids and their effect upon foods are the subjects of the six chapters of this tractate.

There are several considerations discussed in this book. Which liquids can convey the susceptibility? Under what circumstances? What is the relationship between the intent of the owner and the achievement of susceptibility?

This latter question is probably the most interesting. For the owner must either intend to moisten the food for his purpose, or must be satisfied that it is to his benefit when it is done by outside forces. Once again we find this peculiar mingling of the *hok*— the law for which no human reason is given—and very human principles and ideals.

Biblical Source for Makshirin

As to any food that might be eaten, it shall become unclean if it came in contact with water; as to any liquid that might be drunk, it shall become unclean if it was inside any vessel. If such a carcass falls upon seed grain that is to be sown, it is clean; but if water is put on the seed and such a carcass falls upon it, it shall be unclean for you. (Leviticus 11:34, 37–8)

Makshirin 2:7 [1]

If an abandoned child is found there and most of the inhabitants are non-Jews, the child is considered a non-Jew. If the majority are Jews, it is a Jewish child. If the inhabitants are half and half, it is considered a Jewish child. R. Judah said: The determination is made by considering which group abandons more children.[2]

---

1. This is part of a series of digressions dealing with the implications of integrated urban living between Jews and non-Jews, where the majority-minority ratio might play a role in Halakhic decision.
2. R. Judah's view was not accepted as law. The problem posed here has continued to be a real problem in Jewish life. After World War II, for example, many abandoned children were found in Germany near displaced persons camps. These "concentration camp babies," whose fathers were Nazis or even other inmates, were not wanted by their mothers, who were anxious to build a new life. In almost every case, courts held that these children were non-Jewish unless some evidence could be brought regarding Jewish parents. The assumption favored the majority group.

Makshirin 3:1

If a sack full of fruit was put on a riverbank or by the mouth of a well, or on the edge of a cavern pool and the fruit absorbed water, the law of "if water be put" (Leviticus 11:38), applies to all the fruit which absorb water. R. Judah said: It applies to fruit next to the water, but not to fruit not directly near the water.[1]

---

1. R. Judah's view was not accepted as law. The intent of the owner is again a factor here. According to the commentators, he deliberately put the sack of fruit there in order that it might absorb moisture and become larger and heavier. Since it was for his profit, the moisture makes all the fruit susceptible to ritual uncleanliness.

ZAVIM—BODILY DISCHARGES IN ILLNESS

Introduction

The Torah makes a clear distinction between bodily secretions from healthy areas (urine and feces, saliva and mucus, blood, etc.) and those which are connected with an illness—pus, non-menstrual vaginal bleeding, etc. The *zav,* specifically, appears to be the man or woman (*zavah*) with a venereal infection. The Levitical law provides primarily that direct contact with the person suffering from such a malady causes defilement. But the Rabbis, in "erecting a fence about the Torah," added all manner of additional regulations. Contact via clothing, occupying the same seat under certain circumstances, and similar actions could cause the contamination of an otherwise ritually clean person.

Biblical Sources for Zavim

Speak to the Israelite people and say to them:
    When any man has a discharge issuing from his member, he is unclean. (Leviticus 15:2)

SEE ALSO
                    Leviticus 15:1, 3–15, 25–30

Zavim 3:1

If a *zav* and a ritually clean person sat together on a boat, or on a raft, or rode on a beast, even though their garments did not touch, the ritually clean person and his garments suffer *midras* [1] contamination. If they sat together on a plank, a bench, a bed-frame, or on a beam, when these were not fixed tightly, [2] or if they climbed a weak tree or a weak branch of a tree, or if they were on an Egyptian ladder [3] together which was not secured by a nail, or if they sat together on a bridge, a rafter, or a door not held securely by clay, the ritually clean person and his garments become contaminated. R. Judah ruled them ritually clean.[4]

---

1. The word derives from the Hebrew word for "treading upon." It refers to the degree of contamination—an *av hatum'a* (see p. 271) —transmitted via the garments of a ritually unclean person to a ritually clean person when their garments alone touch by accident.
2. So that they swayed and garment contact was possible.
3. A small ladder which leaned against a wall or other object.
4. R. Judah's view was not accepted as law.

TEVUL YOM—POST-IMMERSION UNCLEANLINESS

Introduction

When a person has become ritually unclean for one day, he must bathe. Then he remains ritually contaminated to a slight degree until evening. He may not touch *Terumah;* it becomes invalid. He may not eat of any consecrated foods. But he does not convey defilement to any unconsecrated food products.

This short book deals with problems raised by the specific commandment in Leviticus 22:4–7. Instances are given of the transmission of third-degree contamination to whole objects or to parts of objects. The question of "connectives"—objects which cause contamination to pass from object to object, though they do not touch each other but only the connective—is handled in detail. There is an enumeration of liquids which become defiled by touch, and as always there is a discussion of vessels.

Tevul Yom 4:2

A woman who is *tevulat yom* may knead dough, cut off the *hallah*,[1] and set it apart. But she must put it on an Egyptian basket [2] or on a tray.[3] Then she may bring it near the rest of the dough and declare it as *hallah* offering. For the dough she touched suffered only third-degree contamination, and this is considered ritually clean in *Hullin*.[4]

---

1. See pp. 66–68 for details of the dough offering.
2. This basket was made of twigs, and was not susceptible to contamination.
3. Because a tray does not have distinctive individual receptacles, it too is not susceptible.
4. Until she declared the dough to be *hallah*, it was not sacred at all, but *Hullin*. Since she, as *tevulat yom*, was capable of transmitting only third-degree contamination, the dough did not become defiled.

YADAIM—UNCLEANLINESS OF HANDS

Introduction

The Torah says nothing about the ritual washing of the hands, or about any specific uncleanliness which adheres to the hands. Nonetheless, evolving regulations—all in the direction of more stringency—can be traced to relatively early times. The Gemara (*B. Shabbat* 14b) was probably less than historical in insisting that Solomon instituted the rite of washing the hands before eating. In any event, hand-washing was widely practiced ritually at the beginning of the Mishnaic period. Shammai and Hillel disputed over details of the regulations in the first century. Before the Mishnah was written, it was firmly ruled that hands always constitute a second-degree ritual uncleanliness, capable of conveying third-degree contamination (limited to *Terumah* and sacred things).

But the hands are in good company. Even the Torah scroll is "unclean" in a second-degree manner.

The Dead Sea Scrolls have revealed how compulsive and rigid the whole process of purification by water had become, at least among the Essenes, by the beginning of the Common Era. The New Testament (Matthew 15:2, Mark 7:3–4) relates arguments between Jesus and the Pharisaic scholars on the subject. Over the centuries, the importance of ritual hand-washing did not diminish.

There is a fascinating digression in Chapter 4. The paragraphs begin with the formula: On that day; i.e., the day R. Eleazar b. Azariah was elected Nasi of the Sanhedrin, replacing the deposed Gamaliel II, a number of previous decisions were overturned: the "liberals" had come back into power after a period of domination by the more aristocratic element. There is another digression in Chapter 5, airing open controversies between the Sadducees and Pharisees.

Yadaim 2:1

If a person pours water over one hand with a single rinsing, the hand is ritually clean. But if he pours water over both hands with a single rinsing, R. Meir ruled them ritually unclean unless he had poured more than one-fourth *log* [1] over them.[2]

---

1. A *log* is both a liquid and a dry measure equal to .506 liter, or approximately one pint.
2. R. Meir's view was not accepted as law. Maimonides held, for example, that he could pour water over one hand, then use the same water to pour over the other hand.

Yadaim 4:5

The Aramaic portions of Ezra and Daniel [1] make the hands ritually unclean. If an Aramaic section of the Bible was written in Hebrew, or if Hebrew was translated into Aramaic or written in Hebrew script, it does not make the hands ritually unclean. The Bible makes the hands ritually unclean only when it is written in Assyrian script, on hide, and in ink.[2]

---

1. Just as the Hebrew does. All scrolls of the Bible convey second-degree contamination. This was decreed in order to prevent scrolls from being stored next to *Terumah*. Mice attacked the latter and the former indiscriminately, rendering them defiled. So the scrolls were declared to be second-degree contaminated *a priori*—thus rendering a person who touched the face of the scroll with his hand unfit to eat *Terumah*. These were indirect ways to strengthen the sanctity of Biblical books.
2. "Hebrew" here refers to the early calligraphic forms which evolved from the Phoenician to Hebrew. The writing was changed after the Babylonian Exile to "Assyrian," the script still in use today.

UKTZIN—STALKS AND RITUAL UNCLEANLINESS

Introduction

There is no particular reason for this book to be the last in the Mishnah, or even in this order. Logically, it should come before *Yadaim,* after *Tevul Yom.* For its subject matter continues the concern of *Tevul Yom* with "connectives," the objects which may or may not convey ritual uncleanliness to a ritually clean object from a ritually unclean one. Maimonides stated that it was placed at the end of the Mishnah precisely because it has no Torah origins at all, being composed entirely of rabbinic additions to basic regulations.

Uktzin 2:1

When olive leaves are pickled with the olives, the leaves remain ritually clean, for pickling them was only for appearance's sake.[1] The fibers on a cucumber [2] and the sprouts on the end are ritually clean. R. Judah said: So long as it is still for sale by the merchant, it is susceptible.[3]

---

1. The leaves attached to the olives gave the appearance of recent plucking, therefore of freshness.
2. A parasitic growth of some sort which attached itself to a number of shrubs, but was harmless.
3. He refers only to the cucumber, with its parasites still on it. These growths are part of the cucumber, and as susceptible to contamination as the vegetable itself. The commentators do not indicate clearly the Halakhic decisions, if one was ever finally reached.

Utkzin 3:12 [1]

R. Joshua b. Levi said: The Holy One, blessed be He, will make each righteous person inherit 310 worlds. For it is written: "That I may cause those who love me to inherit *yesh* [2] and that I may fill their treasuries" (Proverbs 8:21). R. Simon b. Ḥalafta said: The Holy One, blessed be He, found no vessel which could hold Israel's blessing, except peace. For it is written: "The Lord will give strength unto His people. The Lord will bless His people with peace" (Psalms 29:11).

---

1. Some editions omit this last paragraph of the Mishnah.
2. The numerical equivalent of the word *yesh* is 310. This is a simple Gematria.

Glossary

Adonay. Literally, "my lords." Used as a substitute for YHVH in speech and prayer, since YHVH is never pronounced. Usually translated "the Lord."

Aggadah. The Aramaic equivalent of *Haggadah,* from the Hebrew "to tell." All non-legal material in Jewish thought and literature.

Agunah. A deserted wife. There is no "legal death" in Jewish law; that is, a specified period of years after which a court can declare someone "dead."

Aliyah (plural *Aliyot*). (1) A pilgrimage, usually to Jerusalem. (2) The honor of being called to recite the blessings before and after the reading of a section of the Torah during synagogue services. (3) A platform or balcony.

Am Ha'aretz. Literally, "people of the land." The peasant, ignorant of anything beyond the most elementary requirements of Judaism, whose actions could not be trusted in ritual matters. Now used pejoratively when referring to an ignoramus.

Ammah (plural *Ammot*). A cubit, defined as the distance from the elbow to the end of the clenched fist of an average adult male (eighteen to twenty inches).

Amora (plural *Amora'im*). Teachers whose opinions are recorded in the Gemara and who lived between 200 and 500 C.E.

Ashkenazi. A person or tradition emanating from Central and Eastern Europe, as contrasted with Sefardi (q.v.) or South European Jewry. *Ashkenaz* is the Hebrew word for Germany.

Av (plural *Avot*). Literally, "father." (1) Mishnaic teachers who set the pattern of Jewish legal interpretation, usually called *Tannaim.* They lived during the last 200 to 250 years before the Christian era and the first two centuries of that era. (2) The ethical maxims of these teachers as recorded in *Pirke Avot* (q.v.). (3) Major categories of objects or principles in law, then subdivided into "children" and even "grandchildren."

Av Bet Din. Literally "father of the court." The deputy of the Nasi, the president of the Sanhedrin. Little is known of his specific duties.

Azaz'el. The place to which the scapegoat was sent during the Temple ceremonies on the Day of Atonement. The origin of the word and the location of the place are not known. The word tended to be linked to the scapegoat itself. Today it has the connotation of "hell."

Bava. Literally, "gate." When the huge Talmudic book on civil law was divided into three parts, each was called a "gate": first, middle, last. (Judges sat in the "gate.")

Berakhah (plural *Berakhot*). "Blessing" or "praise." From the Hebrew "knee" or "to kneel." The generic name for the formula spoken before the performance of many mitzvot, which begins: "Praised be Thou, O Lord our God, Ruler of the world. . . ."

Bet Din. Literally, "house of law," a Jewish court. There were three levels of Jewish courts in the Mishnaic period: three judges, twenty-three judges, and the Sanhedrin of seventy-one. After 425 c.e., only courts of three functioned.

Bikkurim. First fruits, brought to the Temple in Jerusalem on Shavuot. The festival became known both as *Bikkurim* and as *Mattan Torah* (Giving of the Torah) since it also celebrates the Revelation at Mount Sinai.

Dinar (plural *Dinarim*). A coin worth one-half of a shekel. In 1970, a *dinar* would be worth approximately sixty cents or five shillings.

Elohim. A generic name for the deity among many ancient peoples in the Near East. In the Bible, one of the names of the God of Israel most frequently used, along with YHVH and sometimes combined with YHVH. Now translated as "God."

Erusin. Betrothal. In Talmudic times, the first binding contractual undertaking between the fathers of bride and groom, followed by *Kiddushin* or *Nissu'in* (q.v.), the marriage ceremony itself.

Eruvin (singular *Eruv*). 1) The symbolic enclosing of an urban area by the placement of a basket of food, making it possible for Jews to walk two thousand cubits further on the Sabbath. 2) Combining two private domains by the same technique, making it permissible to carry objects between them on the Sabbath. 3) A technique for making it possible to prepare food for the Sabbath on a festival day preceding it.

Etrog. The fruit of a *hadar* tree, used in the Sukkot ritual both in ancient times and now. Usually translated as "citron," a fruit closely related to the lemon.

Ga'on (plural *Ge'onim*). The head of a Babylonian academy during the third to tenth centuries C.E. Used today to denote a world-famous rabbinic authority.

Gemara. A lengthy, discursive commentary on the Mishnah. Gemara and Mishnah together comprise the Talmud.

Gematria. From the Greek *geometria,* "measurement." A form of cryptograph in which a word derives its meaning from the sum of the numbers contained in the Hebrew letters. Widely used in Aggadah.

Get (plural *Gittin*). A legal document used to dissolve a marriage or betrothal, or to free slaves.

Haftarah (plural *Haftarot*). A prophetic passage read in the synagogue on Sabbaths and Festivals, linked to the Torah reading prescribed for that day. It originated in Roman period, when Torah reading itself was prohibited.

Haggadah. Literally "telling," like the Aramaic Aggadah. Used today as the name for the narrative read during the Passover Seder.

Halakhah. The way to walk, the thing to do, the general word for Jewish law.

Halitzah. The ceremony described in Deuteronomy 25:5–10, in which a widow without children released her brother-in-law from the Levirate requirement to marry her.

Hannukah. Literally, "dedication." An eight-day festival commemorating the victory of the Maccabees over the Syrian-Greeks in 165 B.C.E. and the repurification and rededication of the Temple in Jerusalem which resulted.

Hasid (plural *Hasidim*). In Mishnaic times Hasidim were militant, anti-Roman Pharisees. Beginning with the eighteenth century, the term refers to followers of Israel Ba'al Shem Tov in Eastern Europe.

Havdalah. The ceremonial which, through the use of wine, spices, and light, symbolizes the end of the Sabbath.

Issar. A small coin, one-twenty-fourth of a *dinar.*

Kaddish. One of the oldest prayers in the Jewish liturgy. Originally a doxology spoken after a Torah study session, later a memorial prayer for scholars and teachers, now a general memorial prayer as well as a transitional prayer between major sections of the liturgy.

Kavvanah. Literally, "the turning." A directing of the self toward God in prayer.

Kedushah. Literally, "sanctity." Also refers to a specific prayer in the liturgy of morning and afternoon services.

Ketuvah (plural *Ketuvot*). The handwritten Aramaic marriage contract drawn up between the parents of the bride and groom and signed by two witnesses.

Kiddush. From the same root as *Kedushah* and *Kaddish.* Refers to various prayers sanctifying specific events, usually carried on with wine as the symbol.

Kiddushin. One of the two names (*Nissu'in* being the other) for the marriage ceremony.

Kodesh. Any object or animal dedicated to the Temple in Jerusalem in Mishnaic times.

Kohen. A priest, a direct descendant of Aaron, brother of Moses. Though various priestly clans vied for power in ancient times, careful records of descent from Aaron were kept until the fifth century C.E. The Kohen retains specific privileges and duties in contemporary Jewish religious life, and is subject to certain restrictions.

Kosher (noun *kashrut*). Ritually permissible or acceptable. Today used in connection with dietary regulations.

Levirate. An ancient regulation, still enforced in all Ashkenazi and many Sefardi Orthodox communities, which requires the brother of a childless widow either to marry her or to submit to the ritual of *ḥalitzah* (q.v.). Since most communities have been monogamous for centuries, the latter is generally practiced.

Levite. (1) A descendant of the tribe of Levi, including both priests and Levites. (2) The non-priestly branches of the descendants of Levi. They were employed in the Temple in Jerusalem as laborers, musicians, and choristers.

Lulav. Branches of the palm tree, used in combination with willow branches, myrtle branches, and the *etrog* (q.v.) during the Sukkot ceremonies.

Ma'ariv. The daily evening liturgical service.

Ma'aser (plural *Ma'aserot*). Literally, "tenthing," or tithe. There were three tithes, two of which were collected on alternate years, and one each year, for the upkeep of the Temple, for philanthropic purposes, and for the support of the Levites.

Massekhet. Literally, "web," a section or book of the Mishnah, Talmud, *Tosefta,* or other traditional texts.

Matzah. Unleavened bread, required in ancient times in connection with all sacrifices in the Temple in Jerusalem, and in all Jewish homes during the seven (later eight) days of Passover.

Megillah. Literally, "roll" or "rolled scroll." Five books of the Bible are called *Megillot:* Song of Songs, Ruth, Lamentations, Ecclesiastes, and Esther. *Megillah* refers most frequently to Esther, however. Used today in folk language to refer to any long anecdote or story.

Mezuzah. Literally, "doorpost where the *mezuzah* is placed." It is a rectangular piece of parchment, with the following Bible passages hand-written on it: Deuteronomy 6:4–9; 11:13–21. It is customary to place a mezuzah on the right doorpost of every door in any building.

Minḥah. (1) A flour-offering and gift-offering brought to the Temple in Jerusalem. (2) An early-evening sacrifice in the ancient Temple. (3) The afternoon liturgical service, usually conducted late in the afternoon so that the congregation can go on with the evening service after a short interval.

Minyan. The quorum of ten men required for the conduct of a congregational liturgical service.

Mishnah (plural *Mishnayot*). The general name for the classical Six Orders of topically organized Halakhic material. It refers also to one paragraph of material within the Mishnah book.

Mitzvah (plural *Mitzvot*). Literally, "commandment." That which a Jew must do or not do in response to divine command. Traditionally, the written Torah contains 613 specific mitzvot. The potential number of mitzvot is infinite.

Mussaf. The additional sacrifice offered in the ancient Temple on Sabbaths and Festivals. Since the destruction of the Temple, a *Mussaf* liturgy is said on the same occasions.

Nasi. The president of the Sanhedrin. Today, the title of the president of the State of Israel.

Nazir. (noun, adjective *Nazirite*): in Biblical times, a person who vowed to abstain from grapes and all grape products and to abstain from cutting the hair either for a stated period or for a lifetime, as a gesture of sanctity. By Mishnaic times the practice had died out.

Nissu'in. The marriage ceremony, also known as *Kiddushin* (q.v.).

Orlah. Literally, "the uncircumcised." Fruit produced by trees during their first four years of life. Such fruit could not be eaten.

Pe'ah. The corners of a field, the produce of which had to be left for the poor. No area or amount was specified. Today the word appears most frequently in the plural, *pe'ot,* referring to the curled earlocks worn by some traditional Jews.

Pesaḥ. (1) The lamb or kid slaughtered and eaten in ancient times on the first evening of Passover. (2) Passover itself, the seven or eight days of the festival.

Rosh Hashanah. Literally, "head of the year," the New Year festival observed since Biblical times on the first day of the seventh month of the current calendar and, since Talmudic times, on the second day of that month as well (except among Reform Jews, who observe only one day).

Sanhedrin. The high court of ancient Israel, which met in the Temple in Jerusalem until 70 C.E., then in Yavneh and, according to tradition, at a number of other places, until it settled in Tiberias. It was outlawed by Rome in 425 C.E. The Sanhedrin consisted of seventy members plus the Nasi—president—or seventy-one in all.

Seder (plural *Sedarim*). (1) One of the six major sections of the Talmud, Mishnah, and Gemara. (2) The ritual meal of Passover.

Sefardi. A person or tradition emanating from Southern Europe, North Africa, or the Near East. *Sefarad* is the Hebrew word for Spain, the country which dominated Jewish life and thought in those areas for centuries. The Sefardi tradition is contrasted with the Ashkenazi (q.v.).

Sela. A coin worth two shekels.

Shaharit. The morning liturgical service.

Shavuot. From the Hebrew for "seven," because the observance occurs seven weeks after Pesaḥ. Originally a one-day festival, it is now observed for two days among traditional Jews. It combines the commemoration of the Revelation at Mount Sinai with the celebration of the summer solstice and the *Bikkurim,* the festival of first fruits.

Shekel. A coin worth two *dinarim* or one-half a *sela.* The *shekel* was adopted as the symbol of membership in the World Zionist Organization.

Shema. Literally, "hear." The first word of the phrase in Deuteronomy 6:4: "Hear O Israel, Adonay is our God, Adonay is One (or "Adonay alone.") In the Mishnah, the word is used to refer to the morning and evening liturgical services.

Shemitah. Literally, "left fallow." Every seventh year was and is a *Shemitah* year. During the Mishnaic period, fields were not sown, all debts were cancelled, and Hebrew indentured servants were freed. These regulations were modified over the centuries, but the *Shemitah* is still noted in the Hebrew calendar. The year 5728 (September 1967 to September 1968) was a *Shemitah* year.

Shofar. The ram's horn used in Biblical times (1) to announce the "Day of Memorial" on the first day of the seventh month, now Rosh Hashanah, and (2) to summon the people at times of catastrophe or war. Today the Shofar is blown on Rosh Hashanah and at the end of the Yom Kippur observance.

Siddur. The book containing the liturgies for daily and Sabbath services. The liturgy book for Festivals and High Holy Days is known as *Mahzor.*

Simhat Torah. Literally, "joy of the Torah." The annual celebration of the completion of the reading of the Torah and, immediately, the beginning again of the annual cycle of Torah readings. A medieval innovation, it occurs on the twenty-fourth of *Tishri*, at the end of the Sukkot festival, a day earlier among Reform Jews and Israelis.

Sofer (plural *Soferim*). Scribe. In Biblical times, because the scribe had to write legal documents and sacred books alike, he was considered the community scholar and teacher. He was replaced as teacher and scholar by Rabbis, when the title became accepted in the second century c.e.

Sotah. A woman who was accused by her husband of sexual infidelity but who denied the charge. She was subjected to an ordeal which determined her guilt or innocence. In the first century c.e., the practice was abolished.

Sukkah (plural *Sukkot*). A booth originally erected in the fields and groves during harvest season. It was later ritualized as a reminder of the frailty of the housing available to the Israelites during the desert-dwelling after the Exodus from Egypt. It is erected outside homes and synagogues during the Sukkot festival each fall, and meals are usually eaten in it.

Takkanah. A proclaimed change in Jewish law which is not justified or "proved" from Torah text. There is controversy over the differences between *Takkanot* and *Gezerot,* other rabbinical enactments which changed previous Halakhah.

Tallit (plural *Tallitot*). Originally a cloak to whose corners were affixed the *tzitzit,* (q.v.). After the Mishnaic period the *tzitzit* were attached to a separate garment called a *tallit.* Two kinds are used today: the large *tallit,* worn during most traditional services by all men, and the *tallit katan,* or "small *tallit,"* a separate garment worn under the shirt at all times by some traditional Jews.

Tanakh. The Hebrew name for the Bible. It consists of the first letters of the Hebrew names for the three major sections of the Bible: Torah; *Nevi'im* (Prophets); and *Ketuvim* (Writings).

Tanna (plural *Tannaim*). The general name for the scholars whose opinions were recorded in the Mishnah text.

Tefillah. Prayer. The *Tefillah,* in the Mishnah, is the *Amidah,* also known traditionally as the *Shemoneh Esreh,* that part of each service which is traditionally said silently while standing.

Tefillin. Phylacteries, two boxes containing portions of the Torah inscribed on parchment and affixed to the head and left arm respectively with leather thongs in a prescribed manner, as the response of the Jew to the command in Deuteronomy 6:8. They are worn during morning services, except on Sabbath and Festivals.

Terumah (plural *Terumot*). A form of offering usually called a heave-offering. *Terumot* were products of the field brought as gifts to the priests in the Temple in Jerusalem.

Tishah Be'av. The ninth day of the month of *Av.* A fast day, it commemorates, according to tradition, the fall of the First Temple (586 B.C.E.) and the fall of the Second Temple (70 C.E.) Numerous other calamities in Jewish history were linked to *Tishah Be'av* as well.

Tzitzit. Ritual fringes affixed to the *tallit* (q.v.) in fulfillment of the command in Numbers 15:38 ff.

YHVH. The Tetragrammaton, the most sacred name of the God of Israel, pronounced only by the High Priest and only on Yom Kippur, when he entered the Holy of Holies to seek forgiveness for himself, his household, and his people. In prayer, the word is pronounced *Adonay.* Otherwise, a variety of circumlocutions have evolved.

Yibbum. The Levirate marriage (q.v.); the brother-in-law of the widow involved was expected either to marry her or undergo the *halitzah* ceremony.

Yom Kippur (plural *Kippurim*). The Day of Atonement, the tenth day of the month of *Tishri*. It was and remains the most sacred day in the annual calendar, so significant that its Mishnaic book is called *Yoma, "the* day."

Yovel. The Jubilee year. It occurred once every fifty years and was marked by the return of all lands to the original family owners. The *Yovel* was discontinued long before the beginning of the Common Era.

Index